Fortunate Plastic Surgeon

An Autobiography and My View
About the United States

Khosrow Matini, M.D., F.A.C.S.

Another book by Khosrow Matini, M.D., F.A.C.S.

Inside The Minds:
The Art & Science of Plastic Surgery

For Joanie and Lily

Table of Contents:

Preface xv
My Birth at Wrong Time! 1
Pregnancy of My Mother 3
Eczema 4
My Sister Was Born 4
Typhoid Fever 4
Crowded House 5
Water Reservoir of Our Home 5
Electricity 6
Houses in Tehran in 1947 6
School in Tehran in 1947 7
Could I Choose my Food as a Child? 7
Primary School 8
Society of Beneficence and Improvement 8
Acting and Producing Theater 10
Movie Production at Age of 11 10
Bicycle 12
Water Painting Postcards to Buy a Bicycle 12
Persian New Year "Nowruz" 14
My Mother Advised Me through the Stories
   Which She Told Me 16
Family 18
The Most Significant Mother 18
Surgery of my Eye Muscle 20
Swimming and Diving 22
Climbing the Mountains 23
Alborz High School 23
My Classmates at Alborz High School 25
My Parents' New House 27

Olive Oil Lamp	28
My First Sexual Experience	28
My Oldest Brother Gets Married	29
Creation	29
Googoosh (Famous Singer of Iran)	30
Deciding to Go to Medical School	31
Preparation for College or Medical School	31
First Trip to Meshed by Myself	32
Entrance Examination for Medical School of Meshed University	33
Entrance to Medical School	33
Meshed University	34
Lack of Cafeteria and Dormitory	34
Anatomy Course	35
Trapped in the Cadaver's Room!	35
Unusual Event at Termination of Anatomy Course	36
Omar Khayam, Greatest Poet of Iran	37
Lack of Alcoholic Beverages in Meshed	37
Work in the Operating Room of a Private Hospital	37
Swimming and Diving at the Caspian Sea!	38
Political Activity	39
Demonstration and Closure of University	39
Savak (Organization of Intelligence and National Security)	40
Production of Play	41
First Time I Held a Gun	42
At Medical School	42
Planning to Get Married	43
Psychiatric Rotation	44
Distribution of Drug Samples	45
Internship at the Meshed University Hospital	45
Graduation from the Medical School	46

Short Life of the Red Blood Cells of my Mother 46
Army of Hygiene (Sepah Behdasht) 48
Serving in the Military after Graduation 48
Visiting the Three-Star General 48
Military School 49
Guns in the Military 50
Jail Time 50
My Experience at the Military Jail 51
Selection of Village 53
Daman of Iranshahr 54
Medical Practice as a Medical Officer 56
Interesting Patients 57
The Unusual Necklace 58
Trachoma 58
Starvation 59
Unusual Sexual Activity 59
Tuberculosis 59
Second Visit with Governor of Baluchistan 60
Unusual Snake Bite 61
Anal Sex for Money 62
Difficulty of Childbirth 63
Special Food for Car! 64
Acute Appendicitis 64
Hot Weather in Southeastern Iran 64
Leaving Daman 65
Moving to the Northwest 65
Sayed Shekar, Kermanshah 66
E.C.F.M.G. Examination 69
Establishment of Water Reservoir for People of Village 69
Side Effect of Horseback Riding 70

The Effect of Medical Military Physician on the
  Life of the Village's People 71
Endemic Syphilis. 71
On My Way to the U.S.A!. 71
Fortune Teller 71
Leaving Iran 72
Hamburg, Germany 73
Sweden 74
Sweden to the United States 75
Internship at Providence Hospital 76
General Surgery Training. 77
Jewish Hospital Medical Center of Brooklyn, New York 77
My First Medical Doctor Girlfriend 78
New Apartment in Brooklyn, New York 78
Gun Shot in the Jewish Hospital Medical
  Center of Brooklyn, New York. 80
Unusual Event in Brooklyn, New York 81
Thank You Note from the People of Brooklyn, New York!. 82
Worm or Spaghetti!. 82
Importance of Reading the Name of Medication. 83
Second Year Residency in General Surgery 84
University of Louisville, Kentucky. 85
First Lie 86
Second-Year Residency of General Surgery
  at University of Louisville, Kentucky 86
Importance of Surgical Training 88
The Right to Bear Arms. 88
Cause of Death without Burn in a Fire 89
My Research on Platelet Function and Gastric Bleeding 89
New Coagulation Blood Test 91

Platelet Aggregation and Adhesiveness. 91
Presentation of my Research Paper on Platelet. 92
Publications and Presentations 93
Pathology Training at the Mayo Clinic 94
Car Accident in Rochester, Minnesota. 96
Rochester Traffic Court 96
New Chairman of Department of Surgery in Louisville, Kentucky. . 97
Visiting English Professor from Africa. 98
My Vacation to Europe 99
Bullfight in Madrid, Spain. 100
Monthly Conference of the Department of Surgery 101
Unusual Transfer of Injured Patients to the
   Louisville General Hospital by Police Officers 102
Gunshot Wounds in Louisville, Kentucky. 102
Father Shot his 14-Year-Old Son. 103
Wife Shot her Husband Six Times. 103
Who Shot the Wife?. 104
Attempt to Kill a Husband 104
The Fight between a Thief and Police Officer. 104
Unconscious Man due to Gunshot Wound of the Head 105
How to Complete Unsuccessful Shooting of
   a Person in Louisville, Kentucky. 106
Bypass Surgery for Weight Loss 106
Stab Wound of Heart 107
Gunshot Wound of the Heart 108
Early Stage of Cancer of Pancreas 108
Whipple Operation. 108
The General Surgery Residency at the
   University of Louisville, Kentucky 110
Considering Plastic Surgery. 110

Plastic Surgery Training	111
Interview with the Chairman of Department of Plastic Surgery	112
Hand Surgery Fellowship at University of Louisville, Kentucky	113
Plastic Surgery Residency at George Washington University	116
Surgery with Dr. Calvin Klopp	117
First Replantation of Amputated Hand and Wrist in the Washington, DC.	118
Plastic Surgery Residents or Orthopedic Surgery Residents for Treatment of Injured Hand	119
Malignant Melanoma	119
My Second Year Residency of Plastic Surgery	120
Second Successful Replantation of the Amputated Hand	121
Job in Iran	121
Return to the United States and Start of Practice	122
Clinical Assistant Professor of Plastic Surgery	123
Buying a Town House in Old Town, Alexandria	123
Bringing My Nephews (My Second Brother's Sons) to the United States	123
Falling in Love with a Beautiful Dentist	124
Senator Kennedy versus Governor Jimmy Carter	125
Friends from Richmond and Meeting a Persian Woman	126
My First Marriage	127
Interesting Events with My Senior Partner	128
Injury to My Right Hand	128
My Plan to Return and Stay in Iran!	129
Heart Attacks in Iran	130
Enemies of Iran	130
My Practice of Plastic Surgery in Iran	131
Fusion of Joints between the Skull and Jaws	131
The Most Extensive Cancer of Scalp as Result Of Radiation	132

Treating Multiply Injured Patients in Iran:
   Last Demonstration Prior to the Shah's Departure 134
American plan to get rid of the Shah of Iran and
   Replace Him with Khomeini 135
Departure of My Oldest Brother from Iran 136
Request for New President of our University Hospital 138
Leaving Iran Again 139
Returning to the United States 140
Starting a New Life in Alexandria, Virginia 140
Sherwood Hall Medical Center Office Building 141
Difficulty of the Emergency Room Coverage. 142
Membership on the Medical Executive Committee of Virginia ... 143
First Experience in Performing Surgery after
   Returning to the United States...................... 144
Surgical Treatment of Severe Arthritis of Carpo
   Metacarpal Joint of Thumb 145
Gunshot Wound of the Wrist 145
Largest Lipoma (Tumor of Fatty Tissues) of Back 146
My View of Treatment of Skin Cancer 146
The Behavior of Americans in Response to Invasion
   of Their Embassy in Iran by Bunch of Crazy Iranian People .. 147
Arranging to Bring My Nephew Out of Iran
   and into the United States 148
Learning New Reconstructive Muscle and Myocutaneous
   Flaps Techniques 149
The First Muscle Flap Reconstruction in
   the Washington Metropolitan Region................. 149
First Muscle Flap Reconstruction to Save an Arm 151
Breast Reconstruction by Abdominal Skin and
   Underlying Muscle of Abdomen.................... 153

Birth of my Daughter 153
The Crazy Woman Working For the Church 154
Trips to Virginia Beach and Florida 154
Treatment of Longstanding Psychiatric Condition
   by Plastic Surgery 155
Unusual Dog Bite 155
Most Unusual Case of Facial Bone Fractures 156
Disaster to My Daughter's Elbow Due to My Niece's Mistake 157
Selling Our House 159
Possible Heart Attack 160
Vacations with my Daughter 161
My Second Marriage 161
How I Met my Second Wife 162
A New House in Mount Vernon, Virginia 164
My Second Wife 164
My Second Divorce 165
Moving to a New Office Building 166
 Cheating Office Manager 167
Explosion of Sherwood Hall Medical Center Office Building 168
Who Mailed the Explosive Letter? 168
Lightning Strikes My House 169
The Major Fire of a New House Being Built 169
The Successful Achievements of my Daughter 170
How I Fell in Love with a Plastic Surgeon 171
Many Trips with My Plastic Surgeon Friend 172
Trip to Brazil and Argentina 174
Plastic Surgery Conference in Boston, Massachusetts 174
President of Alexandria Medical Society 175
Largest Skin Cancer of Nose 175
Neurosurgery at Inova Mount Vernon Hospital 176

Major Neurosurgery on My Neck 176
My Trip to Turkey and Greece. 178
Cardiac Arrest of Patient during Surgery 178
Successful Use of Muscle Flap for Treatment
   of Unusual Recurrent Fistula of Bladder. 179
The Fantastic Effect of Muscle Flaps 180
Psychiatric Patients in the United States 180
Another Iranian Woman in my Life 181
Prenuptial Agreement 182
Another Persian Woman in my Life. 183
A Wonderful Trip to Africa 184
Other Things about This Woman 187
Travel to New Zealand and Australia. 188
My Last and Best Marriage 189
My Wonderful American Wife 190
Loss of Coverage of Surgical Subspecialty in the
   Emergency Room of Inova Mount Vernon Hospital. 190
My Work as the Biggest Supporter of Inova Mount
   Vernon Hospital. 192
The Truth about Me and Members of My Family 198
My Oldest Brother (13 Years Older Than Me). 198
My Oldest Brother's First Wife 198
My Second Brother (11 Years Older Than Me) 200
Death of my Nephew 201
My Sister and Her Husband 202
Mr. Lewis Johnson 203
Helping my Sister and her Family 204
Difference in the Members of One Family. 206
Cases of Malpractice Brought Against Me in
   36 Years of my Practice. 207

First Malpractice Suit against Me 207
Second Malpractice Suit against Me 208
Appeal to the Virginia Supreme Court 210
Review of Virginia Board of Medicine. 211
The Major Changes of Patient's Care Due to the Legal System. . . . 212
My View about Malpractice in the United States. 213
Retirement of Good General Surgeons Because
   of Increase of Malpractice Insurance Premiums 214
Major Changes in Health Insurance Company
   Payments to the Physicians. 214
Major Changes in the Practice of Medicine in the United States 214
How Religion Can Help 215
My View about the Political System of the United States. 216
American Football is Dangerous 217
Conclusion 218

Appendix
The Biggest Enemies of Iran : Russia and England. A-1
Qajar Dynasty A-1
Fath Ali Shah, 1797-1834 . . . . A-1
Naser al-Din Shah, 1848-1896 . . . . A-2
Mirza Taqi Khan Amir Kabir. A-3
The Constitutional Revolution A-4
Mohammad Reza Pahlavi, the Shah of Iran A-6

Preface

I want to thank my wonderful American wife who helped me write this book.

I want to thank America for allowing me to come and be trained here, and also for allowing me to practice as a plastic surgeon and help a lot of American people.

KHOSROW MATINI, M.D., F.A.C.S.

My Birth at Wrong Time!

I was born in Tehran, the capital of Iran, on August 25, 1941. At that time, there were no systems for providing drinking water, electricity, or heat for houses. That was a particularly bad day for the Iranian People; Reza Shah and Iran's government claimed neutrality in World War II. The Soviet Union situation was so dire that the Allied Forces invaded Iran to use its railroad to help the Soviets. Known as Operation Countenance, this invasion continued for twenty-three days.

This was just the latest in a series of actions conducted by Great Britain and the Soviet Union against Persia/Iran. In the early 1800s, Iran had gone to war with Russia twice; both times Iran had to give up significant territory to Russia when they lost the war. In the mid-to-late 1800s, Nasser al-Din Shah tried to exploit the mutual distrust between Great Britain and Russia in order to preserve Iran's independence, but he was unsuccessful and instead, foreign interference and territorial encroachment increased under his rule. By the late 19th century, many Iranians believed that their rulers were beholden to foreign interests. Things did not improve in the early 20th century. Under the Anglo-Russian Agreement of 1907, Britain and Russia agreed to divide Iran into territories they could each control during World War I. The Russians were to enjoy the exclusive right to pursue their interests in the northern sphere, and the British in the southern and eastern spheres. During World War I, Russian, British, and Ottoman troops occupied Iran. With a coup d'état in February 1921, Reza Khan (who ruled as Reza Shah Pahlavi, 1925-41) became the preeminent political ruler of Iran.

At the time Reza Shah Pahlavi became the king of Iran, Iran was in deep trouble. No one could dare go on a trip from one city to another because it was very dangerous. Reza Shah established the wonderful army of Iran which he sent to every city to get rid of the corrupt people who ran the city and who had used their powers to harm the Iranian people. When he was planning to send the army to the Ahvaz and Abadan (the lands of oil), the Ambassador of Great Britain went to visit Reza Shah and told him he should not send any army to that region. The persistent Ambassador talked with Iranian officials twice more, warning them that they should not go to the oil region. Reza Shah did not listen to the Ambassador and sent the army anyway. They arrested the officials running that region who were the servants of England. The army general told the officials that he did not want to kill them, but in order to avoid execution, they would need to leave the region immediately, which they did. Great Britain became upset with Reza Shah Pahlavi who had not followed their orders like previous shahs had done.

Reza Shah did many good things for Iran. He established the railroad from Tehran to the north, toward Russia. He established several universities. He also formed very good armed forces in Iran. He told the Moslem clergyman that they had to work like other Iranians and they had to wear regular suits, not the Moslem clergyman outfits. The Shah arranged for students to wear school uniforms so that you could not tell which children were from poor families and which were from rich families. He built hospitals and military infrastructure.

Reza Shah changed the name of country from Persia to Iran on March 21, 1935.

Reza Shah was the first shah who ordered Iranian women not to wear traditional Moslem clothing. He banned the wearing of the chador (long sheet of dressing which covered the head, neck and entire body of the woman), and set an example by having his wife and daughters wear non-Moslem outfits when they traveled beyond the palace. Even in 2015, Saudi Arabia continues to force women to wear Moslem clothing and does not allow their women to drive cars until recently.

Reza Shah Pahlavi was the greatest Shah Iran has known. He did fantastic things for Iran and the Iranian people. Unfortunately, one of the terrible characteristics of Iranian people is that they never appreciate

Figure 1: Khosrow Matini at age 1

the good work of any individual; they only remember the bad things.

The same month I was born, August of 1941, English military forces arrested Reza Shah and sent him and his family by ship to Maurice, Africa, which was a colony of England at that time. They replaced him with his son, Mohammad Reza Pahlavi, and told him he had to obey them and be their servant.

Pregnancy of My Mother

When my mother learned she was pregnant, she and my father already had two sons, one eleven years old and one thirteen years old, and one daughter who was nine years old. In early 1941, there was an invasion of Iran by several thousand soldiers from several countries, including England and the Soviet Union. As a result, a food shortage was created. This also introduced new diseases into Iran. While my mother was carrying me, my nine-year-old sister fell ill with typhus fever. The doctor misdiagnosed her with malaria and gave her incorrect treatment, and unfortunately, she died. You can imagine the effect of the death of my sister on my pregnant mother.

In those days in Iran, pregnant women could not go to the hospital for delivery of their baby. During the invasion on August 25, Russian planes bombarded the suburb of Tehran even as I was being born. My brothers were sent to the top of the roof of our house, which was flat, and were told to drum the flat wash-tubs against each other to make enough noise so that my mother would not hear the noise of the bombing planes. Soon after I was born, the Russian bombing was terminated. My mother was glad to have a healthy son and my father claimed I saved Iran!

Iran's birth registration law, enacted in 1918, required all births to be registered within 15 days. My father went to the birth registration organization six days after my birth to obtain my identity certificate card. Although he told them I was born at home on August 25, the clerk put August 31, 1941 in the booklet. To make matters worse, the clerk also wrote my last name with the wrong letter. In the Persian language, we have two letters of T that carry a similar sound, but one originates from the Persian language and the other from Arabic. Matini with a Persian T means "gentle" while there is no meaning of the name spelled using an Arabic T. Unfortunately, my father did not look at the booklet at that time. Everything was in such turmoil after the invasion, everyone was distracted. Years later, my father discovered the mistake and was able to correct the letter T, but the office would not change the birth date to the correct day. To this day, I have some identification materials with the birth date of August 31, 1941, but I celebrate my birthday on August 25 each year. Fortunately, despite all of this drama, my mother had enough milk and nursed me for two years, which was customary.

Eczema

At age two, I developed extensive eczema, a skin disease that causes skin rash and eruptions and which is associated with severe itching. The itching may be so bad that you scratch your skin until it bleeds, which can make your rash even worse and lead to more inflammation and infection. There was no treatment for eczema in those days. Even now, there is no cure for eczema, except for cortisone ointment, which gets rid of it only temporarily. My mother used different ointments that were available at that time and wrapped my arms and legs. People who did not know about my eczema thought I had a massive burn. Fortunately, my condition improved, but I still develop spots of eczema periodically. My oldest brother has the same problem.

My Sister Was Born

Two and a half years after I was born, my sister was born. My mother did not have enough milk to nurse her. Fortunately, our neighbor had also just given birth and had excess milk. I remember this neighbor coming to our house, standing behind the entrance door, and milking her breast to fill up a pot of milk for my sister. Whatever was left over, I used to drink.

After the Iranian revolution in 1979, I brought my sister and her children to the United States a few years later. Her husband promised to come and join them within two years, but he only comes every six months for a couple weeks and then goes back to Iran.

Typhoid Fever

At age four, I caught typhoid fever, an infection of the small intestine. Today we know typhoid fever is caused by Escherichia Coli, but then, its cause was unknown and there was no proper antibiotic for its treatment. When somebody developed typhoid fever, either their body defenses had to get rid of the disease or they died. I was one of the lucky ones who survived. While I was recovering from typhoid fever, one of the muscles of the inner aspect of my left eye ruptured, so my left eye became cross-eyed.

From age six, I wore glasses. I'm not sure why. Today I know that there is no indication to wear glasses to cure a ruptured eye muscle. To prevent the glass lenses from falling and breaking while I was running, the frame of the glasses went all the way around my ear lobe.

Crowded House

We lived in a house which at the time seemed like a big place. My mother's sister, her husband, and their six children also lived with us. My family (father, mother, two brothers, me and my sister) and the family of my aunt totaled fourteen people that lived in the four-bedroom house. We only had one bathroom and no bath. I remember having to stand in line to use the bathroom. All of us went to the public bath outside of our house once a week. I went to the public female bath with my mother, where I remember seeing naked women. At age six, my mother insisted I go with my father to the public male bath; the reason: "Khosrow was looking at those naked women not like a child!" she said.

Water Reservoir of Our Home

Getting water in Tehran was challenging. We didn't have a pipeline. Instead, once a month, my father got up at five A.M. and went outside to pay off some people who sent water to different houses through a narrow, open canal in the alleys. My father gave them money so that we would not be the first house to get the water. The water delivered first from the reservoir was dirty, as it had accumulated all the dirt stored up in the canal. We actually had a huge water reservoir stored at our house. Even though we were not the first house to get the water, it was still dirty. To make it slightly cleaner, my parents added charcoal and some kind of fish to that reservoir. The fish ate lots of parasites.

Because of the parasites in the water, the only place we were allowed to draw water was one faucet deep in the basement. My mother wrapped this faucet with gauze in order to filter the water and prevent those parasites from coming into the containers we used for storage.

Electricity

We also lacked electricity. Every night my entire family sat in the same room to use one kerosene lamp and read by the dim light. My parents were reading books and us children were reading or doing homework. We wrote with sharp pens dipped in ink. A couple of years later, when we finally got electricity, it seemed unbelievable. My aunt and her family finally built their own house and left our house. Then we had one bedroom for my brothers, a bedroom for my parents, and a bedroom for me and my sister, as well as a living room, dining room, family room, and large basement.

Houses in Tehran in 1947

Neither did we have air conditioning or heating in our house. In summer it was very hot, anywhere from 95 to 110 degrees. We stayed in the basement during the day because that's where it was cooler. In the winter, Tehran was cold and had heavy snows. Some winters we had a lot of snow. Because the houses in Iran were all flat-roofed, when heavy snow came, the owners had to go onto the roof and sweep the snow off. They swept it into the backyard of their house or into the nearby alley. One year, there was more than twelve feet of snow which required city workers to make a tunnel through the snow in the alleys for the residents to go to school and other places. As a kid, it was really fun to walk through the snow tunnels.

Families used a korsi to stay warm, a very large stool-like frame of wood which is covered all around with quilts and blankets. Within the frame, there is a large metal container filled with a special kind of charcoal. Our family sat around the korsi until it warmed our legs and the lower portions of our body. Our faces and the upper portions of our body were still exposed to the cold weather, so it was not ideal.

In the summer, I had to take a nap in the basement after lunch each day. Because I was an active boy, that was difficult, but I did what I was told. One day I heard a lot of noise coming from the alley. I wanted to go out and see what was happening. My parents told me I should not go to the alley because it was dangerous and bad people may be there. While my parents slept, I snuck out. The alley was full of kids. I wondered why the kids had gathered and found out they had a cat. They were putting tar into some walnut shells, and then putting the cat's paws into the walnut shells, making them stick. When the kids followed the cat and the cat tried to run away, it slid all over the place because of its walnut shoes, making the kids laugh. It was not funny for me at all.

Another summer afternoon, when I heard noises from the alley and snuck out, I saw that the kids had a live rat which they had put on trial. One kid was reading what this rat had done and why it had to be hanged (he had been sneaking into houses and stealing food). Another kid was the hanging officer. The rat was found guilty and the kids hanged it by the neck until it was dead. Again, it was not interesting for me.

School in Tehran in 1947

Kids started primary school in Iran at age seven. Apparently, because I was so active, my mother begged the principal of the primary school to allow me to go to the first-year class unofficially when I was only six. The principal said yes. At the end of that year, I had done so well that my teacher asked my parents to go to the Department of Education and get a written request for the school to examine me and, if I passed the examination, to let me attend the second-year class the following year. I took the examination and passed, so I was advanced to the second grade.

Could I Choose my Food as a Child?

When I came from school one day, I asked my mother what we were having for dinner. When she told me, I said I didn't like whatever she had said. My mother answered that it was the only food we had. A little bit later, I smelled the food and heard my family eating. I was very hungry, but no one called me to come to dinner. I had trouble sleeping that night. In the middle of night, I went to the kitchen and could not find any food. Those days there was no refrigerator in our kitchen. The next morning, I told my mother I could not sleep because I was so hungry. She said that it was my fault. She told me that she made dinner and I said I didn't like it. She told me that I had to learn to eat any food that was available. She further told me there were many people who did not have any food to eat. That was the best lesson. After that, I never said I did not like any food, even to this day.

Primary School

The primary school that I attended was a good one and I liked it. I was also a good student. The schools were separated by gender, so I attended the boy's school. I must admit sometimes I was a bad boy. We had a woman teacher and I bet with my classmates what color underwear she had. In order to see her underwear, I dropped a pencil on the floor and when I tried to pick it up from the floor, I could see her underwear. Other than that, I was a pretty good kid.

Society of Beneficence and Improvement

When I was about seven, my cousins and I established a society named the "Society of Beneficence and Improvement." Every weekend, we gathered in one of our houses and discussed how we could collect money from members of our family to help poor people. These society meetings were serious matters; we had a president, vice president, treasurer, secretary, etc. Sometimes we created lottery tickets and sold them to members of our family during our monthly dinner parties. The money we collected was spent to buy clothing for poor people.

Many years later, one of my cousins in the society got his Bachelor's degree from Yale University, Master's degree from Harvard University, and Ph.D. from Oxford University in England. When he was twenty eight years old, he returned to Iran to get married. Before his marriage, we gathered together in his parent's house and he found the signboard with the name of our childhood society. We remembered those years fondly and took a picture of the cousins standing next to the signboard.

One summer when I was ten years old, my mother and my oldest brother took me and my sister to a special area named Obe Ask (Water of Ask), LariJohn, where there was a natural reservoir thought to help heal eczema. It was located on the top of a mountain beside a large river.

There was no hotel, so we stayed in tents located beside the river.

To get to the natural reservoir, we had to climb the mountain next to the river. We went every day to that special water reservoir. One day, when I came out of the reservoir, I looked down the mountain at the river and saw our tent. I wondered why I should follow the path down the mountain when I could go straight down to the tent. I started to run downhill. Of course, I did not know that I would quickly reach a tall cliff. I could not stop myself and fell down the mountain about 100 feet. I was lucky; I fell over a young tall tree which bent over and took me to the ground. If I had not fallen on that young tree, I would have died. When I got up, I saw many cuts on the skin of my chest and abdomen that were bleeding. I walked to the shore of the river and washed my cuts with water and also washed my shirt. Then I went inside the tent, changed my shirt, and slept. I never told my mother what had happened. I felt so lucky to be alive!

Figure 2: Reunion of Some Members of the "Society of Beneficence and Improvement"

Acting and Producing Theater

I loved to see movies and I had a big notebook to write about each movie I saw. I put the name of the movie, and the names of the actors, actresses, producer and director. I wrote what I thought of the movie and also put between one to five stars on the top of page to rate the movie. As you can see, from childhood I was interested in acting and making theater. When I was ten years old, I decided to make a play. In those days, Iranian schools didn't have amphitheaters or stages where I could hold my play. I kept looking around our house and neighborhood and finally found an empty old stable that was not being used. I decided to use it for my play. A couple of other kids and I cleaned out the stable, put benches for the audience, and made a stage for performing the play. I don't remember the entire story that I wrote, but I remember a crime occurred and I was a detective. On the first night of the performance of this show, a few of our teachers and many parents and kids attended, filling the benches to watch the show. In the play, when my character arrived at the house of a man under suspicion for murder, I asked him where he had been on a certain day and what happened. He denied everything. I saw a spot of blood on the floor and I asked him, "Where is this blood from?" One of the audience members, a student, screamed, "Your mother had a period." The entire crowd laughed, but I didn't pay attention and continued my acting. When I finished acting that night, many kids and a couple of teachers came to me and said I acted very well. That play was my first experience of acting, editing and directing a play.

Movie Production at Age of 11

In those days, there was no television and the cousins from our family always gathered at one house or another to play together on the weekend. We were very close. When I was 11, I made a movie with my cousins. Video cameras were available but they did not record sound. Therefore, when we made the movie, we recorded the audio and background music on a tape recorder and ran the video and tape recorder simultaneously to play the movie. They were in perfect sync and no one knew they were not from one machine. One of my cousins, who was six months older than me, owned the video camera and was a good cameraman. The movie was an action thriller with policemen and thieves. The story was about a bunch of thieves who went in a big store at night. They broke in and stole a lot of expensive products and, while going home, the police stopped them and arrested them, then took them to prison. Later on, they were tried and were convicted, and then they were put in jail for few years. We gathered the costumes for the movie from our houses. No adult helped us. We showed that movie in many family gatherings and everyone loved it. When we showed the movie, we got money from members of family for the "Society of Beneficence and Improvement." We used the money and bought clothing and dresses and gave it to poor people.

When my videographer cousin turned seventeen, he left Iran to come to California to finish high school in the United States. After one year, he wrote to his father that he was interested in going to movie production school. His father told him that he would not pay a dime for that type of education. That was the mentality of the older Iranian people at that time; they thought that playing in movies, producing a movie, or playing music were low-class occupations. My cousin went to school and became an architect instead. After he completed his education, he got a job in Los Angeles and, while he was working as an architect, he applied to a school to learn movie production. He was accepted. He told me that his acceptance was due solely to the movie he made at age of twelve with me and our cousins.

My cousin graduated from movie production school in Los Angeles and married an American woman. After they had a son, they went to Iran where he made multiple popular movies. Unfortunately, a few years after he returned to Iran, he developed lymphoma[1] of his stomach. It was diagnosed only after it had metastasized to other parts of his body and he died nine months later.

---

[1] Lymphoma of the lymph glands of the neck, throat and groin are found quickly because they are close to the surface of the skin or because they cause a sore throat. The patient can go to the doctor, be quickly diagnosed and be treated by radiation or chemotherapy satisfactorily. When lymphomas start to grow inside of the stomach, they create symptoms only after they become very large. At that time, they have already spread to other parts of the body, making the disease untreatable.

Bicycle

I had many cousins close to my age and we liked each other. On some weekends they came to our house and other times, I went to their houses. Two of my closest cousins had bicycles and I didn't. When I was eleven, I asked my mom to buy me a bicycle. She said if I got good grades for sixth grade, she would do so. I studied hard, got good grades, and my mom told me I won the money for purchasing a bicycle. Since riding a bicycle in our neighborhood was dangerous, she said that instead of buying the bicycle, she would put the money in my bank account. Do you expect an eleven-year-old kid to care about money in the bank? I was very upset, felt betrayed, and was sad when I didn't get a bicycle.

Water Painting Postcards to Buy a Bicycle

In 1906, the first Congress in Iran was established. My grandfather (my mother's father) became a Congressman in the fifth term of the Congress. He was also the first person in Iran to collect stamps and sell the collected old stamps. He was the first person in Iran to establish stores to sell office supplies, writing equipment, school books and notebooks. After his death, four of his sons established the same types of stores in multiple parts of Tehran. I used to go to their stores once in a while. I was attracted to postcards of scenery from different parts of Iran. Some in black-and-white, some in color. At that time, there were no color photo pictures, so one day when I was in the store, I asked one of the salesmen how they got colored post cards. He said there was a guy who used water paints to paint the black and white postcards with different colors. I asked him if the store sold water paints and he said yes. I asked to buy some and he said yes, so I bought a lot of water paint, a painting brush, and thirty black-and-white postcards. I brought them home and tried to paint them with the water paint. My mother thought I was playing, but I was really planning to paint those postcards so well that I could take them to my uncle (my mother's brother) to sell. (I should mention that in those days in Iran, no kids worked in the summer because there was no work for them). After a lot of practice, I thought I was painting the postcards very nicely. I took a bunch of them to my uncle. Before I showed them to him, I asked him how much he paid for color post-

Figure 3: Sample of My Water Painting By Hand at Age 11

cards. He said what was equivalent to 20 cents per postcard. I showed him the postcards that I painted and he was surprised that I painted them. He said I did a very good job. I asked him if I could paint the black-and-white postcards for him in order for me to earn money. said, "Of course," and that was my hobby the rest of the summer. I saved the money I earned in a box at home. When the summer was almost finished, I knew I had enough money to buy a bicycle. I went to my mom and told her I had earned my own money and I wanted to buy a bicycle. When my mother saw the money, she was frustrated and upset because she thought I stole the money. When she asked me where I got the money, I told her I had been painting black-and-white postcards and I showed her some of my work. I said water painting the postcards was my work that summer. She said, "I thought you were just playing with the paint." She asked me who paid me and I said, "Your brother, my uncle." She really couldn't believe that so when she saw my uncle, she asked him and he confirmed that he had been paying me all summer for my work. My mother said that money I made was very valuable and told me that she was going to put it in the bank for me. Then she told me she would come with me and I could choose any kind of bicycle I wanted, with anything on it; she would buy it for me. So, I finally got my bicycle. That made me very happy. I had that bicycle for many, many years. I used to ride it from home to school throughout my middle school and high school years; the schools were a few miles from home. After that, I water-painted many black-and-white pictures of my family members.

Even after I left home for medical school, I used that bicycle during my summer holidays when I returned home. When I finished medical school, I gave the bicycle to our gardener's son; the bicycle was still in good shape after 13 years.

Persian New Year "Nowruz"

Nowruz marks the first day of spring and the beginning of the year in the Iranian calendar. It is celebrated on the day of the astronomical Northward equinox, which usually occurs on March 21 or the previous or following day, depending on where it is observed. As well as being a Zoroastrian holiday and having significance for the Zoroastrian ancestors of modern Iranians, it is celebrated in parts of the south Asian sub-continent as the New Year. The moment the sun crosses the celestial equator and equalizes night and day is calculated exactly every year so that Iranian families can gather together to observe their rituals.

Years after the Arabs invaded Persia and forced the Moslem religion on the people of Persia, Ferdowsi authored the Shah Nameh, "King's Letter," which was epic poetry that explained the legendary history of Persia. His thirty thousand poems were fables which he made up about the history of Persia. In his book, he said the King, Jamshid, took his throne to the sky and created Nowruz (New Day), which was the beginning of the New Year. This New Year was present at time of the Achaemenid kingdom twenty five hundred years ago. The only country which was invaded by Arabs and kept their original language was Persia; this was due to Ferdowsi's poetry, which kept the Persian language alive. To this day, every Iranian is proud of Ferdowsi.

Originally a Zoroastrian festival, and the holiest of all, Nowruz is believed to have been invented by Zoroaster himself, although there is no clear date of origin. Since the Achaemenid era, the official year has begun with the New Day when the Sun leaves the zodiac of Pisces and enters the zodiacal sign of Aries, signifying Spring Equinox. Nowruz is also a holy day for Sufis, Bektashis, Ismailis, Alawites, Alevis, and Babis.

At Nowruz in Iran, the schools were closed for two weeks and everybody got new clothes. In every house, the traditional table setting of Jamshid Nowruz included seven specific items beginning with the letter "S," known as Haft Sin. These items signified life, health, wealth, abundance, love, patience and purity. These items also have astrological correlations to the planets of Mercury, Venus, Mars, Jupiter, and Saturn, and the sun and the moon.

The Haft Sin items were sabzeh (wheat or lentil sprouts representing rebirth), samanu (creamy pudding made from germinated wheat regarded as holy and symbolizing affluence), seeb (apple symbolizing health and beauty), senjid (dried fruit of lotus tree which stands for love), sir (garlic regarded as medicinal and representing health), somagh (sumac berries signifying the color of the sun and the victory of good over evil) and serkeh (vinegar representing old age and patience).

When the Arabs invaded Persia, Persians continued to make the Nowruz table for the New Year and, to silence the Arab invaders, they put a volume of the Koran on the table. The Persian people continue to love and respect Old Persian history and beliefs.

New Year gifts were given by adults to their children and usually were brand new bank notes (money).

Thirteen days after New Year is called Ceesdahbedar. All members of each family leave their homes and go to parks to celebrate. While they are at the parks, they throw away the sabzeh, the wheat or lentil sprouts which had been on the Nowruz table.

I personally loved Nowruz because my parents bought me a new suit, and my parents, older brothers, aunts and uncles gave me brand new bank notes (money). We always gathered at my grandmother's house the first day of spring with our extended family. Before New Year, my parents took me to a tailor to measure me for a new suit. We had to have several fittings so the tailor could make the perfect suit. After Nowruz, we wore our new suit to special occasions and wore the suit from the last year to school. When I became older, I loved Nowruz even more because I found out that our New Year had no relation to any religion.

My Mother Advised Me Through the Stories Which She Told Me

I had one of the best mothers that any child could wish to have. When I was growing up, there was no work for women outside of the house, but my mother performed many jobs in the house. She spent all the money that she and my father made on behalf of our well-being and care. Every success her children had is due to her. She always put her children before herself. When I was a child, every night before I went to sleep, she told me a story. When I got older, I realized she was imparting important wisdom to me in every one of those stories. Through the telling of stories, my mother warned me about bad people and homosexual activity of some men, even clergymen. At that time, homosexual activity was not legal in any part of Iran.

One night, my mother told me a story about two young men named Hamid and Reza who decided to leave their hometown and go and live in another city. A few days after their arrival in their new town, they heard that several young boys were missing and their parents could not find them. One day when they were walking in the street, they saw a large group of men walking together. They started following the group of men and Hamid asked one of them where they were going. The man said they were following their great Moslem clergyman who was going to talk to them about their religion. He said that Hamid and Reza could join them. While they were walking with the group, they heard a tingling bell sound. Hamid asked the man where the sound came from. The man said the clergyman wore bells on his shoes so the ants and other insects would not be crushed under his shoes. Reza held the hand of his friend and told him to slow down, which he did. When they were far enough away from the group, Hamid said, "I bet this clergyman is stealing the young boys who are missing in this city." Reza said, "Are you crazy?!" Hamid said, "No, I am so certain that I'll bet you two pounds of saffron." Saffron is the stamen of a special flower that can be added to cooked rice to give it a special color and wonderful smell. Saffron was very expensive, costing approximately ten thousand dollars for two pounds at that time. Reza said, "I will bet with you, but how you can prove it?" Hamid said, "I will dress you in felt material. I will play the drum and you can dance. Gradually, we will find out where that clergyman lives and we will try to get inside of his house." Hamid listened to Reza and wore a funny outfit made of felt. Hamid played and Reza danced. Some people stopped to watch them and gave them some money. Hamid and Reza finally found the house of the clergyman and stopped to play in front of his house.

One day, one of the servants of the clergyman asked them to come that night to play and dance for the clergyman. When they arrived that night, they noticed the clergyman drinking vodka. In the Moslem religion, drinking alcohol is strongly prohibited. After an hour, the clergyman clapped his hands and several young boys came out of the basement and began to dance in front of the clergyman. At the same time, Hamid was playing his drum and singing, "Please buy me the saffron!" Reza was dancing and singing, "Listen to the trick of the clergyman." After they left the clergyman's house, they went to the police station and told them they found the young boys who had been stolen. The police went to the house of the clergyman and saved all the young boys and arrested the clergyman.

Homosexuality was not accepted between Iranian people at that time. I am sure there were individuals who were homosexual, but in those days they did not dare to admit to homosexuality.

Another night, my mother told me another story which she said was true. She said a few years after Reza Shah became the king, some teenage boys were missing in Tehran. He ordered a special group of police to spread around the city undercover. In Tehran, there were a lot of street vendors who had different sweet foods or desserts. Some of them had a large roll of sweet material. After you paid them, you picked up the end of the sweet roll and broke off a piece. Apparently one of these sellers was a criminal homosexual. When he saw a teenage boy, he gave him some of this sweet material without charging him. Then he told him, "If you come with me, I will show you how I make those sweet rolls and give you a larger piece." When the boy went with him, he raped him. Then he put something in his mouth, tied his hands up and dropped him in a deep well. One day, one of those secret police followed this guy who was walking with young boy. When he took the boy inside his house, the policeman heard the voice of young boy. He broke into the house, arrested the guy, and freed the young boy. The police took that guy to court and he was found guilty of murdering several young boys after raping them. He was hanged in public.

My mother told me this true story so I would be scared and not follow any man to his house.

Family

My grandfather had five daughters, including my mother, and six sons. One son died from tuberculosis when he was young. Another son became a lawyer. The other four sons opened up stores throughout Tehran. I never met my grandfather who died before I was born, but we went to my grandmother's house on many occasion. We had a big family dinner party each month at different relatives' houses with about sixty family members in attendance. The host prepared the dinner for this large group of people. My oldest aunt (my mother's sister) married a man who became the richest person in Iran. Before the fall of the Shah (Mohammed Reza Shah Pahlavi) in 1979, my uncle and his sons owned sixty major businesses in Iran. In 1953, the youngest son was twelve years old when he and his parents left Iran and came to Scarsdale, New York. His parents came back to Iran after two years.

The Most Significant Mother

When my mother married my father in Iran in 1927, her father had made the decision for her marriage and also the marriage of his other daughters. My mother told me she never met my father until the night of their marriage. In those days, arranged marriages were common. My father was twenty years older than my mother. My mother received gifts of jewelry from members of her family on the night of her marriage. My father did not own a house so she moved into the house he was renting. My father worked at the national bank and his job was counting the old money that they wanted to destroy. He typically spent his salary in the first two weeks of the month which meant that he had to borrow money for the last two weeks of the month. When my mother found this out, she decided that she needed to manage the family finances, so she told my father to give his salary to her and she would pay the expenses. She was not used to living in a rented house and decided they needed to buy a house. That was difficult since they did not have a lot of money. A few years after their marriage, my mother bought a house by selling all her jewelry to get a down payment. She also rented half of the new house in order to pay the mortgage. She also started to work inside the house to help pay the mortgage since there was no outside work for women in Iran. I don't remember exactly what kind of work she was doing, but her work at home helped us to have a better life.

My parents had different views of life. My father believed as long as we had a room to sleep in, some food to eat, and simple clothing to wear, that's all we needed. My mother was completely different. My mother wanted to have a good house, good clothing for herself and her children, and nice furniture. She taught me every good thing I learned. I owe every success that I have had in my life to my mom. I respected her a lot when I was a child and missed her greatly after she passed away in 1968.

She was always reading and taught me to memorize poems. The Persian language is a poetic language and she knew many poems. When we didn't have electricity and we all sat in one room, I saw my mother concentrating on the book she was reading. I asked her what kind of book it was and she said the book was for adults, not for children. Of course, that piqued my interest and I had to find out what kind of book it was. After she finished reading that book, I found out where she put it. I took the book and put it inside my school book, so it looked like I was just reading my school book. I started reading that book. It had been translated from English or French into Farsi. The name of that book was Booseh Azra (The Kiss of Mary). This book was all about the horrible things that were done in the 16th century in the churches of Europe. For a young kid to read such a book was very interesting because it was describing how bad priests were using their authority as priests to abuse the women that came to the church asking the priests for help. I cannot forget one part of that book in which a woman came crying to the priest about what was happening at her home. The priest told her he had to examine her and after he touched her body, he said there was a devil inside her body and he had to take it out. He started to have sex with her. He kept saying he caught the devil but the devil ran away. He used that excuse to have sex with her frequently. That book contained stories of many other crimes done by priests in those days. Reading that book shocked me, because I never thought those priests who were supposed to guide and help people used their authority to abuse young boys and women who came to the church.

As a physician, I can tell you that the God who created us created major differences between men and women. Even those individuals who become homosexuals anatomically, hormone-wise, and physiologically have no difference with the rest of people.

When I became older and studied more about Christianity and the churches, I was surprised about the rules of Catholic churches. Although Jesus Christ never said the Christian advisers should not have sex or act as a man, when the Catholic Church was established they made the rule, even though the God who created human beings gave men testes and women ovaries. And, of course, we have a lot of other Christians who believe in Jesus that have nothing in their faith like this. This Catholic rule has resulted in prohibited relationships between priests and women, or priests and boys.

Surgery of my Eye Muscle

When I finished primary school, I asked my mother to take me to the doctor to fix my eye. I told her I would not go to middle school if my eye was not fixed because the kids made fun of me and it embarrassed me.

My mother took me to an ophthalmologist who had been trained in England. He was a professor of ophthalmology and the Chairman of the Department of Ophthalmology of the medical center of the Central Bank of Iran. He agreed that I needed surgery to repair the ruptured muscle of my left eye. I was so happy on the day of the surgery that I was climbing the stairs faster than the nurse who was going with me to the operating room. She told me I was the bravest kid that she had ever seen and that not even adults ran toward the operating room. Well, she didn't know that bravery was not the reason. The embarrassment of having a crossed eye was the reason; I wanted it fixed as soon as possible.

They put me on the operating table. The doctor was going to do the surgery under local anesthesia. When he put the needle around my eye to put in the numbing medicine, it hurt a lot. I remember that I did not move and I just said, "Ouch." The surgeon slapped me in the face on both sides and that kept me completely quiet. The surgery took more than an hour and a half. They wrapped both eyes after the surgery so I could not see anything. The first night that I was in the hospital, I was on full bed rest. The nurse did not raise the side rail of the bed and I fell out. The next morning, the surgeon came and found out that I had fallen out of the bed. He became upset and screamed at the nurses. After he removed the bandages from both of my eyes, he was glad that the fall had not harmed me. He sent me home and told me that I should return to see him within a week to get the stitches out.

The day that I was supposed to get my stitches out, a revolution was apparently festering in Tehran. We did not have a car and there was no cab or bus available on that day, so my mother and I walked to the hospital. As we walked, I saw a large crowd of people demonstrating and I saw multiple tanks coming in to one big square. It was interesting for me to see the demonstration, soldiers and tanks. I had never seen any of those things before and I wasn't sure what was happening. Fortunately, when we reached the doctor's office; he removed the stitches and said everything was fine. I was able to walk back home with my mother. My eyes were fine. That was a critical moment in my life as I was able to gain confidence and look to the future (pun intended).

Years later, when I came to the United States at age 27, I went to a professor of ophthalmology at George Washington University for a check-up and I told him about my previous surgery. After he examined my eyes carefully, he said he never saw such an excellent result for

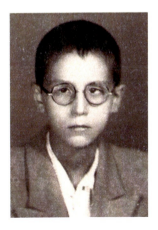 

Figure 4: My Pictures at Ages Ten and Eleven, Before and After Eye Muscle Surgery

muscle surgery in the eye and that if I hadn't told him I had surgery, he never would have known by his examination.

Swimming and Diving

My father was working in the National Bank of Tehran (the largest bank of Iran), which had a sports club with had a swimming pool, diving boards, and multiple clay tennis courts available to employees and their families. In the summer, I swam there every day after teaching myself to swim. There were two diving boards, one ten-feet high and the other sixteen-feet high. I started with the short diving board as I was afraid of the higher one. One day, I asked another kid to climb with me to the high dive and push me off so I wouldn't be scared anymore. At first he refused, but after I kept begging him, he accepted my request and pushed me off the high dive. That was the beginning of my high diving, which I soon came to love. At age 11, I became the champion of backstroke swimming in Tehran, which had a population of two million people at that time.

When we went to see a movie, the theater played the national anthem of Iran prior to showing the film. During the anthem, the theater showed pictures of different places and events in Iran. One day I was surprised to see my own picture taken during the swimming championship, which made me proud.

Figure 5: Climbing the Alborz Mountain of Northern Tehran

Climbing the Mountains

From age twelve, I was climbing the mountains located in northern Tehran with my brothers and cousins. We usually started to climb a mountain located in northern Tehran at five or six in the morning. When we reached the top of the mountain, we sat beside a small river and ate breakfast. We played different games for a while, then at noon we warmed our lunch on the fire and ate our lunch together. In the afternoon we descended from the mountain and everyone went home.

Alborz High School

After primary school, I attended a private high school in Tehran (in Iran, there were no separate middle schools). Alborz High School had 2000 students, all of them boys. Although my family could not afford private school, I was able to attend for free because my oldest brother was a teacher there at that time. It was not only the biggest middle and high school in Tehran, it was also the best.

The Alborz School was founded as an elementary school in 1873 by a group of American missionaries led by James Bassett. The first president of this school was an American. As part of Reza Shah Pahlavi's reforms, in 1926 the school was removed from American ownership and management for which Iran paid two million dollars to the United States. The school was then placed under the auspices of Iran's Ministry of Education.

When I was in seventh grade, there was a lot of political turmoil in Tehran. The Prime Minister, Dr. Mosadegh, was forced to resign. Some people of Tehran demonstrated on his behalf and the soldiers attacked the demonstrators. The government put several soldiers armed with large guns in the lobby of my school and in the hallway of each building. Although I was only twelve years old, I understood the political issues and supported the demonstrations by distributing banned newspapers. One day, while a bunch of kids and I were demonstrating in front of the school to support the cause, a truck full of soldiers stopped. The soldiers got off the truck and attacked us. One hit me forcefully with the back of his gun and I fell into a stream of water, face down on the side of the street. Fortunately, I was not harmed. This was the beginning of political activism in my life.

This school had the best teachers of Tehran; it was a very good school. We had good sports facilities compared to other schools, including a soccer field, and courts for basketball and volleyball.

When I was in eighth grade, jean trousers were not available or worn in Iran. One of my relatives brought me a pair of jeans from America and, when I wore it, everyone looked at me because they had never seen them before. My algebra teacher called me in front of the class to answer some questions regarding the algebra lessons. I answered incorrectly and he made fun of me not only because I answered incorrectly, but also because of my pants. I mention this to show how people reacted to anything new. Now everyone around the world has seen jean trousers and nobody pays attention to them, even in Iran.

Although my brother told the person who scheduling classes not to put me in his class, the scheduler made a mistake and did so anyway. My brother was teaching Persian literature, language and grammar. One of the tasks my brother gave every student was to memorize 25 long poems. I knew that my brother was going to be especially hard on me so that none of my classmates would think he showed favoritism toward me. At the end of each school year, we had two types of examinations, one written and one oral. My brother called ten students and spent about five minutes with each student during their oral examination. I was in the last group.

Although he asked every other student only five minutes of questions, when he got to me, he asked me to recite all of the 25 poems he had asked us to memorize, and then asked many difficult grammar questions. He spent an hour questioning me. I was lucky and passed the examination and nobody accused him of favoritism.

School hours were from eight A.M. to noon, two hours off, and then we returned to school from two to five P.M. During the break, kids who lived far away from school like me brought lunch or ate outside of the school. If we had any free time, we played soccer with a small ball, not a soccer ball. Sometimes older kids in the school took that ball and started kicking it in the air; they didn't allow us to play with our own ball and seemed to enjoy tormenting us. Once I went to a higher class student and begged him to give us the ball back, explaining that we had been having fun. He kicked the ball into the air and didn't give it back to me. I pulled my leg all the way back and kicked him as hard as I could in his shin. Because of the pain, he bent over and could not follow me. I ran away. He never knew who I was and didn't catch me. But I still didn't get the ball back.

My Classmates at Alborz High School

At Alborz High School, students were assigned to classes alphabetically by their last name. As a result, many of us were in the same classes for six years. Some of us became good friends and sometimes we did mischief.

For example, when we got a heavy snow, we asked the strong kids to stand beside a big tree while the small kids like me made snowballs. The high school for girls was near our school and, during lunch break, a lot of girls passed us on their way home. We smaller children hit them with snowballs, then the stronger kids shook the trees and the snow fell down on them. That was really fun for us!

One day we hit the girls with snowballs during lunch break. After lunch, I was standing in front of a new building opposite the school which was not complete and, as the girls were coming back from lunch and walking toward their school, I hit them with snowballs again. One girl stood up and said "Which zoo are you from?" I pointed to our school and she asked me: "This zoo?"

In class that afternoon, a person from the superintendent's office came to tell me that the superintendent wanted to see me, so I went to his office. The superintendent said he knew me, and knew that I had been in the school for six years with no complaints about me. He said that on this day somebody complained that I had been hitting the girls with snowballs. I was going to deny it, but saw that the lower portion of my pants was wet and I knew I could not lie. So I admitted that yes, I did it. He said the headmaster of the girls school called him and said, "Sir, there are girls complaining that one of your students is hitting them with snowballs. The name that most of the girls mentioned was Matini." He told me "that type of popularity would not be good for me." I thanked him for his advice and promised I would never do it again. I left his office and returned to class.

When I was a senior student, there were people near the school who sold cigarettes, chocolate, and gum. We could even buy just one cigarette. We tried to act like smokers because we thought the girls would like that. Just that one cigarette a day got some of us addicted, including me; I became a smoker later on.

Figure 6: Me and My Best Classmates at Alborz High School

My Parents' New House

My mother was a smart lady and bought an inexpensive piece of land in the suburbs of Tehran, many years before she built a house on it. After a few years, when the land became more valuable, she sold half of the land and started to build a house on the other half. I was 16 years old when the building was completed.

When we were packing to move, I offered to help my mother pack the fragile things. She always trusted me and accepted my help. I packed all the china, crystal and glasses myself; some of which were antiques. After the packing was completed, movers came and put everything we owned in a big truck and took our belongings to our new home.

When we came to this new house, I was anxious to open the boxes I had packed to make sure nothing was broken. The electricity was not connected to our new house yet. The truck arrived at six P.M. and I opened the boxes that I packed and found everything was intact. I wanted to take several antique china dishes to my mother to show her that everything I packed was in good shape. Because there was no electricity, it was dark and I missed a step because I was unfamiliar with the new house. Instead of taking three steps, I took two steps and fell face down. Needless to say, much of the antique china was broken. At first, I was afraid that I had hurt myself, but I soon realized that I did not. Then I was worried that my mother would be upset with me about breaking her antique china, so I acted like I was knocked out. This worked well because all the family was concerned about my condition; they were concerned when I didn't answer them and thought I was badly hurt. They forgot about the china and, after a few minutes when I saw they didn't care about the broken china and their concern was just for my health, I gradually opened my eyes. My family was so happy that I wasn't hurt. I never told my mother or other members of my family that I did such a bad thing.

Around our new house, I saw so many varieties of beautiful butterflies which I had never seen before. I started to catch those beautiful butterflies with my hand and put them on the wall of my room with needles after I killed them by electricity. I had a collection of beautiful butterflies on the wall of my room.

Olive Oil Lamp

I also started to make night lights using the skin of a tangerine and olive oil. I cut the skin of a tangerine in the middle and carefully took off the upper and lower tangerine skin. Then I made multiple holes in the upper portion, and poured olive oil inside of the lower skin in which I had put a large stick in the center. I lit the large stick and it resulted in the most beautiful night light with a wonderful smell. It could be used for several nights.

My First Sexual Experience

I was sixteen years old and still a virgin, which was not uncommon for adolescents in Iran at that time. In fact, most Iranians only had their first sexual experience on the night of their marriage. One night, one of my sister's classmates, who was also her friend, stayed overnight in our house. After dinner and doing my homework, I went to bed and fell sleep. Suddenly, I smelled a nice smell and felt someone touch me. When I opened my eyes, it was my sister's friend. I asked her why she came to my room and she said, "Keep quiet, I love you and I came here to have sex with you." I had no idea what to do. Apparently, she realized that and told me, "Be quiet, I'll show you what you have to do." She took her clothes off and took my clothes off and started to hug and kiss me. She put my hand on her breasts and taught me what I had to do. Nature took over from there. I didn't see her again until my sister got married. We both acted like it had never happened.

Figure 7: Family Member Orchestra at the Marriage of My Oldest Brother

My Oldest Brother Gets Married

When I was sixteen years old, my oldest brother got married in the city of Meshed, where his wife was from. The marriage took place on Persian New Year. I went with other members of the family on a bus to Meshed. This was one of the best weddings I ever attended. There were about thirty members of our family who came from Tehran to Meshed for the wedding. We all stayed in the large kindergarten school where my future sister-in-law worked as the principal. We ate together and sang and danced every night for twelve nights.

Creation

I was very good at writing compositions during my senior year. We had a teacher who gave us a topic to write about every week. He was an open-minded teacher. He told our class that they should put the name the student on the blackboard whose composition they most wanted to hear. One day, he gave us a topic which was interesting: If you were the creator, how would you create your creature?

Since most of the kids knew I wrote compositions well and that topic was interesting, they put my name on the blackboard to hear my essay. When the teacher came to the class, he called me to read it.

The composition I wrote at age seventeen went something like this: The creation is very difficult and unbelievable; however, when we look at the history of creation, we know that at first there was a creature with just a few cells, and then later on little fish, then frogs, birds, and gradually bigger animals, then a monkey and eventually human beings. Even the first human beings who were created were not similar to the human beings of today. Human beings of every generation are better than the previous generation. The creator is improving his work. I am sure that the creator does not enjoy creating creatures and then getting rid of them. Therefore, the creator probably has not been able to keep creatures alive forever or have them stay young permanently. When we see a wonderful young boy or girl who gets sick and dies, it is definitely not the desire of the creator (God). I am sure death is not under his control. Every religion believes in heaven and hell, but I believe when we die, we are gone for good. Maybe one day God will be able to keep human beings healthy, young and alive forever.

At that point, the teacher told me to stop and sit down. He did not allow me to finish reading the rest of my composition. My classmates asked my teacher why he wouldn't let me finish. My teacher asked if they would like to see their teacher be taken to jail because he was allowing a student to talk against God. The kids started to laugh.

That was one of the most interesting things that ever happened to me in high school. I still believe what I wrote. I did not believe after we die we would be brought back to earth as promised by prophets of many religion. This tenet has been a good marketing campaign for every religion. All religions have tried to tell people that their lives are a trial of their performance. I did not believe that philosophy then, nor do I believe it today.

If God was able to keep us forever young and healthy, he would also be able to make us good people without any bad behavior. In that case, there would be no reason to get rid of us and then one day bring us back again. I believe today what I wrote at that time.

Googoosh (Famous Singer of Iran)

While still in high school, I went to ski in the mountain suburbs of Tehran called Damavand, about an hour and a half drive from home. I did not have a car so I usually took the bus. On one of those days, the bus's tires went flat and we had to stop so the driver could change the tire. The bus driver asked all of the passengers to get off the bus. We had to stand outside in very cold and windy weather. One passenger had a bottle of vermouth and gave a shot to everybody so they could warm up. Everybody thanked him. He had a 5-year-old daughter that he put on the hood of the bus; then he asked her to sing. She started to sing and, because she had a wonderful voice, she got the attention of all the passengers. Later on, that girl named Googoosh became the most famous singer in Iran for years and years. About thirteen years ago, she finally came to the United States to give multiple concerts. I was able to attend two concerts, one in Washington, D.C. and the other in Las Vegas. In 2012, she came back to Washington again. I was able to attend her concert along with my American wife, who liked the concert a lot in spite of the songs being in the Farsi language. Music transcends cultures.

Deciding to Go to Medical School

When I was in high school, I loved flowers and was thinking of becoming an agriculture engineer to raise and sell flowers. I was able to talk to a couple of agriculture engineers who worked for the government. They suggested that if I wanted to be an agriculture engineer and raise flowers that either my parents should be rich or I should own a lot of land. Neither of these was true for me.

About that time, I saw a movie called "The Men" in which Marlon Brando played a paralyzed man in a wheelchair who had sustained a severe injury to his back when he was an army soldier. The movie was about several paralyzed individuals who could not stand on their feet or walk. That movie affected me so much that I decided to become a doctor and later a neurosurgeon to try find a way to correct paralysis and help paralyzed people live better.

Preparation for College or Medical School

I was not a top student in high school. When I started 12th grade, one day my oldest brother, a teacher at my high school, asked me to come to his room so we could talk. He indicated that he wanted to talk to me about my future. He said that many of our cousins went to the United States or Europe for further education when they became 17 or 18 years old, but he said that unfortunately, my parents could not afford to send me to those places for education. He said a good education was available in Iran (at that time it was paid for by the Government), but there weren't many universities and there was incredibly stiff competition for the spots. Because it was so hard to gain admission to the colleges, many families sent their children to foreign countries for their education. He said if I want to go to college, then I really had to study hard in 12th grade and in the summer after graduation. Only then would I have a chance to pass the entrance examination for the different universities.

He said if I didn't go to college, the military would draft me for two years. After that, I could get a job making $30 to $40 per month. I thanked him for his advice and left his room, then sat down to ponder what he had said. I decided that I had to study really hard if I wanted a good future. From that point on, I studied every night and, during the summer after I graduated from high school, I studied about 16 hours a day to prepare myself for entrance exams. At that time, each college in Iran had a separate examination; even the medical schools had different and separate examinations. The university which I applied to for medical school was located in the city of Meshed, about eight hundred miles from Tehran. I also applied to Agriculture Engineering School and the School of Dentistry in Tehran.

First Trip to Meshed by Myself

When I went to Meshed to take the entrance examination of the medical school, it was the first time I had traveled by myself outside of Tehran. My second brother went to buy the train ticket for me and when he came home, he said unfortunately the only ticket available was a third-class one. I took a taxi and went to the train located in the southern part of Tehran. After I showed the ticket to the train attendant, he showed me my seat, which was located next to the window. Seven other adults and two children were seated in the same room. A lady sat opposite me, also next to the window. She started to ask me questions, including why I was going to Meshed. She seemed about thirty years old and was pretty. When the evening started and the weather become darker, she started to hold my hand and sing love songs to me. Later on that night after dinner, when all the other passengers were asleep, she asked me to lie on the floor of that train room. I do not know why I listened to her, but I did what she asked.

After I lay down, she came and quietly laid down over me. She quietly opened the zipper of my pants and started to have sex with me quietly. That was the second time I had sex and I started to understand why people liked sex so much!

Entrance Examination for Medical School of Meshed University

For the medical school at Meshed University, one thousand students took the entrance examination that year and only 81 students were accepted. I was number seven on the acceptance list.

Entrance to Medical School

The medical schools in Iran were completely different from medical schools in the United States. When I graduated from high school in 1959, there were only six medical schools in Iran. There were so many high school graduates who wanted to be doctors and, with only six medical schools in Iran, the total number of students accepted was less than 750 per year for the entire country. Also, there was another difference between Iran and the United States. In Iran, a student did not have to have a college degree before going to medical school. After we passed the entrance examination and were accepted, we had to study for seven years to become a doctor. The first two years we spent in classes or laboratories, in the second and third year we studied anatomy and learned anatomy in French, Latin, and Farsi languages. From the third to the sixth year, we worked mostly in hospitals with just a few hours a day spent in class. In the last year, we became interns and had rotations in internal medicine, obstetrics and gynecology, pediatric and surgery.

My parents could not pay for me to live in another city, so my wonderful brothers decided to help me. For seven years, they paid me every month to be able to live and go to school. For this reason, I was very careful about how I lived. A lot of my classmates played poker once in a while. I never did that. I didn't want to take a chance on losing the money my brothers had sent me. I respected my brothers. My roommate for six years played poker and lost a lot of money. He didn't seem to care that his wonderful parents (who were not rich) had to support him financially.

Meshed University

Meshed University was established about ten years before I attended. It did not have a formal dormitory nor a cafeteria. The medical school rented one floor of a two-story building where it could cheaply rent rooms to non-married students. There was no heating, air conditioning, nor baths in the building. The only thing we had were a few toilets with sinks. The size of each room was 10 by 10 feet and two students lived in each room. In the first week after I arrived, I went to a store and bought a small kerosene heater. I was planning to use this heater to keep the room warm when the weather was cold and also to cook. Fortunately, I had learned how to cook from my mother. When I was about sixteen, I used to go to the kitchen and help her. Although she told me cooking was for women, she seemed glad to have my company and taught me cooking.

The first time that I turned on the kerosene heater, I create a problem. After a few minutes, the heater started to smoke, so I had to open the window. As soon as I opened the window, the heater started to work perfectly. I realized there was nothing wrong with the heater; it just didn't have enough oxygen in that small room. Thereafter, for the seven years I lived in that room, I had to keep the window partly open all year long. The winter was very strong in that city and many times we had two or three feet of snow, but the window was always kept partially open. After I graduated from medical school, a new big and modern dormitory was completed.

Lack of Cafeteria and Dormitory

The lack of a cafeteria was a big challenge since restaurants were very expensive for students to eat in. During the first month, I gathered all the students living in our building and told them that I knew about cooking, and that we should hire a cook to make us lunch. I told them we could choose what kind of food we would like to have for each day, and then we would make a schedule. One student each morning would go with the cook and buy items needed for that day's lunch. Another student would stay with the cook while he was serving lunch to make sure the cook did not steal the food. All the students agreed to my proposal. I found a cook and talked to him about our plan. He accepted my offer and payment. I planned each day's meal and told the assigned student what they had to buy every morning. This program was very successful. The food was excellent and cheap. Two years later, when the university decided to build a cafeteria for the university, they called me and asked me to be a consultant for the project.

Anatomy Course

We started learning anatomy during the second year. We had anatomy class for three days a week over a two year period. Before I started anatomy, one of the students who was two years ahead of me told me that it was much easier to learn anatomy dissecting a thin cadaver, rather than a fat one. He also said if you pay the guy in charge of the anatomy lab, he would give you a thin cadaver. I knew seven students were going to work with me on one cadaver, so I talked with them and asked them for money to give the guy so we could get a better cadaver. After I collected the money, I went and talked to the guy and paid him. He said he was going to leave the door of the cadaver room open for me and after I finished my classes, I could go choose a cadaver. He said the cadavers were kept in a pool and I could put my name on a tag on the cadaver I wanted.

Trapped in the Cadavers Room!

At six P.M., after all my classes were finished, I went to the basement of the anatomy building where the cadaver room was located. I had never seen a cadaver in my life prior to that night. I looked inside of the pool and found a skinny female cadaver. I put my name on a tag and stuck it on the head of that cadaver. When I went to the door of the room to leave, I found it had locked behind me. I screamed a few times and then sat on a concrete seat. Every ten minutes, I went to the door and hit it and also screamed at the top of my lungs. For a person like me who had never seen a dead person, it was very unnerving to sit near several cadavers.

Around nine P.M., I got lucky because the guy in charge had forgotten something that he needed and had returned to the building to pick it up. He heard my voice and opened the door cautiously; it seemed like he was wondering if one of the cadavers was screaming. When he saw me, he could not believe what had happened and seemed quite relieved to find a live person.

My medical school class had 80 male students and only one female student, who was the daughter of the Professor of Obstetrics and Gynecology. Sometimes she went to the anatomy lab earlier than the other students to work on the cadaver by herself. Our anatomy classes started at seven A.M. and when she came earlier, it was still dark. One day, apparently one of our classmates set up the sheet which was covering the cadaver in such a way that when you pulled the sheet off the cadaver, the hand of the cadaver hit whoever pulled off the sheet. So when she pulled off the sheet, the cadaver's hand hit her. She fell down and passed out cold. When we came to anatomy lab a little later, we found her on the floor. Fortunately, she was all right.

Unusual Event at Termination of Anatomy Course

At that time, few students had cameras. One day, a man from a photo shop came to the anatomy lab to take pictures of the students, both with our professors and standing beside multiple dissected cadavers. I asked the photographer to take a picture of me while I was holding an arm and leg of a cadaver; it looked like I was playing a cello.

A few days later, one of my classmates and I went to a photo shop to see the photos and order prints. When we got to the photo of me playing cello using the arm and leg of the cadaver, we started laughing and another customer saw the picture. He became very angry and almost tried to hit us. He was angry that we were playing with a dead body.

I wrote in my will that I am going to donate my body to the anatomy lab of Howard University. I did this because I tried all my life to help people, therefore, even in death I could help the medical students learn anatomy. Another advantage is that my wife and daughter need only call Howard University and they will send somebody

Figure 8: Playing Cello with the Arm and Leg of the Cadaver at the End of the Two Year Anatomy Course in Medical School

to pick up my body free of charge, thus eliminating the cost for burial.

In the third year of medical school, seven of us become close friends. Anytime we had a chance, we got together to play soccer. Afterward, we sat around and joked with each other. The third year of medical school was the most difficult. We had to study anatomy, biochemistry, biology, parasitology, physiology, bacteriology and histology. That year, nine of the 81 medical students failed and had to repeat the third year. Three of our seven friends were among them and I really missed hanging around with them after that.

Omar Khayam, Greatest Poet of Iran

The author of Robaiyat is buried in Neishabour, the neighbor city of Meshed. Many times I visited the grave and read Omar Khayam's poetry.

Figure 9: Me in Front of Omar Khayam's Grave in Neishabour

Lack of Alcoholic Beverages in Meshed

In Meshed, there were no alcoholic beverages available to buy or drink at restaurants. The only place people could drink was in their homes or hotel room. I found out there was a restaurant far away from Meshed which had good rib-eye steaks and served vodka. Once a month, I gathered a few friends and we went to that restaurant mainly to drink vodka, but also to have a good dinner.

Work in the Operating Room of a Private Hospital

During my time in medical school, in addition to working in the university hospital, I worked in the operating rooms of a private hospital at night for no pay because I was interested in surgery and wanted to be an expert at it.

Swimming and Diving at the Caspian Sea!

The Caspian Sea was located between northern Iran and southwestern Russia (Soviet Union at that time). Although it was only a three hour drive from Tehran to the Caspian Sea, I never went there until I was 21 years old. My classmate and roommate at medical school invited me to go to his family's villa, which was located on the beach of the Caspian Sea.

The first day that I arrived, I made a horrible mistake not knowing any better. Since this was the first time I had ever been to the beach, I thought the tall lifeguard chair was a diving board. Of course, there was no guard sitting there when I saw it. I climbed the tower and dived into the water. I didn't realize how shallow the water was near the chair. I hit my hands and head on the sand beneath the water. And I mean I hit hard! Afterwards, of course, my head and hands were hurting very badly. My roommate's father immediately came over and, after examining me, told me to lie down in the sand and then he buried my neck, hands and wrists under the warm sand for several hours. Of course he came to visit me frequently and gave me some water to drink. Fortunately, by nighttime I felt much better. My roommate's father told me a girl made the same stupid mistake a couple of weeks before and she was paralyzed from the neck down. I was lucky!

After that I went to the Caspian Sea beach frequently and sometimes rented a boat. My friend and I went swimming for four to five hours continuously in the sea and the boat followed us closely for safety.

One day when I returned from a long stretch of swimming in the sea, I was lying down in the chair next to the swimming pool of the hotel where we were staying. I saw a middle-aged man encouraging his wife to swim in the swimming pool. When his wife jumped in the deep water, she started drowning because apparently she did not know how to swim. Her husband did not know how to swim either and was hitting his head with his hands in fright. I jumped in the water and saved the heavy-set woman. Her husband came over to thank me and invited me for dinner. When I asked him what happened, he said he thought his wife, who had been taking swimming lessons, had learned how to swim. The husband said he was not planning to kill his wife.

Political Activity

I was not always so smart. I was elected president of my class in my second year of school. Then I was elected as president of the entire medical school when I was a third-year student. I made a big mistake that year. I was interested in the politics of the government and I was against the Shah of Iran and the government at that time. One night, I met one of my close friends in the dormitory and I suggested that, since there were a lot of demonstrations against the government in Tehran University, we could do a similar demonstration at our university. He said this was not possible, because the students in our university were not interested in politics. I told him wait and see.

Demonstration and Closure of University

Our classes started at seven A.M. When the first class finished just before nine A.M., we usually went to the small cafeteria in the school for fifteen minutes until the next class started. Starting at nine A.M., every hour on the hour, the main radio of Tehran broadcasted brief news of the world. By the time we arrived in the cafeteria, the radio was announcing news about the demonstration of students at the University of Algeria and said that fifteen students had been killed. I immediately repeated the news about the killing without mentioning that it was in Algeria. I said that if radio Iran was saying fifteen students were killed in Tehran University, probably more than one hundred students were killed. Then I said that we had to go on strike to support the students of Tehran University. My lies worked very well. We did not go to the next class and started to demonstrate in the school, closing several classes. I sent a friend out and he bought a large speaker and brought it to the school. I started to speak against the government of Iran. A few minutes later, the medical school was surrounded by police. And a few minutes later, they cut off the electricity to the school.

After they cut the electricity, I ran toward the anatomy lab which had its own generator. At the lab, the associate professor of anatomy blocked my way and said that I could not enter the lab. I pushed him back and went into the lab. I connected my speaker to the electricity there and continued my speech. A few minutes later, the police turned off the generator in the anatomy lab but by then, the students of other schools of the university had heard my speeches, joined us, and closed their schools. This demonstration continued for the whole day. In the afternoon, I did not go back to my dormitory because I knew Savak (Organization of Intelligence and National Security) was coming for my arrest. Instead, I went to my brother's house. He was the Vice President of the Faculty of Letters.

When my brother came home, he sat down with me and told me that what I did earlier in that day was wrong. I told him that with all respect I was planning to continue the demonstration and planned to go to the Office of the Governor of the State of Khorasan tomorrow. He again said that this was wrong and I would be arrested. Of course, with youthful stupidity, I did not listen to him.

The next morning, I woke up late because school was closed. My brother and his wife had already left the house. I put my clothes on and went to the door to leave the house. The door was locked. I started to think. I knew my brother loved me and he locked the door to stop me from going to the Governor's office. I decided not to go. Later on that day, I heard the students who went to the Governor's office were arrested and taken to jail. Unfortunately, they stayed in jail for three months. As a result of this strike, the President of the University, Dr. Samirad, resigned and was replaced by a new President. This was unfortunate because Dr. Samirad was a great pediatrician and he was the one that opened that medical school. He was a great guy and I did not want him to leave. His daughter and son were my best friends.

I did not plan to close the university because I was a student, loved my education, and wanted to be a doctor. There is always stupidity of young ages, and I consider myself guilty. I did not know that the demonstration of the students would cause the closure of the university for three months.

Savak (Organization of Intelligence and National Security)

When the university reopened, the new President called several students, including me, to his office. He told us that our names had been given to him by the Savak and we had to contact the Savak office. The only way we could return to school was if the Savak told the university to take us back. This was the worst news in my life. I called the Savak office and made an appointment. I truthfully told them everything I had done. They did not believe me. They told me they heard from another student that I was far more involved and had extensively planned the strike. The only person I talked to before the strike was my best friend and I could not believe he had told them anything. Of course, I never mentioned him. I told the Savak that I was young and had made a mistake. I told them I was sorry and would never do such thing again. After I signed a statement to that effect, they allowed me to return to medical school. From that point on, I only paid attention to my education.

Production of Play

When I was still a third year medical school student, the Vice President of the medical school came to us and said the Prime Minister of Iran, Dr. Eghbal, was coming in three days to visit the university and we had to have an entertainment program for him. He asked us who had experience with acting in the theater. I raised my hand because of the stage show I had made when I was in primary school. I described how I had written the story, recruited and prepared the actors, and even made a theater hall in a stable. I told how I successfully performed the play in front of my primary school teachers, fellow students, and their families. I also shared that I had participated in the production of a movie with my cousins when I was eleven years old. So, I had more experience than anyone else in the medical school.

The Vice President of the medical school put me in charge and told me to arrange for this entertainment using other students I could recruit. In three days, I was able to find a Russian play we could use where I could act as a Russian major in uniform. I convinced some of my fellow students to play with me. We practiced several hours together and were able to pull off the play very successfully to much applause from the faculty, students and the Prime Minister of Iran. When I finished acting that night, the Vice President of the medical school asked me what I was planning to do after I finished medical school. I told him I was planning on becoming a neurosurgeon. He said "I think you look much better in a uniform, so you'd better join the Army."

First Time I Held a Gun

One of my brother's friends, also a professor of literature, invited me to his summer place, located about an hour from Meshed. I traveled by bus. It was a beautiful place and had a big river at the bottom of a large mountain. I went in the river and fished with his sons. One day, he said he was going to get me up early to take me to the mountain for quail hunting. I had never been hunting in my life.

He woke me up at four A.M. and we started climbing the mountain. When we reached the top of the mountain, there was a beautiful natural fountain. I saw he had created a small room using rocks with some holes in its walls. He opened his bag and brought out a quilt made with different colored material which he hung over one of the walls next to the fountain. I thought he did that to attract the quails. We went into the room and stayed quiet. A few minutes later, a large group of quails (about 40) came over to the fountain to drink.

He gave me his shotgun and told me to shoot the quails. I held the gun in my hand, but realized I could not shoot those beautiful birds. I gave the gun back to him and told him I could not kill those beautiful quails. He used the gun himself and shot several quails and took them home.

At Medical School

In Meshed, there was no night club, nor was there any place for dancing. It was a religious city; no alcoholic drinks were served in restaurants or elsewhere.

I was lucky to find friends at the medical school who had rich families. Many had either a foreign mother or a father who had been educated in Europe or the United States. Fortunately, I became friends with this group. Some of the students attended college, a few went to medical school, and some were still in high school. Every three or four weeks, there was a party in one of the houses to which I was invited. I did not have any house or apartment to invite them back.

We danced a lot, which I loved. Two of the girls in the group were medical students one year behind me; one was the daughter of the president of the Meshed University. She finished nursing school in London, England before coming to the medical school. The other one's mother was from Germany. She and I become interested in each

Figure 10: Chairman of the Department of Surgery from Europe, Nurses from France and Me and My Classmates

other and gradually became close friends. Unfortunately, we were not able to sleep together. She was living with her parents and I was living in a tiny room in a dormitory with another medical student. That year, two of our professors built a private hospital. Since I was working at night in one of the professor's private operating rooms, they allowed me to stay overnight at their new hospital as an intern. A few weeks after I started to work there, my girlfriend went to them and asked them if she could work there at night, too. They told her they had only one room and I was staying there. She told them she was a close friend of mine and we could share the room. They allowed her to stay at night in my room. Therefore, not only did I have to work as intern and take care of patients, but I had to go to bed with her at night and do the other duty!

Planning to Get Married

This woman and I decided to get married. She told her parents and they agreed. We traveled by train to my parent's house in Tehran and I told my parents about our engagement. Twenty-four hours after our arrival, I invited a bunch a close friends to a restaurant; however, I did not tell them about our plan to get married. I had intended to surprise them with the news at the restaurant.

The restaurant had live music and, after we ordered drinks, my fiancée got up from our table and went to another table. She sat next to a guy who was with an older lady who might have been his mother.

After a few minutes, she got up and was dancing with him, and then they started to kiss each other. I was shocked and saddened, but at the same time was happy that I had not told my friends about our plans. The only person who knew about our marriage plan was my first cousin, who was with us that night. She recognized my shock and told me quietly that she knew about the relationship between my fiancée and that guy. She had not told me before because she thought they had quit seeing each other. She told me she had frequently seen my fiancée and that guy together because he lived across the street from her. I was lucky to find out about this lady before I married her.

Psychiatric Rotation

Our university did not have a psychiatric unit; therefore, for our rotation in psychiatry, nineteen other students in my class and I went to the psychiatric house (a place for psychiatric patients to live) in the city to learn about psychiatry. The first day when we arrived, we waited for our professor, then followed close to him because we had always heard that crazy people could be dangerous. When he stopped in the hall to talk to someone, I couldn't help looking at one particular patient who was a muscular short man that was standing in the hallway near us close to the wall. The patient put his finger in front of his nose (the signal in Iran to be quiet). I forced myself to look away from him so I could listen to the professor. That patient suddenly came toward me and the other students and I started to back away. He used that space to come behind our professor and slapped the back of his neck so hard that our professor fell two steps forward. Our professor did not show any reaction and continued talking. For the first time, I thought psychiatrists were not normal people either.

They told us that every third night we had to stay in that psychiatric unit. One night when I was checking the patients assigned to me, I entered the room of one of those patients. I did not see the patient who was hiding behind the door. As soon as I came into the room, he closed the door, which scared me. He asked for a cigarette, which I did not have and I told him so. Only then did he allow me to leave the room.

Another day, a patient asked me and my classmate to play a coin game with him. In the game, one person put a coin on the back of his hand and covered it with his other hand. The other player had to guess which side of the coin was up. If he guessed right, he got the coin, otherwise he had to pay a similar coin to the other player. We were told if patients liked or trusted us, they would open up and tell us what was on their minds. Because of that advice, we agreed to play with the patient. During our play, if the patient was right he took the coin, and if he was wrong he did not pay. Later on, I told my classmate that this patient was smarter than us when it came to gambling!

Distribution of Drug Samples

During the last two years of medical school, I was hired to represent different drug companies to practicing physicians and provide them drug samples. While I was doing this work, I learned the advantages and side effects of different medications and I could explain them to different physicians in different specialties. It was a good experience for a future doctor.

Internship at the Meshed University Hospital

In the seventh year of medical school, we were called interns. We rotated through the medical, surgical, pediatric, obstetrics and gynecology services. In the obstetrics and gynecology services, we were taught how to deliver babies. I delivered 62 babies and all of them, including a set of twins, were boys. Thereafter, when a woman came for delivery and wished to have a boy, the nurses told them to let Matini deliver the baby.

My last three months of rotation were in the pediatric service. Doctor Samirad, the chairman of the Department of Pediatrics, who had been Dean of the medical school, came one day and made a round with us to see the pediatric patients. After the round, he came to the intern room and asked why we were not happy. We looked at each other and did not know why he was asking us such a question. Then he said "You should appreciate what you have. In our country, thirty to forty per cent of children of each family do not survive; you are one of the sixty to seventy per cent who made it. Also, only twenty per cent of our children finish high school; you are one of the lucky ones who accomplished that, too. Every year, only 700 high school graduates could pass the entrance examinations of six medical schools in Iran, and you are one of those 700. Ten percent of your classmates could not reach the last year of medical school (internship) as you did. You are on the last month of your internship, and next month you will be a doctor. Therefore, you should be very happy and proud of your accomplishments." I told him he was absolutely right. In my family, my parents lost two of their six kids. I told him I was very happy and thankful of our accomplishments. I thanked him for establishing the medical school, university and for teaching us how to take care of children.

Graduation from the Medical School

The year in which I graduated from the medical school of Meshed University was the first year the university allowed us to wear caps and gowns.

Figure 11: Medical School Graduation

Short Life of the Red Blood Cells of my Mother

When I was 25 years old and had just finished medical school, my mother was feeling weak. She went to her family doctor and was diagnosed with anemia and sent to a specialist. Her hematologist, trained in the United States, could not find anything wrong with her except anemia. My mother was worried that she had leukemia because a few years prior to this, my cousin died of leukemia at age 27.

I suggested that my mother go to New York, where her sister lived, and consult with a well-known hematologist. She listened to me and went to the Department of Hematology at New York University Hospital. She was examined and given several tests. Finally, after two weeks, the Chairman of the Department of Hematology told her she was an interesting patient for the University and, because of that, they would treat her free of charge and study her case. My mother told him that I had just finished medical school and had started military duty and I was the one who had recommended that she come to New York to see him. After a couple months of treatment, the hematologist sent her back to Iran, along with a letter which was written to me.

When my mother returned home I read the professor's letter. I was surprised. He said my mother was the fiftieth person in the world with her condition. He wrote that the normal life of red blood cells, which are made in the bone marrow, is ninety days but for my mother the cells only survived for 45 days. He explained that there was no cure for this condition but taking testosterone, which stimulates bone marrow to make more red cells, helps to compensate for their short life. He wrote she had already responded to this treatment in New York, yet only half of the patients with this condition had a normal life and the other half developed leukemia (cancer of the blood cells) and died early.

A few months before I came to the United States, my mother was going to her hematologist for a routine follow-up. I knew her hematologist was trained in the United States where I wanted to be trained; therefore, I went with my mother to the hematologist's office. I introduced myself and asked him where I should go for training in the United States. He drew blood from my mother and gave it to his nurse. Then he advised me about different things in the United States. After a while, his nurse came back to his office and said sixty per cent of the blood cells were malignant. The doctor thought she was talking about another patient, but the nurse said that it was my mother's blood. He took me to the laboratory and we both looked at the slide and saw many malignant white cells (leukocytes). Based upon that test result, my mother was diagnosed with leukemia and he started treating her right away. After two months, all the malignant white cells of her blood disappeared. I was very happy that she was in recovery; if she hadn't been, I would not have dared to leave Iran. I promised my mother that after a few months, when I settled down, I would send her a ticket to join me. After she had spent time in the United States, she came to love it and wanted to live in America.

Army of Hygiene (Sepah Behdasht)

When I graduated from medical school, I ranked number two in the class. All the physicians were drafted for military service for eighteen months, including me. This was a program that the Shah of Iran established many years before. It was a wonderful program for the people in the villages because the government sent the doctors to the small villages that for many, many years had never had a physician.

One of the three divisions the doctors could join for their military duty was the Army of Hygiene (Sepah Behdasht). Every three months, the government sent thirteen crates of free medicine to the doctors for use in these villages. The government also sent two high school graduates to help the doctor, as well as a four-wheel drive jeep and a driver to help them get around.

There had never been a military person in our family, except for one of my uncles (my mother's brother), but I had never seen him in a uniform because he quit working in the military when I was a child.

Serving in the Military after Graduation

I really didn't want to go into the Army. Instead, I wanted to come to the United States for training as soon as possible. I went to one of my professors who really liked me in medical school and asked if he knew any top echelon military people who might help me avoid the military service. He was nice enough and gave me the name of his close friend, a three-star general and the head of the Department of Gendarmerie of Iran. He told me he was going to call his friend and let him know I was coming to visit him. I was very happy and I thought, "That's it!"

Visiting the Three-Star General

I went to the office of the three-star general and saw that he was one of the top ten military generals in Iran. He welcomed me and said that one of his best friends had sent me to him, so I just needed to tell him what I wanted and he would do what he could for me. I said that it was not a big thing; I did not want to go to the army, which all graduates of the medical school were required to do at that time. He looked at me and said "You don't want me to be killed, do you?" I said of course I did not want him to be killed. I asked him why he asked that question. He said the policy of the Shah of Iran was that if any military man interfered with the military service of those who were required to join the military after their education, the military man would be crucified in a military court. I told him that I didn't want any harm to come to him, so he recommended that I join the military and do my service. I shook his hand, thanked him, and left his office.

I had to go to a large stadium with my fellow physicians and college graduates of different universities to be drafted. None of my fellow physicians was interested in military service. We felt it was a waste of our time. It didn't matter what we thought; we all had to join the military. Of course, we had to go to military school first. There were few choices for us. I chose to continue work as a military doctor after I finished four months training at the military school. After the training, I was assigned to join the division of the Sepah Behdasht.

Military School

I did not touch a cigarette for seven months prior to going to military school, but on that day, I started to smoke again because I was so depressed. They told us what we had to do. We had to wear a military outfit similar to the outfit of a regular soldier. The place we had to stay was like a dormitory. We were treated like the lowest soldiers during the four months of training to become officers. Again, because I had no previous attachment to the military and had no friends or family in the military, I had no interest in the military. Those things that we had to study, I didn't study hard. At night, when we had free time, I drank vodka and played backgammon in the dormitory. Of course, bringing vodka to the military campus was prohibited completely, but a couple of my friends and I (because we got to go home once a week for 36 hours and then spent the rest of the week in the dormitory) brought two or three bottles of vodka in our bags when we came back from our leave. Every day, the military school personnel checked our bags in the dormitory to make sure there were no drugs or alcohol in them. Where do you think we hid those bottles of vodka so they couldn't find them? We hid them in the water tanks of the toilets. Because we had bad attitudes, we lined up the empty bottles of vodka in front of the dormitory the next morning. They never found the bottles of vodka in our dormitory during the entire four months. There were a few of us who played backgammon, drank vodka and didn't study hard.

The rule of military school was that after three and half months, whoever got the highest score on our examination had priority in choosing the village where he would serve his duty. We had to stay inside of the military school five and half days and nights each week. They choose me as the secretary of the unit. Again, because I had no previous attachment to the military and had no friends or family in the military service, I had no interest in the military. We had to study the rules and regulations, and military laws. Most of my work as secretary was paperwork during the day. Most of my colleagues studied military rules and regulations at night to prepare them for the final examination. Unfortunately, because of my lack of interest, I did not study hard.

Guns in the Military

The officers at the school taught us how to break a gun down into parts and then put it back together. This was the second time in my life that I had held a gun in my hand. Of course, there were no bullets in those guns. Every few hours at night, one of us had to guard the camp unit and walk around the compound with one of those bulletless guns. To me and many others, it seemed crazy to guard the unit with a gun that had no bullets.

One day, they put all of us in multiple buses and each of us had a gun with bullets in it. They took us to a place where we climbed to the top of a hill. Then, the officers told us to lie down on the ground, face down. They instructed us to shoot a target on the opposite hill when they gave the word. A friend of mine and I lay down on the hill and I held the gun pointed toward the target. When the officer said shoot, I pulled the trigger and the bottom of the gun hit my shoulder really hard. I thought I had shot myself and started looking for blood, which I could not find. When I told my friend that I thought I had shot myself, he laughed at me and said when you shoot, if you are not holding the gun tight, the bottom of the gun kicks back on you. That was the only time in my life that I used a gun.

Jail Time

While I was at military school, I registered for the Educational Commission for Foreign Medical Graduates (E.C.F.M.G.) examination (the exam that foreign physicians take in order to be accepted as a medical doctor in the United States). Because of the amount of studying required at the military school, I did not have enough time to study and prepare myself for the examination. I wrote a letter to the American Embassy to postpone the date of my E.C.F.M.G. examination.

On the day we were supposed to go home for the weekend, each of us picked up our bag from the dormitory and ran to catch the military bus. Our bags all had a similar shape and were light blue in color. It was about two miles from the dormitory to the bus station. One time, when I reached the bus station, I realized that I had taken somebody else's bag, so I had to run back to the dormitory to get my bag and then run back to the bus station. When I got back to the dormitory, they announced that we had to wait until the head of the military school, a colonel, come to give us a speech. Unfortunately, that day I was anxious to leave as soon as possible so I could send my letter to the American Embassy to inform them I would not be taking the E.C.F.M.G. examination in the coming week, and asking to reschedule it. We waited and waited and the colonel did not show up. One of my friends could tell I was upset and asked why. I said, "We have been here day and night for five and a half days. Why didn't the colonel come and talk to us during that period? That is why the people do not trust the military officers!" Apparently, one of the lieutenants overheard me and asked, "Who said that?" I told him I said it. He ordered the sergeant to take me to the jail of the military school. Before they took me away, I called my sister, told her the story and asked her not to tell my parents. She had a classmate whose father was a full colonel and I asked my sister to talk to her friend to see if her father could help me.

My Experience at the Military Jail

At the jail, I was given a pillow and a blanket. They kept whatever I had in my pocket and briefcase. As soon as I arrived at a cell, I met a group of prisoners. I greeted everyone. One of the prisoners said, "Welcome here, doctor. Please call one of your colleagues; I need something for pain." I was really scared by then; I did not know what was going to happen to me. I called the physician on call and explained the situation to him. He said not to worry about it, that he would bring the pain medication for the prisoner, and he did.

After the prisoner received the pain pill, he became friendly and said he wanted to tell me why he was there. He said when he was 18 years old he was drafted. One day, while he was working as a soldier in the military compound, an officer came and used abusive language to him and his family. He could not stand it and slapped the face of the officer. The officer ordered the sergeant to take him to solitary confinement. Later, they told him he had to serve two additional years in the army, so he escaped from the army and, instead, started to sell drugs and make a lot of money. He got married and had a son. He continued to make a living by selling drugs. They arrested him again and he claimed he was a soldier; therefore, the police brought him to the military compound and put him back in military jail. After a few months in the military jail, he escaped and started to sell drugs again. He made so much money that he could send his son to Europe for his education. He was arrest again, told them he was a soldier, and was again put back in military jail. He told me he would escape again soon.

Figure 12: Second Lieutenant Matini

I was lucky because the uncle of my sister's friend was a general and was the head of the military school. He told his niece he would talk to me the first day after the weekend, so I remained in jail for 38 hours. On Saturday (the first day of the week in Iran), they came and took me to the general's office. He asked me what had happened and I told him the truth. He said I had to be careful what I said while I was in the military. He told me that he would forgive me if I promised to be good. I promised I would.

Later on, I found out I was very lucky because the military officers had heard that the physicians in the military school planned to boo the Shah when they were scheduled march in front of him the next week. For this reason, the military officers were planning on making an example of one physician by punishing him badly.

I had never been against the military, and I always respected military officers because they sacrificed their lives to protect people against the enemy. I understand that military men, in general, who are supposed to defend their country against an enemy have to use guns and have to learn how to take a gun apart and then put it back together. But it was a waste of time for a physician, who would not be allowed to buy a gun and use a gun, to learn how a gun functions and how to shoot. In those four months, it would have been more helpful for us to learn how to treat patients in a big fire, earthquake, or war.

Selection of Village

After completing military school and passing the final examination, I became a second lieutenant in the army. The military gave me the names of the villages where I could choose to practice in the Sepah Behdasht.

I chose a village, named Daman, twenty two miles from the city of Iranshahr. Because of my lack of knowledge about my country's geography, I didn't realize how far that city was from my hometown, Tehran, and I didn't understand what kind of city it was. I was assigned to Daman. I said goodbye to my family and flew from Tehran to Zahedan, the capital of another state named Baluchistan, about a

Figure 13: Meeting with the Governor of Baluchistan (Three Star General)

four-hour flight from Tehran. I went to a meeting, and met the governor of the state of Baluchistan.

I stayed overnight and attended a meeting where we were told our duties and responsibilities. My driver then picked me up from my hotel and drove me toward the village in the land rover car that the government had provided for our use. We had to drive about six hours on poor roads and through mountains to reach Daman.

Daman of Iranshahr

The village of Daman was beautiful. It was covered by many date trees, which looked like coconut palms.

The region was very dry. The houses in the village were small and impoverished. I had never seen the type of clothing the men and women of that village wore. The medical building, built two years prior, was great compared to the houses in the village. When the people of the village heard the sound of our car, they came toward us. My driver had worked with the previous physician in that village, so the villagers knew my driver and were not afraid to approach and talk to him.

We finally arrived at the medical building and the size of it surprised

Figure 14: Climbing a Date-Palm Tree in the Village of Daman, Iranshahr

Figure 15: Two Visiting Physicians and I, Two Sergeants and Driver in Daman, Iranshahr.

me. There were multiple bedrooms, two large examination rooms, a pharmacy, kitchen, full bath and a couple of bathrooms. There was also air conditioning in it. The accommodations were much better than I expected when I first arrived. When I went to my bedroom and lay down, I was thinking that during four months at military school, they taught us useless material. They never taught us what we should do in the event of an earthquake, storm, major fire or other disaster.

I thought that if a patient came to see me and required surgery, I would send him or her to the hospital in Iranshahr, twenty miles from my clinic. When I was sitting with two sergeants (high school graduates assigned to assist me) and my driver at dinnertime, I asked the driver if I had a patient who needed to be hospitalized, how I would send him or her to the hospital in Iranshahr. The driver laughed and told me that there was no hospital there. He said that there was no difference between our village and Iranshahr. He said there was no hospital, restaurant, movie theater or anything else in that town. This information shocked me. I was wondering why nobody during the four months of military school talked to us about the different villages. They only talked about military rules and regulations, even though we were not going to be working as military officers.

After dinner, I went to the pharmacy room with the two sergeants.

I classified all the medicines and put them on different shelves, then compared those medications with the notebook which listed them. I found a lot of discrepancies, which I wrote down and later mailed to the central office. I also emphasized to my assistants the importance of looking and reading the name of the medication before giving it to a patient. I told them the type of work they were going to do starting the next day and said that it would be the most valuable work they had done in their life so far. I said our work would help the poor people of our country and that treating them was the best thing any Iranian could do. The appreciation from the villagers would be the best payment for their services.

The people of that region rarely saw snow and rain. There was no river. I realized that I did not know much about the country of Iran. I was surprised that there were no real roads in that region, even though Iran was the fifth country in the world from the standpoint of military equipment (such as planes, tanks, and other advanced military equipment).

The village was large with seven thousand population and there was a school with five hundred students. Students came from other villages to this school.

Medical Practice as a Medical Officer

For the first time, I was practicing medicine without other colleagues. There were no professors and no other physicians to consult. There were no computers and no cell phones. The only things I could reference were a few books that I had brought with me. In this village, I was only the second physician that the people had ever seen in their lifetime. Sometimes it was difficult for me and the patients to understand each other because their dialect was different from mine. Two days a week, I saw patients in that village; two days a week I went to a village further north and saw patients there, and two days a week I went to a village in the south to see patients. This duty was the most unusual that anyone could imagine. I was available 24 hours, 7 days a week for the villagers.

There was no entertainment or anything available for me to take a break. There was no television. The other challenge of this village was that it didn't have much meat. As I mentioned, it was dry land and there was nothing for sheep or cows to eat. I found the butcher of this village and told him that anytime he had an animal to sell, I would buy the whole thing. Once in a while he brought me a goat and we ate goat meat. But the goats I was able to buy were so skinny and thin that they didn't have much meat on them.

The weather of the area was very warm. After breakfast, if I was seeing a patient in the village, we started at eight A.M. and continued until we were finished (about six P.M.) with a half hour lunch break. If an urgent care case came after six P.M., we still had to see the patient. The days when I saw patients in other villages, we traveled, saw patients and then return to Daman. The people in the villages sometimes didn't know how to take medicine. I found out that sometimes when they came to me complaining of a cough and I gave them a bottle of cough syrup, or if they had a parasite like Ascaris and I gave them a bottle of syrup to kill the worms, many times they crushed dry bread and put it in a pan, then poured the bottle of syrup on the bread and ate it like soup. They didn't know anything different because they weren't used to having medicine.

Interesting Patients

During the first week of my practice in this village, a young lady eighteen years old came to my office complaining about vaginal discharge. I learned in medical school that when a patient came with this complaint, I had to do a pelvic examination. I had no nurse in the village; it was just me and the patient. It was routine in Iran that when you did a pelvic examination, the patient covered her face with her skirt or the lower portion of her dress. The same thing happened with the young lady in the village, so I thought all was well. After I did a pelvic examination on her, I took a culture of the discharge. I talked with her and gave her some antibiotic capsules, then instructed her how to take them. I told her I'd like to see her the next week. She said that she would not return. When I asked her why, she said something I couldn't understand. So I wrote what she said on a piece of paper and put a circle around it so that I could ask my driver, who was more knowledgeable of the local dialect.

At lunch time, I told the driver what this lady had said and asked what I did wrong that made her say she would not return. He told me,

"Dr. Matini, you should never do a pelvic examination here!" When I asked him why, he said "These people don't know anything about pelvic examinations; I bet she thought you had sex with her." I could not believe what he was saying, but when I asked him if he was serious, he said, "Yes." Therefore, that was the last pelvic exam I did during my military duty in the villages. Also, I found out there was no laboratory we could use, so that was the last culture I took.

The Unusual Necklace

The same woman came back the following week and said she was not better. I gave her a different antibiotic. She came back a week later and said it was not better, so I gave her another type of antibiotic. This continued for five weeks. After six visits, she again said she was not better. I was looking at her chart and saw that I gave her every type of antibiotic we had in those days. It was unusual to find a bacterium which was resistant to all these antibiotics when I was the second physician in the village and not many antibiotics had been given to the villagers. I was puzzled. I kept looking at the chart, then looking at her and, one time when I was looking up at her, I saw something on her chest. I noticed that she had a very interesting necklace. When I looked at it more carefully, I saw that she had made a necklace by passing the string through the antibiotic capsules which I gave her instead of taking them. They were pretty as a necklace because the capsules are usually in two different colors. That was unbelievable to me. I started laughing and told her that the reason she was not getting better was because she was not taking the medicine. She started to laugh with me. That was one of most unusual things I ever observed in my life.

Trachoma

In the first week I was in this village, I saw a lot of students from the school who complained about problems with their eyes. I went to the headmaster of the school and told him that I would be glad to come to the school once a week to see students with eye problems. A common problem for the children of this village was an infection of the conjunctiva, called trachoma. The head of the school agreed to let me come to the school.

Starvation

One day when I was seeing the students who had eye problems, one student told me he had a sore throat. I asked him to open his mouth. When he did, I saw his tongue was green. I had never heard of any disease that caused green discoloration of the tongue. I circled his name on my paper. A few other students came with the same complaint. When I asked them to open their mouths, I saw more green tongues. At that time, I thought I was discovering a new disease and I would become famous. I was dreaming in my head as I continued to see the students. After I saw three of four more green tongues, I started to look at every mouth and found that every tongue was green. I asked one of the older kids what he had for breakfast. He looked at me, and then put his head down. I asked him again and he said "We don't have any breakfast, Sir." I said, "So when you come to school, you don't eat anything?" He said, "No. We eat whatever grass or leaves are on our way to school." That's why their tongues were green. All my dreams of a new discovery and fame suddenly collapsed.

Unusual Sexual Activity

One day I saw a seventy year old man in the office who introduced himself as the mayor of the village. He said he had four wives, and he had sex with each one every night, but recently some nights he could not have sex with every wife. He asked me if I could help him. I told him I never heard of any person at his age who could perform sex every night with so many women. I told him I was not aware of any medication that could help him.

Tuberculosis

There was a lot of tuberculosis in the area involving the cervical or groin lymphoid glands of young people, even many children. I was surprised that we had so many cases of tuberculosis. I started to do some research and talked with the elders and teachers of the village. They said the government sent a group of medical technicians to do tuberculin tests on the people in the village one year ago.

Usually, after giving a tuberculin test, medical professionals had to wait for five days, at which time they examined the place of the injection and, if they saw no reaction to the tuberculin injection, the test was negative and the patient was given BCG vaccine to prevent tuberculosis.

I asked these people if the technician who gave the original shot came again and examined the people who received the injection. Their answer was no. I sent a report to the central office of military health and also sent a copy to the governor of Baluchistan. I told him that I didn't know what was going on, but that I was treating many patients who had tuberculosis and I needed more medication for their treatment. I said I wasn't sure what type of medication had been given to the population the year before, but my investigation showed it was not a routine tuberculin test. I guessed they had given the BCG shot to everyone without checking who really needed it. There had not been any follow-up.

Second Visit with Governor of Baluchistan

One day when I was going to another village in the north, and as my driver was driving, we saw another car coming toward us, which was unusual in that region. We drove as far to the right of the road as possible so that the car could pass. It was a big black car. We stopped and that car stopped. The driver came out and asked "Are you Dr. Matini?" I said yes. He said that he was bringing the governor of the state to my office. The governor got out of the car and we shook hands.

I returned to my office with the governor. Forgoing the trip north that day, I explained the situation of the village's health care to him. I told him the number of patients with tuberculosis are high and involved both children and adults. According to the elder people of the village, they did not have that many patients a couple of years ago before they had a military physician. The governor was surprised to see that I had made a chart for every patient. He said the previous physician did not make charts. He told me that he appreciated my work. I showed him how many patients with tuberculosis I was treating. He said he was going to investigate this issue. After a few hours, he left and I went ahead to the other village since they were expecting me.

About two weeks later, the governor sent me a letter. Apparently, he had assigned a group to investigate the testing done the previous year. The investigators found that the technicians were in a hurry, so they took a shortcut and didn't give the tuberculin test, but just gave everyone the vaccine. Because the tuberculosis bacteria were already in the bodies of many villagers, this caused more of them to develop tuberculosis. Instead of helping the people, by taking a shortcut, they ended up harming the people. The governor ordered more medication for the treatment of tuberculosis.

Unusual Snake Bite

One night, we heard frantic knocking on the door of our clinic. One of my assistants opened the door. After talking to the people who were banging on the door, he came to me. He said there was a very sick patient. Apparently it was customary in that village that when a patient was very sick, and they were worried he was dying, they put him in a coffin, even though he was not dead. They brought in a completely unconscious young man.

We transferred the young man to the table in our clinic for examination. He remained unconscious and would not respond to anything. I started an intravenous (IV) fluid and put a Foley catheter in his bladder. There was very little urine in his bladder. I performed several tests and there was no evidence of diabetes, kidney failure, or anything like that.

I asked the people who had brought him in if he talked to anybody to say what might have happened to him before he passed out. One guy said this young man went to the woods to cut some wood and when he came home, he told his mother a monster bit him. I thought that he was talking about a snake so I looked at the skin of his body from head to toe, inch by inch, looking for a snake-bite wound but I couldn't find anything.

Since there was no evidence of any other disease, I thought it must have been a snake-bite even though I could find no evidence. Fortunately, we had anti-venom serum, so I injected half of it intravenously and half of it underneath of the skin of his abdomen. I gave him bottle after bottle of IV fluid and watched to see if any urine came through the Foley catheter. I had to give him eight liters of the IV fluid before we saw urine coming through the Foley catheter. Fortunately, the next morning, the young man woke up. He wondered where he was. I told him that his family brought him to the clinic. I asked him what had happened the day before. He said he was cutting wood and suddenly a large red snake appeared and wrapped around his neck. He said that when he saw the snake he screamed, and the snake bit him inside his mouth. I understood why I did not find any snake bite during my examination of the skin of his entire body. Getting a snake-bite in the mouth is very dangerous because it's so close to the brain. He was very lucky that I treated him properly for a possible snake-bite even though I couldn't find the site of the bite. Although he lost weight overnight, he completely recovered and went home in good condition.

Anal Sex for Money

In the same village, one day the military police (Gendarme) brought a 12-year-old boy to my office along with a registered letter, which I had to sign for its receipt. The mail was an official letter. The father of this boy was suing another man for having anal sex with his son. The military police sent the boy to me for examination to find out if the accusation was true or not. This was the most difficult case for me because I had never examined a person who had anal sex before.

I recalled that during a medical school forensics class we were told that if a young man or boy was complaining that someone had anal sex with him, the only way you could prove it was to have him sit naked on a tray full of flour-type powder. If the anus had been invaded, the wrinkles of the anus would be changed from what was normal to something abnormal and those changes would be permanent. In order to understand the results, I should have seen what was normal versus what was abnormal. I had not seen this, so couldn't perform the test.

This was very bothersome to me. I didn't know how I could find out if the kid had anal sex with someone. Since I knew I could not correctly evaluate the situation, I decided to talk with the kid. I started to talk to him on another subject so he could get comfortable talking to me. I asked him to tell me about the village, the weather, and asked him if he'd seen snow there. After talking with him about different things for about thirty minutes, he became very relaxed. I asked him if a man had sex with him and he said, "Yes." I asked the name of the man and he said the name of the accused man. I asked him if this was the first time he had sex with him and he said, "No." He said he had anal sex with him many times for money, but the last time he had anal sex with the man, he didn't pay him. Then I was so relieved that I could report back and tell them the truth, that yes, the young man had anal sex and it was not the first time. Previously, he never complained because he received money and this time he complained because he was not paid.

Difficulty of Childbirth

Another day when I was in the office, three people came to my office and asked me to go with them to their village far away. They said there was a woman had not been able to deliver her baby for the last three days, and they were worried that she would die. Immediately I asked my driver if he knew where they lived. My driver took me outside of the room and said those people lived about three or four hours' drive from our clinic. He said they didn't live in a village, they lived in tents. Further, he said they were very dangerous and had guns. I told him I was a doctor and they had a sick patient, so they were not going to hurt us because they needed us. I had to talk to the driver for a long time until I convinced him to drive us to their village.

When we arrived at that region, I saw a lot of people in the village laying on the ground with guns in their hands pointed at us. Then, the head of the village came and told them we were there to help them. He came to welcome me and thanked me for coming. I asked him where the patient was and he said the patient was his daughter. He then showed me her tent. He said he was the head man of the village. I told him that I needed to tell him something important, that I would need to examine his daughter's pelvic area and I knew that they were religious people, but that's the only way I could treat her. He said there was no problem as long as I saw his daughter in the tent and nobody else was around us. I said OK.

I examined her and saw that she was trying to deliver her baby. There was nothing physically wrong, but she was so weak that she didn't have any power to squeeze her baby out. I gave her some medication for that problem intravenously and within 20 minutes she delivered her baby.

I came out and told the father that her daughter had delivered a son; I brought the baby to her father, and the entire village raised their hands to the sky and thanked their god. Then they insisted that I have lunch with them. I didn't want to have lunch with them because I didn't know what they ate. My driver told me it was a bad insult if I didn't have lunch with them, and convinced me to stay. We all sat down and they put a big round tray full of rice and lentils in front of me. I never saw that type of rice before; it had the same round shape as the lentils and they were eating it with their hands. They gave me a spoon and I ate some.

Special Food for Car!

When I was getting ready to leave, I saw there was a package in front of our car. I asked my driver to tell the people that I could not accept a gift from anybody. He started laughing and said the people of the village had never seen a car, and said that they go everywhere with their horses. He said they thought the car was our animal so they brought some food for our "horse!"

Acute Appendicitis

One day an interesting patient was brought to my office. She was a 35-year-old woman who had abdominal pain. When I examined her, I knew she had acute appendicitis. There was no hospital or surgeon nearby. I admitted her to my office, put her on intravenous fluids, put a nasogastric tube in her stomach, and started intravenous antibiotics. I did not feed her and called the nearest hospital which was about 6 ½ hours away in the Zahedan capital of the Baluchistan state. The Chairman of the Department of Surgery at the hospital said that as soon as I could find a bus bringing passengers to the north, I should put the patient on that bus and they would take care of her as soon as she got to the hospital.

It took three days for a bus to come. When it finally did, and after all the other passengers were loaded, we put the patient on the floor of the bus in between the seats. I told the driver and the passengers to take care of her and told them that she was very sick. She was fortunate that they took her to the hospital where they performed an appendectomy, and she survived. I received a lot of thank you notes from her and her family.

Hot Weather in Southeastern Iran

The air-conditioning unit of our clinic broke down and there was no technician or anyone who could fix it. This was during the month of February when the weather was so hot. I poured a bucket of water on my mattress because of that heat and one hour later the mattress was completely dry. The heat made it difficult to live in that village. I wrote a letter to my second brother asking him to try to get me transferred somewhere else.

Leaving Daman

I was lucky. Apparently, another doctor who was in a village in the northwest of Iran (a good region, good weather, and good villages) had an argument with the head of the military health organization in Kermanshah. During the argument, the doctor punched the face of the head of Sepah of Behdasht of that state. They wanted to punish him by sending him to a bad place. So, they decided to transfer him to the village I was working in and send me to the village where he was working.

The day that he came to stay at the village and I was leaving, he said I was lucky. He explained that he and his friends studied hard in military school so they would get their top choice of destinations when they finished. They all decided they wanted to go to one particular place so they could see each other every weekend. He told me he wasn't sure how his friends would treat me. I responded that I would try my best to be accepted by his friends. He gave me the name of the hotel where his friends stayed on the weekend.

That physician who replaced me in Daman came to the United States after finishing his military duties and became an obstetrician and gynecologist, practicing in New York City. He got married and had three children. He had a sudden heart attack and died when he was only fifty-five years old.

Moving to the Northwest

When they issued my transfer to the northwest part of Iran, they gave me a few days off. In those days, there was no telephone so I could not call my parents and tell them I was coming home.

My driver brought me to Zahedan, the capital of the state of Baluchistan, where I went to the airport and flew to Tehran. When I arrived at the Tehran airport, I got a cab and went home. When I reached home and knocked on the door, my mother opened the door and didn't recognize me for a few seconds. Apparently, she didn't recognize me because I had lost so much weight in those two months and had also grown a mustache. I found out later that my brothers told everyone not to tell me how skinny I was because I might worry about it.

Sayed Shekar, Kermanshah

I flew to Kermanshah, located in northwestern Iran that weekend with my second brother. It was the first part of the spring season and that region was very beautiful. All the hills were covered by naturally blooming flowers. Most flowers were corn poppies and they were beautiful. There were ancient statues of the Persian Empire that were more than twenty five hundred years old located in the city of Kermanshah.

The taxi took us to the hotel where the doctor who had replaced me advised me to go. I met all the doctors who were working in the different villages of Kermanshah. I introduced myself and told them I was very sorry that the Army had sent their friend to the village where I was working. Within a short period of time they accepted me.

I was lucky to be transferred from Daman to a much better village, Sayed Shekar in the northwest of Iran.

Figure 16: In Front of an Ancient Persian Statue (Residual of Persian Empire More than 2500 years ago), with my Sister and the Daughter of the Owner of the Village

Figure 17: With Colleagues In Front of an Ancient Persian Empire Wall

E.C.F.M.G. Examination

I was preparing to pass the examination necessary to acquire the E.C.F.M.G. certificate (which granted the title of medical doctor for foreign medical graduates) to come to the United States. After I saw patients all day, I studied until midnight to prepare myself. When the time came to go to Tehran to the United States Embassy to take the exam, several feet of snow fell in our village. Even my four-wheel drive jeep could not drive through that heavy snow. I had to hire 20 people to clean the road so I could get to the airport. Fortunately, I was able to fly to Tehran to take the eight-hour examination at the American Embassy the next day. I passed with a high score.

One advantage of living in the village in the northwest of Iran was its availability of food and especially good meat. My friends and I would go every weekend to the city of Kermanshah, only twenty-five miles from where I was working. We stayed overnight in a hotel with a bunch of other physicians who were working in other villages. We had a good time together and bought different types of foods for the entire week. I was thankful to have been interested in cooking since I was a teenager, because the two high school graduates who were helping me at work and the driver didn't know anything about cooking. I was not only a physician, I was also a cook!

Establishment of Water Reservoir for People of Village

Besides medical care, the other thing I did for the people of Sayed Shekar was to establish a better water system. There was a natural spring fountain on the top of a very tall hill above the village. The women had to climb the hill to get the water and then carry it in a leather bag down to their homes.

I sat with the people of the village and told them I could cover the natural spring fountain and pipe the water all the way down to the village in order to create a reservoir. Everyone could go, open the faucet, and get water. The funds for this project were provided by the government. To make the people of the village responsible for the project, I suggested that every day, three people should come and help the plumber and construction workers. Everyone agreed. Another condition I suggested was that every person who lived in this village should pay a small amount of money equal to three dollars per person to better appreciate and take care of the water reservoir and what we were doing for them. In spite of their agreement to these conditions, every morning I had to come and pick up the three people who were supposed to help the construction workers and plumbers. They would not come by themselves.

Figure 18: The Clinic, Where Me, my Assistants, and my Driver Lived in Sayed Shekar Village.

Side Effect of Horseback Riding

There was a horse in the village that I occasionally rode for fun. One morning, I was trying to round up the three people who were supposed to help the workers, but one of them did not show up. I rode the horse around the village and the surrounding countryside looking for the guy. The horse was climbing over the hill rapidly and dangerously as I held onto the neck of the horse. My hat flew off of my head and I lost control. I thought that was the last day of my life, but I was fortunate that one of the farmers saw me and came to stand in front of the horse. The horse reared up and I was able to drop myself off the horse; if the farmer hadn't done that, I could have died.

The Effect of Medical Military Physician on the Life of the Village's People

The headman of the village told me that before the military doctor program started, the villages of that region lost 300-500 kids a year due to complications from measles. After the program began, there were no deaths. Every three months, doctors got 13 crates of medicine to supply patients free of charge. Also, patient consultations were free of any charge.

Endemic Syphilis

For one month, the military sent all physicians who worked in the villages of the state of Kermanshah to the city of Ahvaz, located in the south of Iran for one month. After we arrived in Ahvaz, we were taught how to perform a blood test on the adult residents of that city in order to check for syphilis.

On My Way to the U.S.A!

I finally finished my military duties, passed the E.C.F.M.G. examination, and was eligible to come to the United States. I applied for an internship at Providence Hospital in Washington, D.C., and was accepted. Then I applied for a passport in Tehran.

Fortune Teller

While I was back in Tehran, prior to leaving for the United States, I borrowed the car of my second brother and went to my Aunt's house where her two daughters, younger than me, asked me for a ride to a place where they could get Turkish coffee, then have fortune teller look at the coffee cup residue and guess their future. I said "Are you trying to find out if you can find a husband?!" They laughed and said no, but begged me to take them. They asked me not to make fun of them and to participate instead. I went with them to the fortune teller. A guy who I never met before asked my first name and gave me a cup of Turkish coffee. After I drank the coffee, he turned the cup over, waited a few minutes until the inside of the cup became dry, and then he turned the cup back over. Looking inside of the cup to read my fortune, he told me that I was planning to go somewhere very far away, although he did not say where. He said it was almost impossible for me to go. But if I could surmount all the difficulties of going on this trip, I would be a very successful man. He also said one of my loved ones would die soon. He then guessed the future of my cousins.

When we left his office, I told my cousins that I had already passed the E.C.F.M.G. examination for the United States and had obtained an internship position. I had already applied for a passport, but this fortune teller said I would have difficulty in trying to go.

Leaving Iran

I went from Tehran to Meshed (the city where I went to medical school) to see my oldest brother. He had become the Vice President of the university. I wanted to say good-bye to him since I was going to the United States. After three or four days, my second brother called me from Tehran and said I needed to return to Tehran because the government had refused to issue me a passport. He said I had to go to the office of the Savak.

I immediately returned to Tehran and went to the office of the Savak. The officials there wanted to know about my political activity in medical school. I told them what I did and said I didn't belong to any particular political party. They said they didn't believe me because I was the only student leading the demonstration that had caused the temporary closure of the university, yet I was not arrested. I told them it was the truth that yes, I had created the demonstration which caused the school closure, and that I knew what I did was the wrong thing. After that event, I had not participated in any political activity. I further told them that my brother was a Vice President of the Faculty of Letters when I was a medical student. After the demonstration, instead of going back to the dormitory, I went to my brother's house because I knew the Savak was coming after me in the dormitory. Apparently, due to their respect for him, they never came to arrest me in his house. The Savak officers didn't believe me.

A friend of my second brother who worked for the Savak looked at my file. He said the general who was the head of the Savak in Meshed had put a note on my file that for the next 15 years I could not leave the country. I thought the fortune teller apparently was right and I could not leave Iran.

I went to the office of the Savak every day. On the 30th day, I was really fed up, so I said either you think I'm against the Shah of Iran or

I'm on his side. I told them that I received a letter from the Shah's office that recognized me as a top officer of the Sepah Behdasht in Iran. The officer was surprised and asked me if I still had the letter. I said yes and he asked me to bring the letter to him, which I did. That letter saved me. After he read it, the officer allowed me to get a passport and come to the United States. The Shah's office issued the letter, apparently, because of my excellent medical and social work performed in the villages of Iran. In that formal letter from the Shah's office, they called me a distinguished, super-qualified, privileged member of the health military corps (Sepah Behdasht).

Hamburg, Germany

When I came to the United States, I traveled through Munich and Hamburg, Germany then through Stockholm, Sweden. This was the first flight and first trip for me outside of Iran. I was excited!

During this first trip, I had to take my aunt to Hamburg because she wanted to visit her son. Her son was living in Los Angeles but was coming to Hamburg to see her. When the plane took off from Tehran airport, I noticed that my aunt kept playing with a little radio that she had. She complained that it didn't work. I told her the radio would not work when the airplane was in the air and there was nothing wrong with her radio. Then she told me that she had a large bag of tea which her friend had asked her to mail to her son in Munich.

When we were getting close to landing in Munich, where we had to change planes for Hamburg, I told her we didn't have much time to mail the package and if we mailed it from Hamburg it would be better. As soon as we arrived in Munich and passed through customs, I told her to stay in one place so I could figure out where we had to go to catch the connecting flight from Munich to Hamburg. We had a very short time to catch the next plane. I ran to find out where we needed to catch the next plane and then ran back to my aunt to take her to the gate. As soon as a customs official saw I was talking to my aunt, he told me that we could not go anywhere. He had asked my aunt to let him check her box and she refused. My aunt, who did not speak German or English, showed her package of tea to the customs officer and said the word "post," which in the Persian language means mailing. The custom officer became suspicious when she wouldn't let him examine the package. I told her she had to give them the package of tea, which she would not. I insisted and she finally gave it to them. They opened the package and checked it gram by gram looking for drugs. After they finished checking the tea, they allowed us to leave, but by then we had missed our flight. We had to wait for three hours for the next flight. I was so upset that I went to the bar in the airport and requested a triple vodka. We finally got on the plane and flew to Hamburg.

In Hamburg, I went to a very good restaurant and ordered a delicious dinner. After dinner, I needed to use the bathroom but didn't understand the German words for female and male on the doors of the bathrooms. I waited, hoping to see someone go into the bathrooms so I could understand which one was for men and which one was for women, but unfortunately, nobody went to the bathroom. I finally couldn't wait any longer and just went into one of bathrooms. It had multiple stalls and I had to put money in a box to use the toilet. I went into one of the stalls and, as soon as I finished, I opened the door of the stall very slowly. I saw four women standing against the mirrors, so I very slowly closed the door and sat back, scared, especially since I didn't know the German language. I thought they would arrest me! I waited and finally the four women left, so I could escape. I decided I needed to understand the word for "woman" and "man" in any foreign language to stay out of trouble in the future!

Meanwhile, my aunt was waiting for her son to arrive. The day after we had arrived in Hamburg, she wanted to go to a store, so I took her. She said I didn't have to stay with her, instead I could just pick her up at a certain time. I left her in the store, but I was looking to see what she was doing. I saw that she went to the bra section and spoke to the salesperson with her hand over her breasts to indicate she needed a bra. That scene made me laugh from far away.

Sweden

Three days later, I flew to Sweden. At the airport; I bought a large bottle of tax-free whiskey, which I put in my briefcase. At that time you could bring liquids on the plane. I arrived in Stockholm and loved it. The buses were so clean and nice, and were always on time. They ran twenty-four hours a day so you didn't need a car to live in

Stockholm. I also found out that in Stockholm you couldn't drink and drive and, if you were arrested even one time, they would take your driver's license for good. If a person had a party, the host had to ask the guests for their car keys in order to serve them alcoholic beverages. The reason was that if a person attending the party had drinks, drove, and then had an accident, the hosts of the party were liable and could be arrested and lose their licenses, too. I loved Stockholm and thought it was beautiful. In every park you could see different shows and listen to music. Of course, I was there in the summer. If I was there in the winter, I probably would not think that way.

I thought of staying in Stockholm instead of going to the United States for medical training, and visited a university hospital and showed them my credentials. I told them I was planning to go to the United States, but after I visited Stockholm, I decided I would rather stay there, if possible. The hospital officials said my credentials were good, but that I would have to learn the Swedish language to stay. I asked how long it would take to learn the Swedish language and they suggested a minimum of six months, during which time I would not get paid. I decided not to stay in Sweden. Now I'm very happy that I continued to the United States.

Sweden to the United States

The plane from Stockholm to New York City was big but carried only twenty passengers. I sat next to a young American student who was going home. She was friendly and I was happy to have somebody to talk to, which made the flight more pleasant. We talked and chatted and ordered a drink, which was very expensive for a young man like me. Because it was such a long flight and because I had a bottle of whiskey in my briefcase, I poured the whiskey in our glasses and we kept drinking all the way to New York City.

When we arrived in New York City, we were both drunk. We said goodbye to each other, passed through customs, and I gave the cab the address of my aunt's apartment in New York City. The roads, bridges, and highways in New York were interesting to me. I had never seen such highways or bridges. After three days, my aunt took me to the bus station to catch a bus to Washington, DC where I would begin my internship at Providence Hospital.

When I arrived in the bus terminal of Washington, DC, I saw a few huge black people for the first time in my life. During twenty-seven years of living in Iran, I had never seen a black person. Later on, I noticed that I had been standing and staring at those black people for an hour.

Internship at Providence Hospital

I started my internship at Providence Hospital. When there was a lecture and the medical staff asked questions of us, I found out that I knew more than most of the other interns. That really surprised me because I thought I had come from a small university in Iran which would put me at a disadvantage compared to interns from Harvard, Georgetown, George Washington University and other top American schools. That gave me great confidence.

I chose eight months of surgery and four months of medicine for the year of my internship and asked the chief resident of surgery to put me in the operating room with neurosurgeons. He was surprised. He said nobody typically likes to do that but he listened to me and frequently put me in the neurosurgical operating room.

I discovered that the only thing the neurosurgeons said during surgery was "suck" and "cook." Suck meant to suction the blood and cook meant to stop the bleeding blood vessels using electro- cautery. Usually, neurosurgical cases took five to eight hours. When I visited the patients the next day and tried to talk to them, they couldn't answer. I was surprised. Many of these patients were in comas for days and, even when they woke up, they weren't normal. Because of that, I gradually lost interest in neurosurgery, even though I went to medical school intending to become a neurosurgeon. Of course, I had not known that most surgeries could not fix the problems of paralyzed patients. I finally decided that neurosurgery was not for me, and changed my plan to become a general surgeon instead.

Two and a half months after arriving in the United States, my second brother called me to tell me he was traveling to Japan and Korea for his business. He said he missed me and was planning to come and see me for a few days before returning to Iran. That, of course, made me very happy. He told me he was arriving at Washington Dulles International Airport. I checked with my friends and they gave me directions to the airport. I had just bought a car two weeks before his arrival. At that time, there were no buildings on either side of the access road leading to Dulles Airport.

I was so happy to see my brother and we went to different parts of Washington DC, which was challenging since I did not yet know the city or how to get around. He also brought a letter from my mother. She had written a small portion of the letter and the rest was written by my older brother and my sister.

After a few days, my brother received a call from Iran saying that our mother was sick and that it was terminal. I wanted to go and see her but he told me our mother would be sad if she saw me back in Iran, knowing I was supposed to be in medical training. He also said that was why she could not write more in that letter. He flew back to Tehran and three days later I was told by phone that my mother had passed away. When the physicians at Providence Hospital heard the news, they told me I could stay home for a week. After 24 hours, I decided to return to the hospital because sitting at home alone and thinking about the loss of my fantastic mother was terrible.

General Surgery Training

At Providence Hospital, there was an intern who had completed his general surgery training in England, but when he decided to immigrate to the United States, he was told he had to repeat general surgery training. I was concerned because I thought that when Providence Hospital selected two first-year residents for general surgery, when these two residents finished their third year of residency, the hospital would choose one of the two residents as Chief Resident. I knew he had a better chance of being selected because he was already a certified general surgeon. Because of that, I applied to more than seventy hospitals in the United States for a first-year residency of general surgery.

Jewish Hospital Medical Center of Brooklyn, New York

I chose the Jewish Hospital Medical Center of Brooklyn for my first-year residency. It was located close to a park and used to be in one the most beautiful and famous areas. However, at the time I went for my residency, it was one of the most dangerous neighborhoods. No insurance company would give car insurance to people living there. There was an apartment building, which belonged to the Jewish Hospital, where they rented rooms to the residents. When I began my residency, they didn't have any rooms available, so I had to stay in a small room inside the hospital building, which lacked windows. From the standpoint of learning, the residency in that hospital was great.

My First Medical Doctor Girlfriend

One of my neighbors in the hospital building was a physician from Germany. She was a first-year resident in internal medicine. We became close friends and, after a while, she told me that she was going to move to one of the best neighborhoods in New York City. Apparently, a rich German lady living in the United States who had a lot of property wrote in her will that her properties could be rented only to German citizens at a low price.

Any night that I was off and I didn't have to stay in the hospital, I stayed with my new girlfriend in her apartment. We had a nice time together from every standpoint; however, she criticized everything about the United States. I never argued with her because I thought the medical training in Germany must have been inferior, and that is why she came to the United States for training.

One night, when I was in her apartment in the middle of winter, there was heavy snow outside. She started to complain about her training in the hospital. I said, "I thought you came to the United States because you knew the training here was better than Germany. Now you're saying the training is also better in Germany?" She was fixing coffee and was boiling some water. She got so upset that she threw the pot of hot water toward me. If I had not moved quickly, I would have been burned badly. I decided to leave right then. I put on my overcoat and walked in the heavy snow toward my car. She came out without any coat or shoes, running behind me to apologize. I was worried about her behavior and suggested that she go back to her apartment. I told her that we weren't a good match.

New Apartment in Brooklyn, New York

I finally got one room in the apartment building that was located within walking distance of the hospital. In that building, the trash closet was right next to my apartment door. One night around midnight, I took the garbage out of my room. It was the middle of summer, so I only had underwear on because I was planning to go to bed when I got back to my room. I opened my door and then opened the door to the garbage chute, and dropped the garbage in. As soon as I closed the door to the garbage chute, the draft also closed my apartment door. There I was, only in underwear, and locked out of my apartment. I had no key with me. I had no choice but to go to the manager of the building. I thought nobody would be in the elevator at that time of night. At first I was alone until I got to the first floor, where some people entered the elevator. They looked at me with surprise and I explained there was nothing to worry about; I just had some bad luck. I knocked on the door of the manager's apartment and had a hard time convincing him to open the door. Finally he did, and he gave me a key to open my apartment door.

My aunt lived in New York City and I visited her once in a while. One night she invited me for dinner. After we had eaten and watched a movie, I left her apartment and drove toward my apartment in Brooklyn. While parking my car in the street next to the apartment, I saw a person running toward me. It was around midnight, so it scared me. I drove the car away and went back into Manhattan. In those days, there were no cell phones, so I went back to my aunt's apartment building and called her from the lobby. She had a hard time believing it was me, but I finally convinced her, so she let me in her apartment and I stayed there overnight.

There was no parking lot for the physicians at the Jewish Hospital. There were only five parking spaces for senior physicians, including a general surgeon with whom I worked frequently. He bought a brand new Cadillac and parked it in the parking space at the hospital. Two days after he bought the car, apparently a tow-truck operator came to the front of the small parking lot and told the manager that the doctor who bought the Cadillac had some problems with it, so he was towing it to the repair shop. The manager tried to call the doctor, but the doctor was in the operating room and could not be reached. The manager looked at the paperwork which seemed in order, so he let the tow-truck operator tow the Cadillac. When the general surgeon came out of the operating room, he realized his car had been stolen. He never found his car.

Sometimes top criminals came to the Jewish Hospital. One arrived with a gunshot wound. He had surgery and then was admitted to the hospital. The entire wing was controlled and protected by hoodlums with machine guns, who checked anybody who was going into that wing; they were powerful enough to do that.

Gun Shot in the Jewish Hospital Medical Center of Brooklyn, New York

When you came off the elevator on the second floor of the hospital, there was a female ward on the right and a male ward on the left. Between the elevator and one of those wards was the entrance to the operating room and the office of the Chairman of the Department of Surgery. One day, when I came out of the operating room to go to one of the wards, and I was practically in the center of the area near the elevator, a man pointed a gun at me! I put my hands up and noticed there was someone behind me. I realized the gun was not for me so I dropped to the floor face down. I heard the gunshot. The man behind me was shot and the gunman ran away.

As a first-year resident, when a patient came to the Emergency Room and the Emergency Room physician thought the patient needed a surgical consult, he or she called the first-year resident of general surgery. After the first-year resident examined the patient, he or she would call the Chief Resident and they would look at the patient together. That process provided me with great learning experiences.

One night when they called me to see a patient, I found a young lady with a sudden onset of abdominal pain and fever. After I examined her, I found out she didn't have the typical signs of appendicitis, but I couldn't tell what was causing the abdominal pain and fever. I called the Chief Resident who came and examined the patient and said it was a very unusual type of acute appendicitis. He said in this patient, the appendix was behind the large bowel instead of its usual location in front of the large bowel. He told the patient she had acute appendicitis and we took her to the operating room for removal of her appendix.

The Chief Resident allowed me to do the surgery. This was the first time I cut the abdomen of a living patient. Of course, the Chief Resident was standing near me and helping. When I opened the abdomen, there was a large amount of pus in the abdominal cavity and we tried to suction it out. This was unusual for acute appendicitis. We saw that the appendix was not inflamed and was present at its usual location in front of large bowel. The Chief Resident agreed that the patient did not have appendicitis, but he couldn't tell where the pus was coming from. He told me to lengthen the cut to try and find where the pus originated. Suddenly, his glasses fell inside the patient's abdomen. For many seconds, nobody said a word and nobody moved. The Chief Resident finally fished out his glasses and went to wash them off and change his gloves. The reason for her abdominal pain was an infection of both uterine tubes. We washed her abdomen out with ten liters of normal saline and admitted her to the hospital. We gave her antibiotics intravenously. She did very well and, after few days, was discharged from the hospital.

Unusual Event in Brooklyn, New York

At one A.M. one morning, I was called to the Emergency Room to see a patient. The patient was a 42-year-old black man with multiple superficial stab wounds of his face. The way he got hurt was very unusual. This man was married and had finished his work at eleven P.M., then went home. He found his wife having sex with another man in their bedroom. The man who was having sex with his wife got out of bed and hit the poor husband with his fist. When the husband fell down, the man used his knife to cut the husband's face, making multiple superficial stab wounds. It took two hours for me and another resident to suture all those cuts.

During my first-year residency, I was sent for two months to another hospital in Brooklyn where the majority of patients were Spanish and didn't speak English. That hospital had a lot of unusual and interesting cases for me. For example, when a patient came to the Emergency Room and required a surgical procedure which could be done in the Emergency Room, the only people who could help me were the family of the patient because the hospital was short of medical personnel. If the person needed an x-ray, I had to take the patient myself to the radiology department where a technician took the x-ray. I had to review the x-ray myself and make a diagnosis. There was no radiologist in the hospital at night. If I had to do something like reducing a displaced fracture, I had to ask the family of the patient to help me.

Thank You Note from the People of Brooklyn, New York!

One night they called me to see a patient because of a laceration of his wrist. I found blood shooting out of the wound which meant the main artery of the wrist was cut. I asked her family member to help me as I tried to suture the laceration of the main artery of wrist. I had to stop the blood flow to the wrist temporarily with a blood pressure cuff around the arm in order to find the location of the laceration. I was able to find the laceration of the artery and repair it under local anesthesia in the Emergency Room. After I put the bandage around her wrist and removed the blood pressure cuff, I wanted to write a prescription for her. Then I noticed that her family had stolen a gold pen from my uniform pocket while I was repairing the laceration of the artery. I had received that pen as a gift after I finished medical school in Iran.

Another time, a patient arrived late one night to the Emergency Room and I was called to attend to her. When I saw the patient, I immediately called the Chief Resident to come and see her as well. The patient was a gorgeous 16-year-old girl who had broken up with her boyfriend. He was upset that she broke up with him and had snuck in to her apartment and shot her three times between her legs while she was sleep, then he ran away. We had to take the patient to the operating room and, under general anesthesia, explore the multiple gunshot wounds. She was lucky that none of the bullets entered her abdomen or hit main arteries or nerves. She had multiple big wounds that had to be debrided. The wounds were washed, cleaned and packed with gauze. After surgery, one of my duties was to change her dressings every day. One of the residents teased me and said that I liked to do that work because I got to go between the legs of this beautiful girl every day!

Worm or Spaghetti!

One time they brought a nine-month pregnant woman to the Emergency Room. She was not able to breathe well and was severely sick. I asked her what happened and she said she was climbing the stairs and then fell down. When I listened to her chest, I could not hear any breathing sounds on the left side of the chest. I asked for an x-ray of her chest. The left lung could not be seen in the x-ray and a lot of fluid was present in the left chest. I called the Chief Resident right away.

The Chief Resident thought that the patient had a huge abscess in the left chest, causing her to have shortness of breath. He decided to put a chest tube into the left chest to drain the pus and allow the lung expand. When he put the chest tube in, the fluid coming out of the chest tube contained some long yellow tube-like things. The Chief Resident thought it was some type of parasite; maybe a worm called Ascaris. I pulled a couple of the items out of the drainage bottle and examined them myself. I said they were not worms, they were spaghetti. Apparently, the poor patient received a major trauma to her chest and abdomen, and the diaphragm (the structure that separates the chest cavity from the abdomen) was ruptured, so the stomach moved through the opening from the abdomen into the chest. The tube he put in the chest was actually going into her stomach. We had no choice at that time but to operate on the patient to fix the hole in her stomach, bring the stomach back to the abdominal cavity, and repair the ruptured diaphragm.

The patient was fortunate that although she was nine months pregnant, she tolerated the surgery well and was fine. The next day I went to her and asked her to tell me the truth of what happened to her the previous night. She said she would as long as I promised not to tell her husband, and I agreed. She said that when her husband came home from work, they argued and her husband kicked her in the abdomen then pushed her down the stairs. She was afraid to tell the truth, thinking that her husband would be angrier with her. This patient went home after a week.

Importance of Reading the Name of Medication

We had a young lady patient with a condition we call recurrent infection of the presacral region (the region is located right above the buttock in the lower portion of the spine). Skin and subcutaneous fatty tissue covers that region of spine. If this infection reappears, there is no other treatment except to cut out all the infected skin and soft tissues of that region, leave the area open, pack it, change the dressing of that area every day, and give the patient antibiotics. Gradually the area fills up with the patient's own granulation tissue and heals.

My job was to change the patient's dressing every day. Because of the location of the wound, I had to ask the patient to lie in a prone position (abdomen down) on the table to change the dressing. Because I was doing this for many days, the patient and I chatted about different things during the dressing changes. Usually after I removed the packing out of the wound, I picked up a bottle of hydrogen peroxide from the shelf of the cabinet, opened the bottle and poured the peroxide solution in the wound, left it for a few minutes, then dried out the wound, and repacked the wound with gauze moistened with salt water.

One day, when I poured the liquid from the bottle (which I thought to be hydrogen peroxide) in the wound, she screamed. I looked at the bottle and found out I had made a mistake; the bottle was not hydrogen peroxide, but acetone. The bottles were similar in shape and color. Of course, I was very sorry and started to wash the wound with a lot of normal saline. I called my Chief Resident and told him what I did. He said there shouldn't be any problems and that I should just continue to repack the wound on a daily basis.

That event taught me an important lesson: that you never use any medication or solution without first looking at the label on the bottle. That lesson remained with me for the rest of my medical practice.

Second-Year Residency in General Surgery

I choose the Jewish Hospital Medical Center of Brooklyn for my first year residency in general surgery because they had taken ten first-year residents a year for second-year residencies, usually two for orthopedic surgery, two for urology, two for neurosurgery and four for general surgery. I thought there would be no competition or lay-offs in this residency program for general surgery. With my bad luck that year, all ten first-year residents wanted to go into general surgery, so the Chairman of the Department of Surgery, who was very nice, called six of us together in his office before Christmas. He said that all ten residents wanted to go into general surgery that year and that they only had positions for four. He said he chose six out of the ten (I was one of the six), but that he couldn't choose four among the six of us because we were all excellent. He told us that if any of us found a better place for our second-year residency, he would be glad to write us a great recommendation. As I looked at the five other residents, I saw that four out of the five residents had been in the Jewish Hospital as an intern the previous year. I thought they had a better chance than me to stay there.

I started looking for a second-year residency opening in general surgery anywhere in the United States. I applied to more than fifty hospitals and the only hospital that offered me a second-year residency was Providence Hospital in Washington, DC where I had done my internship. Because I didn't have any other options, I signed a contract with them.

University of Louisville, Kentucky

One week after I signed a contract with Providence Hospital, I got a call from the University of Louisville asking me to interview for a second-year residency position in general surgery. The University of Louisville had an exceptionally wonderful general surgery residency program, so I flew to Louisville. I spoke to Dr. Rudolf Noer, the Chairman of the Department of Surgery and a famous surgeon. After a few minutes of talking to me, he said I was accepted into the program. I thanked him and mentioned that I had a couple of questions and he referred me to his Chief Resident to answer them. When I was leaving Dr. Noer's office, he said he wanted me to know that in 175 years, I was the fourth foreign resident to have been accepted into the Department of Surgery of the University of Louisville. He said two of those other three foreign residents had also been Iranian. Of course, after hearing this from the Chairman of the Department of Surgery, I was proud to be the fourth foreign resident of general surgery at the University of Louisville during the 175 years and proud to be an Iranian at that time.

After the interview, I went to the Chief Resident and told him I already signed a contract for a second-year residency with Providence Hospital in Washington, DC. Because I wasn't a U.S. citizen, I needed approved training in order to get a visa to stay in the United States every year. The Chief Resident said it was no problem. Because the University of Louisville was so powerful, I just had to sign a letter of resignation and that would take care of the problem.

First Lie

I wrote a letter to the Chairman of the Department of Surgery of Providence Hospital saying I had to go to Iran so I was not coming for the second-year residency after all. Two weeks later, I received a letter from the University of Louisville saying that they needed Providence Hospital's agreement to my resignation before the University of Louisville could issue the documentation to extend my visa in the United States. Of course, this was unbelievable for me. I didn't know how to get Providence Hospital's approval when I had lied to the Chairman of the Department of Surgery. There was a pediatrician named Dr. Mahalati at Providence Hospital who was the one who gave me the application for the internship there. I called him and told him the truth and he said he would intercede on my behalf with the Chairman. Two days later, he called me and said, "The Chairman of the Department of Surgery of Providence Hospital was upset when I told him that you are not going back to Iran, and that you had lied." Dr. Mahalati said that because I lied, the Chairman wouldn't do anything to help me further.

I thought I was not going to have a second-year residency anywhere. I kept begging Dr. Mahalati to help. Finally, after a month, he said he had to lie to the Chairman of the Department of Surgery telling him the reason I was not going to Providence Hospital was that I got paid more for the second-year residency at the University of Louisville and since I got married, I needed more money. A few days later, I received a letter from Providence Hospital agreeing to my resignation which I promptly mailed to the University of Louisville. My visa was issued, and my ordeal was over. I thanked Dr. Mahalati profusely and told him I would never lie again. I learned my lesson.

Second-Year Residency of General Surgery at University of Louisville, Kentucky

The first day I started my second-year residency, we made rounds with a senior professor of surgery. I could not understand a word he said during the rounds because of his accent and nasality. After the round, he took all the residents into a conference room and asked me the first question. I couldn't understand the question and asked him to repeat it, but still didn't understand. I thought that was the end of my residency. After that meeting was finished, I went to my Chief Resident and said, "I think I have to leave because I didn't understand a word this professor said." The Chief Resident said, "We are American and we cannot understand him either because he talks through his nose. Don't worry." So that was another break for me. The work at the University of Louisville was hard. For every forty-eight hours, we were on duty thirty-six hours and off duty twelve hours.

The University of Louisville gave us a list of residents and their rotations. I found my name under the list of second-year residents in the booklet, but my rotation was like that of the first- year residents. This upset me; I thought there had been a mistake. I went to the Chief Resident and asked him why I had the rotation of a first-year resident when I was a second-year resident. He said that the Chairman of the Department wanted it that way. I thought there had been a mistake.

I went to talk to the Chairman who had hired me and found out that he had retired the day I started my residency. The Acting Chairman was Dr. Phil Harbrecht; he was one of the nicest people and the best surgeons that I have ever known. Of course, at that time I didn't know him.

After we finished grand rounds at one P.M. on Saturday, I went to Dr. Harbrecht and asked if I could speak to him. I told him that I was hired as a second-year resident in general surgery but had been put into the rotation of a first-year resident. I told him I came from Iran and this was the third year I was in the U.S. I told him I wondered why when a big university like the University of Louisville hired someone as a second-year resident they would give him a different rotation than one given to other second-year residents.

He said in this program the first-year residents learn about surgical patient care at Louisville General Hospital, and they leave until their third-year residency, when they practically run the show, so it's important to learn about this hospital in their first year. He said, "Because you were not here as a first-year resident and didn't have that experience, you have to catch up." Then I asked him why I didn't get the pathology rotation at the Mayo Clinic or the hand surgery rotation in Louisville. He said he would check on those and let me know.

After a couple of days, he called me and said he could send me to the Mayo Clinic for the pathology rotation, but since I needed the other rotations to learn everything I needed to know, there was no time for the hand surgery rotation.

Importance of Surgical Training

The surgical residency program was unbelievably busy. In the thirty-six hours we were on duty, we worked continuously. If we were able to sleep three or four hours, we were lucky. The good thing about it was that we saw all different types of patients and performed many types of surgery. Shortly after we were taught something, we were allowed to do smaller parts of that surgery under supervision. In spite of the fact that it was very, very difficult work, I loved it.

There was a relationship between the University of Louisville and the Mayo Clinic. The surgical residents at the University of Louisville spent three months at the Mayo Clinic learning pathology.

In December of my second-year residency, I became sick. My liver was enlarged, my neck lymph glands were enlarged, I had no appetite, and I had a fever. I was hospitalized at Louisville General Hospital. After a couple of days, I called one of the medical residents and asked him if he could talk to one of the professors to do a bone marrow biopsy to see if I had leukemia (blood system cancer). The next day, a Professor of Hematology came and saw me, examined me and said she was requesting multiple blood tests. After she reviewed the results, she would talk to me, but at the present time, she believed I had infectious mononucleosis. Her diagnosis proved to be correct, and there was no treatment except rest. Eventually I recovered.

The Right to Bear Arms

One day when I went to the operating room, I saw a professor who was Chairman of the Department of Anesthesia in a scrub suit with a gun right over his scrub suit. I thought something bad had happened, so I asked him what was happening and why he had a gun. He explained that I should buy a gun, too, and he would show me where to go to learn how to shoot. He said that once I had a gun, if a bad person came to the door of my apartment, I could shoot him, then bring the body inside, and say that he had been inside my apartment when I shot him.

I was shocked to hear this. In Iran, nobody had a gun. Even the police officers and military officers who had guns at work had to give back their guns each night when they left work. The only individuals who could take guns home were generals. That was why occasionally we read in the newspaper that a general's wife was killed with a gun by her husband. When I became a second lieutenant and had to go to a village in the southeast of Iran, I asked the military if I needed permission to buy a revolver. The answer was that I could not own a gun. Of course, that was the law in Iran before President Carter removed the Shah and brought in Khomeini. I do not know what the law is in this regard now.

Cause of Death without Burn in a Fire

One day at the beginning of my second-year residency when I went to the operating room, I met the head of the Department of Anesthesia, a very knowledgeable man. He was the first researcher in the world to find that people who died in fires who were not burned were killed by inhaling the smoke. His research work started by anesthetizing some german shepherd dogs, and after they were anesthetized, using a torch inside their throats. After using the torch, he killed the dogs and did an autopsy. He found out that the lungs of the dogs were not burned. He was the first to identify the cause of death in a fire was due to victims inhaling toxic materials in smoke and not as a result of heat.

My Research on Platelet Function and Gastric Bleeding

One of my professors, Dr. Mohammad Atik, was born in Afghanistan and came with his family to Iran where he finished primary school. Then they came to the United States where he finished high school and college. After that, he went to Harvard Medical School. When he graduated from Harvard Medical School, he went to Ohio University for his residency of general surgery, and then he started to work in the Department of Surgery at the University of Louisville. When I met him, he was a tenured professor and had published some original papers based on extensive research he had conducted.

There was a patient who came to the hospital because he was bleeding from his stomach. I put a tube in his stomach, irrigated the stomach frequently and also gave him blood transfusions. I did blood tests to ensure he didn't have a bleeding problem. All his blood tests were normal. Despite all of this, the bleeding did not stop. So after talking to my professor, Dr. Atik, we decided to take him to the operating room to find the source of the bleeding and fix it.

Dr. Atik was scrubbing with me and when I opened the stomach, we found no ulceration in the stomach. We noticed bleeding came from the entire surface of the stomach. I asked Dr. Atik where the bleeding was coming from and why. He said he didn't know. I thought he was joking because he was a renowned professor and I asked him again to please tell me where the bleeding was coming from. He repeated that he did not know. He said if I was interested in finding the cause of the bleeding, I could do research and find the reason.

Because there was no ulceration, we removed ninety per cent of the stomach and then anastomosed (connected) the remaining part of the stomach to the small bowel.

Dr. Atik told me that he believed that in patients like this in which bleeding didn't stop, there was something wrong with the blood clotting and that our current available blood tests could not recognize the problem. He said that if I was interested in researching this, he would put me in charge of any patients with gastric bleeding that were admitted to his service. He said we would not give blood transfusions from the blood bank to those patients. Instead, we would ask the patient to ask his or her family members to donate their fresh blood to him or her. In those days, when someone donated blood, the blood bank kept the whole blood in the refrigerator.

I accepted this challenge and Dr. Atik told our colleagues that I would be responsible for any patients who presented with gastric bleeding and who were admitted in his service.

For some of these patients, the level of hemoglobin was very low, but we did not give them the blood from the blood bank as we had done previously. When one member of the patient's family donated blood, we transfused that fresh blood into the patient. To my surprise, when we did that, the gastric bleeding stopped and no surgery was required.

I collected records on more than thirty patients who had massive gastric bleeding. All the available blood tests for blood coagulation were normal. We were able to stop their gastric bleeding just by giving them the fresh blood donated by their family members. At that point, Dr. Atik and I still thought the problem was that there was not a blood test available to recognize their coagulation problem.

New Coagulation Blood Test

I next went to the head of the laboratory of the University of Louisville and told him my challenge. I asked him to think about creating a blood test that would tell us the problem with the coagulation of the blood due to a possible abnormality of the platelet function in those patients. He said that there was no such test. I told him that I knew there was no such test, but that I thought there was something wrong with the patients' blood coagulation and platelet function that we could not detect with currently available blood tests. If he could create a test, we might be able to solve this problem. He didn't believe I was serious, but when I told him I was working closely with Dr. Atik, who was well-respected, he said he would think about it.

Two weeks later, he called and said he had developed a blood test that we could do on patients who had no bleeding and also on patients with the massive gastric bleeding to see if there was any difference. We started to do this new blood test, called platelet aggregation and platelet adhesiveness, on both types of patients.

In the blood of every human being, there are red blood cells, white blood cells, platelets, and serum. Platelets are the cells that stick together and plug a hole in the blood vessel to stop the bleeding when there is a hole or a cut in a blood vessel. When somebody gets stabbed or otherwise cut, these platelets immediately stick together to seal the hole and stop the bleeding.

Platelet Aggregation and Adhesiveness

The head of the laboratory developed a test to determine if the platelet function was normal, which meant that the platelets could stick together normally. The test explained why patients with massive gastric bleeding who got fresh blood stopped bleeding, but those who got blood from the blood bank continued to bleed. The platelets in the blood that was kept by the blood bank lost their effectiveness (in sticking together) over few days. The test was positive on patients who came with massive gastric bleeding which stopped after they received fresh blood. We compared fresh blood with the blood bank blood with regard to platelet adhesiveness and found there was a difference between the two blood sources. The platelet adhesiveness and aggregation disappear in the blood which is kept in the blood bank. Also, an infection or aspirin could interfere with platelet adhesiveness and platelet aggregation so platelets could not stick together and stop the bleeding.

Presentation of my Research Paper on Platelets

I sent my research paper on platelets to the Clinical Congress of the American College of Surgeons. They accepted it for presentation and scheduled it during their 57th annual meeting to be held in Atlantic City from October 18 through 22, 1971. It would be presented during their "Forum on Surgical Problems." This portion of the American College of Surgeons meeting only covered new ideas and new techniques

When I went to this meeting, I was a third-year resident of general surgery. The title of my paper was "**The Significance of Low Platelet Adhesiveness in Massive Gastrointestinal Bleeding**." The authors were me and Dr. Atik.

The majority of the audience consisted of big shot professors. I told them that in the beginning, I found a significant change in the quality of stored blood in blood banks. That is why the transfusion of blood bank blood to patients with severe gastrointestinal bleeding did not help the patient, but transfusions of fresh blood did stop the bleeding. I explained this was due to the destruction of platelets in blood saved in blood bank. I told them that if we separated the platelets, plasma, and red cells from each other in any unit of donated blood, and kept the plasma and platelets frozen and separated in the blood bank, the function of the platelets and plasma would not be disturbed as long as we kept them frozen.

During our research, we also discovered that aspirin reduced the adhesiveness and aggregation of platelets. Patients who have heart problems are told to take aspirin every day to reduce the blockage in the blood vessels of the heart that might cause heart attacks. Aspirin can also be used to prevent the blockage of blood vessels of the heart in patients over age fifty.

The majority of the professors did not believe me. Dr. Atik got up and said, "Whatever Dr. Matini said is accurate and I recommend that when you return to your practice, you try to measure platelet function in your patients without gastric bleeding and in those patients with gastric bleeding. I am sure you will find that whatever Dr. Matini said is accurate."

After research done at other universities confirmed my findings, blood banks across the United States started dividing donated blood into three parts (red cells, plasma, and platelets) and kept the platelets and serum frozen. When blood banks freeze the platelets, it keeps their function intact so you can give them to patients with bleeding to stop the bleeding. I was lucky that I had a great professor like Dr. Atik on my side and I am proud of my research which benefitted people around the world.

After this research, many people over age fifty take one aspirin tablet a day to reduce clotting and blockage of their coronary arteries of the heart. Also, patients with bleeding from their stomach respond well to a platelet transfusion which causes their bleeding to stop. With the help of the director of the laboratory at the University of Louisville who responded to my request and created a new blood test to measure the function of platelets, now we can better understand about the malfunction of platelets.

Physicians in every specialty eventually retire or die and their patients may remember their good work, but even those good works will eventually be forgotten. My accomplishment of identifying the function and response of platelets based on the effect of aspirin or infection will never be forgotten, even after I die.

Publications and Presentations

I presented papers at several medical conferences and wrote an article regarding my work on platelet function.

"**The Significance of Low Platelet Adhesiveness in Massive Gastrointestinal Bleeding**," Presented at the *Surgical Forum of American College of Surgeons*, Oct 1971, Surgical Forum, 325, 1971. (First such paper in the world.)

"**A New Approach to the Problem of Massive Gastrointestinal Bleeding**," Presented at the *40th Annual Assembly of the Southeast-*

ern Surgical Congress, Washington, DC, March 27, 1972.

"**Platelet Dysfunction: An Important Factor in Massive Bleeding from Stress Ulcer**," *The Journal of Trauma*, Vol. 12, 884, 1972.

"**A New Approach to Massive Bleeding from Acute Gastroduodenal Ulceration**," Presented at the *15th Annual Conference of University Surgical Residents*, Houston, TX, April 11-14, 1974.

Pathology Training at the Mayo Clinic

At the end of December, I had to drive to Rochester, Minnesota for my pathology rotation at the Mayo Clinic. Because the trip was so long, I planned to stay one night in a motel midway through the trip, but while I was driving, I heard on the radio that there was going to be a significant snowstorm overnight and the road would likely be closed. So I decided not to stop.

I arrived in Rochester safely and went to a Marriott Hotel, taking a room on the first floor. After I had dinner, I was tired and went to bed. When I woke up at ten A.M. the next day, I looked outside the window and saw it was still dark. I knew that Rochester was in the same time zone as Louisville, but because it was dark, I got confused and called the front desk to ask what time it was. The clerk said it was 10 A.M. I then asked why it was so dark and the clerk responded that the first floor rooms were buried in snow. She said there was a heavy snowfall the previous night. The snow was so heavy that it covered the windows of the first floor rooms and also my car.

In Rochester, I was impressed that they were able to clean the snow from the streets within two hours; therefore, I was able to get out of the room at noon. There was a nice lady at the front desk who told me that since I was new to the area, I should know that the weather was very cold at night. She said I should empty the radiator of my car and fill it with 100% antifreeze, which I did.

The Mayo Clinic had one of the best pathology departments in the United States, with 36 operating rooms on one floor. The pathology residents had to take specimens removed from patients' bodies during surgery from the operating room to the laboratory on the same floor for a frozen section examination, a procedure also performed by the pathology residents.

There are two techniques for pathology examination of any specimen. The most common type is a permanent section in which the specimen which was removed from the body is put into a paraffin solution and dyed. After three days, it is cut into multiple thin layers and examined under a microscope for diagnosis. The other technique is a frozen section in which the specimen is marked with different colors of dye in a clock orientation to color the tissue. The tissue is then frozen immediately in a special machine, then cut into thin layers and examined under the microscope. When you do a frozen section, it is more difficult to make a diagnosis. The policy in the Pathology Department of the Mayo Clinic was that every specimen that came out of a patient had to be examined via frozen section. This policy enhanced the training of the pathology residents.

We examined any tissue which had been removed from patients in the operating room using frozen sections regardless of whether or not the surgeon requested it. As soon as the surgeons removed tissue, the operating room nurse pressed a button which lit a light in the pathology lab showing the number of the operating room where the specimen was removed. When this happened, one of the pathology residents would go to the operating room to retrieve the specimen along with its written surgical diagnosis which indicated which part of the body the tissue came from. After preparing and examining the frozen section and making a diagnosis, the resident returned to the operating room and gave the written pathology diagnosis to the surgeon.

The Mayo Clinic has one of the most sophisticated medical libraries in the world. When I visited it, I saw so many young people, even younger than eighteen years old, in the small rooms of the library surrounded by multiple books and studying. Seeing them encouraged me to prepare my paper on the gastric bleeding research. The library was incredibly helpful. Because I didn't have to work at night in the Mayo Clinic during my residency, I had time to research and prepare my paper. The paper was later published in the general surgery journal and was even referred to in a textbook of surgery. My experience in Rochester proved very valuable. The pathology training at the Mayo Clinic taught me frozen section examination which helped in my practice as I eventually performed numerous skin cancer surgeries. In the operating room, I put the specimen on a piece of white paper and marked twelve, three, six and nine o'clock around the specimen. The operating room nurse or physician's assistant took the tissue to the pathologist right then while the patient was still in the operating room. Sometimes I took the tissue sample myself, prepared the frozen section and examined it under the microscope. Many times the pathologist would tease me and say that I didn't need him since I could diagnose it fine by myself. The training eventually allowed me to help many of my own patients.

Car Accident in Rochester, Minnesota

One cold and icy day, I was driving out of the hospital parking lot in Rochester where I had to cross the main road. I saw that the road was clear, and began to cross the main road when suddenly, a car exited its parking space and forced me to stop. When I did that, another car that was coming down the main road could not stop and struck the side of my car. I saw a state police car coming toward us. The state trooper stopped. The trooper told me that he called the local police to come and take care of the problem. When the local policeman came, he took me and the other driver into his car and gave me a citation to go to court. I told him I was fully stopped when I was hit, then asked him how I could be guilty. He said that the law of Minnesota stated that in any accident involving a car crossing the main road, the driver of that car was at fault.

That seemed wrong to me so I decided to contest the ticket in court. When I went to court, the judge asked me if I was guilty and I said I was not. He said I had to come to court four months later. I told him I was only in town for a total of three months, so he gave me an earlier date.

When I came to the hospital the next morning and told my colleagues what happened in court, all of them laughed at me for going to court to fight the police. They all thought I was crazy and made fun of me.

Rochester Traffic Court

I went to court on my assigned day. The police officer testified and also brought the state trooper as a witness. After the state trooper finished his testimony, I was allowed to ask him questions. I asked him if he was driving when he saw the accident. He answered yes. I said I had no further questions. I told the judge that when a police officer was driving instead of stopped, he could not see clearly what happened.

In the end, the judge asked me to defend myself. I went to the board and drew a picture of the parking lot and the main road, my car and the other car, and showed how the accident happened. I mentioned that the policeman told me that Minnesota law stated that if anyone had an accident while crossing the main road, it was always his or her fault. I said if this was the law, it meant that if a child was crossing the main road, a driver crossing that road had to run over the child because that was the law of the State of Minnesota. I mentioned that I had to stop to avoid hitting another car, and, although I was sure the other driver tried to stop too, because of the ice causing the road to be slippery, he was unable to stop and hit the side of my car.

The judge said I was not guilty and the driver of the other car which hit my car was guilty. When I was leaving the court, the local police officer came to me to apologize. I told him it was no problem; I was just truthfully defending myself.

When I got back to the hospital the next day and told my colleagues that the judge found me not guilty, they said I was lucky. I told them this was not luck. It was because I was truthful and, in telling the truth, convinced the judge that I was right.

New Chairman of Department of Surgery in Louisville, Kentucky

When I finished my second-year residency of general surgery, everyone was happy with my work, including the Acting Chairman of the Department of Surgery, the faculty members of the Department of Surgery, the Chief Resident and other senior residents for surgery. Then we got a new Chairman of the Department of Surgery. His name was Dr. Haram Polk and he was originally from Mississippi. He was very young and replaced the Acting Chairman of the Department of Surgery, Dr. Harbrecht.

At the first faculty meeting Dr. Polk held with members of the Department of Surgery, he said that the first thing he was going to do was get rid of all of the foreign residents. At the second meeting, just a couple of days later, he mentioned that he was going to fire Dr. Matini. Dr. Harbrecht got up and asked, "Why? Have you ever seen him? Have you ever worked with him?" Dr. Polk said, "No, I haven't seen him and I haven't worked with him." Dr. Harbrecht said, "Well, then there is no reason to fire him. Between the four third-year residents that we have now, he is the best." He also said that every professor of the program would resign if he fired a resident just because he was a foreigner. All the doctors in the Department of Surgery stood up and supported Dr. Harbrecht's statement. Dr. Polk backed off and did not fire me. I didn't hear this story until I finished my Chief Residency.

Visiting English Professor from Africa

When I was a third-year resident in general surgery, we had a lecture by a visiting English professor who had lived in Africa for many years. The title of his lecture was "Carcinoma and Diverticulitis of the Large Bowel and Their Relation to Diet."

He began his lecture by showing a picture of a toilet full of stool in Africa. He said the stool belonged to a native African man. The next slide showed another toilet filled with stool, but a whole lot less stool than the previous one. He said this belonged to an English man. The professor said there was no large bowel cancer or diverticulitis (inflammation of diverticula which is an abnormal pocket formation of the large bowel) in native Africans, but when Africans changed their diet to be more like the diet of Europeans, they can develop large bowel cancer or diverticulitis like the Europeans. He said the reason for the lack of large bowel cancer and diverticulitis in native Africans was their diet. Because they ate a lot of fiber in their food, the volume of their stool was double or triple that of our stool.

The professor's research showed that if we increase the amount of non-absorbable fibers in our diet, it reduces the chance of getting cancer of the large bowel and diverticulitis. His landmark research gradually changed how we eat, and today, we are eating a lot more fiber in our food.

Prior to the research of this professor, the treatment of large bowel diverticula was a low residue diet (a diet with more easily digestible foods). However, after his research, this was changed and today a high residue diet (one high in dietary fiber) is recommended for the treatment of diverticula, and to prevent the development of diverticula or colon cancer.

My Vacation to Europe

While still a resident in general surgery, I had a vacation and decided to go to Europe with my brother and his family. We made arrangements to meet in London. I asked my brother which hotel he was staying in so I could come there when I arrived, but he said he would come to the airport to pick me up.

I made my reservation to fly from Louisville to Philadelphia and then catch an international flight to London. I told my brother the flight number and the time I was scheduled to arrive in London.

When I flew from Louisville to Philadelphia, I got to Philadelphia on time, but there was heavy rain and we were kept on the tarmac for a long time prior to proceeding to the gate. When we finally were allowed to proceed to the gate and disembark from the airplane, I had missed my connecting flight to London. The airline customer service agent told me it was best to go to New York that night and then leave from there for London early in the morning. I explained to the agent that my brother was waiting for me at the airport in London and I had no way to contact him to let him know the change in my plans. In those days there were no cell phones. The agent said he would send a message to the airline staff in London and ask them to find my brother to let him know I would be delayed. I flew to New York that night, stayed in a hotel near the airport and caught a flight to London the next morning.

When I arrived at the London airport, I saw my brother, which made me very happy. He said nobody told him I would be delayed. He said when he didn't see me at the time I was supposed to arrive; he asked an airline agent if my name was on the passenger list. The airline attendant said it was, but said I was not on the plane. My brother ended up staying overnight at the airport waiting for me since he didn't know when I was going to arrive. It was lucky for me that he waited for me because otherwise I wouldn't have known where to find him.

I had a lot of relatives at that time who were living in London. I decided to invite them for dinner to a restaurant. Since this was my first trip to London and I didn't know any restaurants, I looked around and found a restaurant that appeared to be nice, so I made a reservation for ten people, which included my brother and his family. When we arrived in the restaurant that night, I saw pictures of the political leaders of both England and America on the walls of restaurant. Later on, I found out it was one of the most expensive restaurants in London.

When I was sitting at the table and all the guests had arrived, my brother, who is eleven years older than me, announced that although I invited them for dinner, because I was still in training, everyone would be his guest that evening, instead of mine. Although my brother was trying to help me, I was insulted because this was the first time I had invited those relatives for dinner. I decided to punish him, so I drank many dry martinis, which cost him a lot of money. I thought that was good punishment. He was a good businessman and was very wealthy, so it was not a big deal to him, but I remember seeing his eyes open wide in surprise when they brought the bill to him.

Bullfight in Madrid, Spain

The last portion of the trip was interesting because after my brother and his family went home, I went to Madrid, Spain by myself. It was a Saturday night and I went to the concierge of the Hilton Hotel to ask how I could get a ticket for the Sunday bullfight. He asked me which Sunday. I told him, "Tomorrow," and he laughed. He said the bullfight was all sold out and that normally you had to get a ticket two or three months in advance. I told him I would only be in Madrid for a couple more days, so I could not go.

I came to my room and a few minutes later the phone rang. It was the concierge. He said I was lucky. He told me that there was an American lady who came every few months to Madrid. This American lady liked bullfighting and bought season tickets for herself and a friend. She had just called him to say that her friend couldn't go to the bullfight and she was willing to sell that ticket. He told her that I had just inquired about getting a ticket and she was happy to sell it to me.

It was lucky for me to sit next to the American lady because she knew everything about bullfighting. At the bullfight, I saw lots of things I had never seen before. She told me that there was a young bullfighter fighting that day who would become a matador if he won two more bullfights, both of which were to take place that day. The spectators had white handkerchiefs which they waved to cheer the bullfighters on. The first fight had a famous matador. People were throwing flowers and wine in leather containers for him in to the bullring. When the fight began, I found out that the bull had been stabbed multiple times prior to the fight so it was mad to start with and weaker than normal because of blood loss. The famous matador was very close to the edge of the ring when the fight started. When the bull came after him and the matador tried to move backward, there was no room for him to move. The bull gored him and threw him up in the air. When he fell back down on the ground, bullfight attendants quickly pulled his body on the ground and out of the field. They didn't even use a stretcher. Next, the younger bullfighter came out and was able to kill the next two bulls. Everyone raised their white handkerchiefs to signal their approval and their vote that he should become a new matador.

The next day, I saw in the newspaper that the matador who was gored had a perforated bowel, but he survived after surgery. After watching one bullfight, I had no interest to see any more bullfights. I wondered how people could watch such a horrible event. I was glad to hear recently that bullfighting was banned in several cities in Spain.

Monthly Conference of the Department of Surgery

Every month, we had a mortality and morbidity conference at which the professors put the Chief Resident of Surgery "on trial." The entire faculty of the Department of Surgery attended along with the medical students and interns who rotated in surgery, and all the residents of general surgery. I don't believe this type of meeting could happen now because of the legal environment. At this conference, they explored why some patients had complications after surgery or why patients died. The Chief Resident had to defend himself. This was a fantastic educational program. The Chief Resident prepared himself well and discussed all the issues about every patient who had complications or died. At the end of the presentation and discussion, the professors decided whether the complications or death of a patient were caused by the patient's condition, by disease, or by the error of residents in the diagnosis, or in the surgical or medical treatment of the patient. Because all the residents were in attendance, this was a very effective way to learn from cases.

Unusual Transfer of Injured Patients to the Louisville General Hospital by Police Officers

During my general surgery residency at the University of Louisville between 1970 and 1973, there was a policy in the city of Louisville that I had never heard about. The policy was that when there was a major accident or gunshot wound victim, or even a seriously wounded patient, the police would bring the patient directly to the operating room of Louisville General Hospital after they called the operating room nurse in charge to alert her they were on their way. As soon as the operating room nurse received the call, she paged the Chief Resident of general surgery to the operating room and every other resident of general surgery when they heard that page also ran to the operating room. Because of this policy, I think we saved a lot of severely injured patients. If they had been taken to the Emergency Room, many of them would not have survived because their injuries were too severe and needed immediate treatment.

When a patient was brought directly to the operating room by the police officers, the Chief Resident and all the residents of general surgery worked together as a team. Of course, the head nurse of the operating room also helped us. We started an intravenous line in a major vein; and took the blood for a type and cross match for a blood transfusion and blood tests. We also put a catheter into the bladder to check the urine and see how much urine the patient produced. This group of residents and nurses cut the clothes that the patient was wearing and examined the patient together. When we did not know which part of the body was injured, many times the only way we could find it was to cut off all the clothing of the patient. Within three minutes, we had to complete the examination and make a diagnosis of what was wrong with the patient.

Gunshot Wounds in Louisville, Kentucky

We had many patients with gunshot wounds. Every month, between seventy and ninety such cases were brought to Louisville General Hospital. One professor asked why they were sending physicians to Vietnam when they could come to Louisville and see more gunshot wounds. Most gun fights were between family members. In the three years I was in the general surgery residency, only two patients with gunshots were either thieves or police officers; the rest were people who had been shot by another family member. Apparently everyone in Louisville had guns, and when they got upset, they shot their loved ones. Of course, they were immediately sorry, but it was too late then.

Father Shot his 14-Year-Old Son

One father shot his 14-year-old son with a shotgun at such close range that we found the shell of the shotgun in the son's liver. As soon as the father shot his son, he was so sorry and knew that he had made a bad mistake. He hit his forehead against the wall so many times that he cut his forehead badly. Instead of one patient, we had two. Unfortunately, the 14-year-old's liver wound was so severe that he died.

Wife Shot her Husband Six Times

Another night, the police brought a patient directly to the operating room who had six gunshot wounds. The patient happened to be one of the radiologic technicians of Louisville General Hospital. He was a nice guy who was married and had children. Fortunately, he was still able to talk. I asked who shot him and he said his wife had done it. Under general anesthesia, we opened up the area of each gunshot wound and found he had major injuries to the kidney, stomach, bowel and pancreas. It took me six hours of surgery to repair all the wounds in the organs. We kept him in the intensive care unit and kept transfusing blood, intravenous antibiotics, intravenous fluid, and pain medications.

When I came out of the operating room around two A.M., I was being paged. When I answered the page, I found out the patient's wife wanted to speak to me. I could not believe that the wife, who shot her husband six times, was not arrested and, instead, was in the hospital wanting to talk to me! In Louisville at that time, when someone was shot, unless they made a complaint, the assailant was not arrested. I talked to the wife and asked her what she wanted. She said she wanted to know if her husband would still be a "man" after receiving multiple gunshot wounds. I told her that if her husband survived after all of his injuries, he would not have any problem with sex. The patient was in the hospital for six months, but unfortunately, despite our best treatment, he did not make it and died because of pancreatic failure.

Who Shot the Wife?

One night at midnight, the police brought an overweight 50-year-old woman to the operating room because of a gunshot to the left upper corner of the abdomen. After our routine preparation for exploration of the abdomen, I asked the lady who shot her. She said she shot herself by accident. I was surprised at her response and asked her how it happened. She said she was looking for one of her dresses and apparently a gun was in her closet where she was looking and she accidentally shot herself. I did not believe her at all. Under general anesthesia, I explored the abdomen and I found the bullet missed the major blood vessel of the abdomen by only one half of an inch. Fortunately, the bullet did not injure the large bowel or any important structure of the abdominal cavity. I'm still convinced to this day that the patient did not tell the truth.

Attempt to Kill a Husband

On another occasion, they brought in a 50-year-old African-American man who was awake and alert. We asked what had happened and he told us that his wife hit him with a hammer over his head several times. We got an x-ray of his skull in the operating room and found out that a major portion of his skull did not exist. We asked him if he had any injuries to his head in the past. He said yes, he had a gunshot wound to the head which required surgery and removal of a large portion of his skull. So the wife knew that her husband didn't have a full skull and hit him with a hammer several times right on the brain. Somehow hammering his brain did not kill him. He survived and left the hospital in satisfactory condition after a couple of days.

The Fight between a Thief and Police Officer

One night they brought two patients to the operating room: a thief and a police officer who had shot each other. The condition of the police officer was stable; he had a gunshot wound of the abdomen, but he was not bleeding and his vital signs were stable. The thief had multiple gunshot wounds of the abdomen, was bleeding severely, and his blood pressure was falling. I had no choice but to take the thief to the operating room first.

After I finished his surgery and stopped all the bleeding, I took the police officer to the operating room. He had a gunshot wound to the large bowel, so I had to divert the stool at that time to a colostomy (dividing the large bowel at the level of gunshot wound and bringing the proximal portion of large bowel outside of the abdomen). This was a temporary colostomy and, after a month, I brought him back to the operating room, and put the divided large bowel back together. After the second operation, the patient became completely normal.

At the monthly meeting in which I discussed the surgical cases, I presented the case of the thief and police officer. After my presentation of facts, Dr. Polk, the Chairman of the Department of Surgery, stood up and said I did the wrong thing by operating on the thief first. My response was that, with all due respect, when I finished medical school, I took a vow as a physician to take care of patients as best I knew how without regard to other issues; therefore, my priority was the patient's survival. I was one surgeon with two patients: one stable and one dying. If I operated on the police officer first, the thief would have died. I saved the thief's life and the police officer also survived. I said I didn't think I did anything wrong. The Chairman of the Department could not comment further because the other professors agreed with what I did.

Unconscious Man due to Gunshot Wound of the Head

One night, they brought a young unconscious man to the operating room with a gunshot wound to the head. As usual, I started an intravenous line and the head nurse of the operating room, who was very experienced, started cutting the patient's trousers from the ankle up. She stopped cutting the pants at the knee level and asked me to finish the job. I was very surprised that she asked me to finish cutting the trousers. As soon as I got the scissors and held the edge of the trousers up, I found out the reason she asked me to finish it up. It was because the length of this patient's penis was very unusual. Even while he was unconscious, the tip of his penis was right above his knee. Unfortunately, despite our best efforts, he died the same night. Besides wanting to save his life, we were all hoping that this patient would survive so we could see how long his penis would get with an erection.

How to Complete Unsuccessful Shooting of a Person in Louisville, Kentucky

They brought a patient to the Emergency Room who had a gunshot wound to his right thigh, and called me to examine him in the Emergency Room. I found out the gunshot had not struck any main arteries or nerves so we scheduled him for surgery later that day. An hour later, I received a call from the Emergency Room physician. He said that the patient was dead. Apparently someone had told the assailant that the man who was shot was in the Emergency Room, and that he was fine and was talking. The assailant got his gun and came to the Emergency Room to finish the victim off. The Emergency Room physician saw the assailant and asked him why he had a gun in his hand. The assailant pointed the gun at the physician, who promptly jumped behind a desk, then proceeded to locate the victim in the Emergency Room. He shot and killed his intended victim, then walked out.

Bypass Surgery for Weight Loss

Near the end of my chief residency in general surgery, there was a new operation presented at one of the national meetings. It was a new bypass technique for patients who were extremely obese and could not lose weight by strict diet and exercise.

We had a patient who weighed about 350 pounds. We put her in the hospital and did a bunch of tests; we couldn't find anything to explain the cause of her obesity. We put her on a 500-calorie diet every day for a week and we did not see any significant weight loss. We thought she was a good candidate for this new bypass surgery, which had only been done a few times so far within the entire country.

When I suggested this operation to her and told her all the details, she said she would like me to come back that afternoon and talk to her husband. I returned that afternoon and she introduced me to her husband, who weighed about 160 pounds and was very short. Apparently, the patient noticed my surprise at seeing her tiny husband. She said that was the best type of husband to have because he knew if he did anything against her, all she had to do was pick him up and put him on the shelf and he couldn't come down! I explained the operation to her husband and he said he was for it and he would pray that all went well.

All night I was thinking about how I could put such a huge body on the operating table. I thought I could bring other operating tables into the operating room and wire them together. I went to the operating room early the next morning and the nurses helped me to get another operating room table and wire the two tables together. When the patient was placed on these two wired-together tables, I realized that I could not reach the abdomen because the tables were too wide after being wired together. We unhooked the table and put the patient on just one table with each side of her body hanging off the table. I performed this operation and, fortunately, it came out fine. The patient was in the hospital for three weeks and lost about 35 pounds. She was discharged in good condition. She ended up losing 150 pounds total.

Stab Wound of Heart

One day, the police brought in a patient that they had found lying on his back in the street. They shook him, he opened his eyes, and an officer asked what was wrong. He said he didn't know, but that he felt all right. They brought him directly to the operating room because they thought something was seriously wrong.

When I put a needle in the major vein of his neck to start an intravenous line, instead of intravenous fluid going in the vein, blood was coming back into the intravenous tube. This was a bad sign and meant that there was a hole in the heart and that blood was coming out of the hole every time the heart pumped. The blood accumulated underneath the sheath around the heart, and was squeezing it. When we examined him, we couldn't find any cut or stab wound. At the same time, the resident of anesthesia was putting an endotracheal tube in to put him to sleep, when suddenly the patient's heart stopped.

I immediately put sterile gloves on and opened his chest with a sterile knife. I cut open the sheath around the heart and suctioned blood that had accumulated around his heart. Immediately the heart started to pump and, of course, with each pump of heart, the blood was shooting out from a stab wound of the heart. I was able to suture the stab wound of the heart quickly and stop the bleeding. This patient did well and went home within one week. The reason I could not find the stab wound because it was very tiny and located in the junction of chest and upper abdomen. Most probably this stab wound was done by an ice pick.

Gunshot Wound of the Heart

One night, the police brought a patient with a gunshot wound to his chest. After I started a central intravenous line, the anesthesia resident put him under general anesthesia and I opened his chest. Then, I opened the sheath around the heart and blood was shooting out from the hole created by the gunshot. I found the bullet, removed it, closed the hole, and the bleeding stopped immediately. This patient did very well and was discharged one week after surgery. The only reason this patient survived was because the police brought him directly to the operating room right after he was shot. Such was the success of this unusual and wonderful procedure of the police system of Louisville.

Early Stage of Cancer of Pancreas

When I was Chief Resident, one of my patients was a 35-year-old man with a diagnosis of a duodenal (first portion of small bowel) ulcer. The pre-operative x-ray showed nothing could go from the stomach to the duodenum. This patient had no other abnormality in his x-rays or his blood tests. I thought the cause of obstruction was the duodenal ulcer. When I opened the abdomen and looked inside, I found a small round tumor, slightly larger than a ping pong ball, in the head of the pancreas, located next to the duodenum. That mass pressed against the duodenum, causing a total obstruction. I took a needle biopsy of the tumor and sent it to the pathologist for frozen section examination, so that I could find out what kind of tumor it was. My initial diagnosis was adenocarcinoma (cancer) of the pancreas. The pathologist called me in the operating room and said that my initial diagnosis was correct.

Whipple Operation

The surgical treatment of cancer of the pancreas is the most difficult and complicated operation in the field of general surgery. I had read about the technique of this operation but I had never observed or performed it. Therefore, I contacted the on-call professor for that day, the Chairman of the Department of Surgery. On the phone, he tried to give every excuse for not coming and helping me with the surgery, but I finally convinced him that this was a rare occasion. I told him this patient was lucky that I discovered his pancreatic cancer accidentally in its early stage since it had not yet spread to any part of the abdomen. I told the professor that we could save the patient's life if we perform the Whipple operation. A few minutes later, the chairman came to the operating room and looked at the tumor. He agreed that this operation had to be done. After ten minutes of working with me, he said he had to go and I could do this operation myself, although I told him I had never observed or performed this operation before. I spent seven hours and did this complicated and difficult operation alone. This procedure involves a resection of the head of the pancreas, the entire duodenum (first portion of small bowel), a part of the jejunum (second portion of the small bowel), and the distal part of the stomach; a transection of the pancreatic and biliary ducts; and an anastomosis of the pancreatic and bile ducts to the jejunum, and the lower portion of the stomach to the jejunum. The patient did very well after surgery and his recovery was excellent.

Ten days after this difficult surgery, we had our monthly meeting to discuss surgical outcomes of our cases. Dr. Ellison, one of the greatest professors of surgery, who was particularly famous for his work on the pancreas, was our visiting professor and attended our monthly meeting. I presented this unusual case and said I accidentally found carcinoma of the pancreas. I said I had never seen this operation in the past but was able to perform this difficult surgery by myself. Dr. Ellison asked me when the patient died. I said the patient was alive and was doing very well and, as a matter of fact, was sitting in the front row of the conference room. The professor got up, went to the patient and asked him few questions. The professor pulled the patient's gown up and looked at the surgical wound, which was completely healed. The professor asked me if I had done this operation before. I said I had never done it before and had never even seen it done before. Dr. Ellison congratulated me for doing this very difficult operation by myself. He told me I would be a great surgeon. I was proud that I could save the patient's life.

The General Surgery Residency at the University of Louisville, Kentucky

The general surgery residency at the University of Louisville was one of the best training programs in the United States. They trained us so well that when we became Chief Resident (fourth year residency of general surgery), we were able to do any type of general surgery, peripheral vascular surgery, head and neck surgery or trauma surgery of the chest without supervision. Of course, in those days we did not have so many threats of lawsuits. Today, I am sure no resident could perform any surgery without the presence of his or her professor because of the risk of lawsuits, but then the Chief Resident was given permission to do all kinds of surgery by himself, and if he needed assistance, he could call the professors anytime and ask them questions or ask them to come and help him.

Considering Plastic Surgery

In the middle of my last year of residency of general surgery, I found out that if I practiced general surgery, I would not be doing such major and complicated surgeries as I was performing during my general surgery residency. I learned that the most common procedures that general surgeons performed were hernia repair, gall bladder surgery, hemorrhoid surgery, colon surgery and surgery for peptic ulcers. None of those appealed to me. Two cases I had recently seen made me think about plastic surgery training.

During a three-month rotation at the Veterans Administration (VA) hospital in Louisville, Kentucky I made a round with the Chief Resident who was just finishing his rotation there. He introduced every patient, and told me their diagnoses, what kinds of surgery was performed and what their status was. He also talked about those patients who had not yet had surgery. We walked in to a room in which a male patient was sitting and the middle portion of his face was covered by a black sheet. When I asked the Chief Resident what was going on, he said he would talk to me later. When we came out of that room, the Chief Resident said that the patient had cancer of his left cheek, which required a wide and deep excision, resulting in being able to see inside of his sinus. That is why they covered the middle portion of his face with a black sheet. He also said they were looking for a nursing home that had blind patients, so that he could be transferred there and nobody could see him. Later on when I examined him, I thought if we had a plastic surgeon, the defect of his face could be reconstructed.

Another afternoon I was presenting the cases for the next day's surgery to Dr. Harbrecht, the Chairman of the Department of Surgery at the VA hospital. One patient had a large skin lesion, similar to skin cancer, on the dorsum of the upper portion of his nose. Dr. Harbrecht asked me how I wanted to do the surgery. I said I knew I had to remove the entire skin cancer, but I did not know how to reconstruct the defect of the upper portion of the nose after the excision. He told me that I had better find out that night because we could not send the patient home with a hole in the dorsum of his nose. I went to the library that night and reviewed the technique for reconstruction of the defect of the upper portion of the nose using a skin flap from the lower portion of the mid-forehead. The next day, Dr. Harbrecht asked me if I knew how to fix the defect and I said yes. I did the surgery successfully.

Plastic Surgery Training

In 1973, there were only forty-two residency programs for plastic and reconstructive surgery in the entire United States. Each program accepted only one or two residents per year. There were a few programs that accepted four residents per year.

I applied for every plastic surgery residency program in the United States and only five of these programs sent me application forms. Since I had applied for the plastic surgery residency late in the application cycle, I was not able to apply for the cycle beginning right after my general surgery residency ended. Since I was applying for the following cycle, I would have to wait for a year. I knew there was no time to spare to secure my plastic surgery residency. After I completed the application forms and mailed them back I made several telephone calls. The University of Detroit accepted me, and the University of Chicago, University of St Louis and George Washington University gave me appointments for interviews.

Interview with the Chairman of Department of Plastic Surgery

Each of these four programs accepted one resident per year. When I went for the interview to the University of Chicago and met the Chairman of the Department of Plastic Surgery, he told me that every resident who finished his or her general surgery residency had good recommendation letters from the Chairman of the Department of Surgery, or other professors of surgery. He said the recommendations about me were quite different and he asked me what I had done. I told him that besides my surgical residency work, I did research and published the first research paper about the effect of aspirin and infection on the function of platelets which had resulted in gastric bleeding. This was the first paper in the world about this subject. As a result of my paper, blood banks now separated the platelets from the serum and red cells of donated blood. He said that he now understood why my recommendation letters were different. He asked if I had any questions. I asked what my chances would be for being accepted in his program.

He said seventy-five general surgeons had applied and I was one of the top five. He told me he would have difficulty choosing between these five top applicants.

When I went for an interview at George Washington University, after first meeting with the Chairman of the Department of Plastic Surgery, Dr. Lewis Thompson, I was sent to a famous general surgeon, Dr. Calvin Klopp, who was doing breast cancer surgery and head and neck cancer surgery. After I spoke to Dr. Klopp, he asked me to give him the list of operations I had performed during my chief residency of general surgery. Since I had the list with me I gave it to him.

Dr. Thompson asked what time I was flying back to Louisville. When I told him 7:30 P.M., he invited me for dinner before my flight, which I accepted. At dinner, he told me he had accepted me for the residency of plastic surgery at George Washington University. He told me he had sixty-eight applicants, and he had chosen me, which was a great triumph and honor.

Hand Surgery Fellowship at University of Louisville, Kentucky

The first few months after the completion of my general surgery residency, I continued to work in Louisville as the first assistant to general surgeons in private hospitals. Those general surgeons who knew me usually asked me to do the surgery on their private patients when I was working with them. During this period, I scrubbed a few times with a general surgeon who booked patients for repair of a hernia, but he only cut the skin of the lower abdomen then did not repair the hernia. He closed the skin and told the nurse he had repaired the hernia. I was surprised and went to the Chairman of Department of Surgery of that hospital and told him what I observed about that surgeon. He said unfortunately he could not do anything about it.

After three months, I saw Dr. Polk one day and I told him I was not happy because I felt like I was wasting my time. He said I could get a hand surgery fellowship at the Dr. Kleinert Hand Surgery program, which was also in Louisville. In those days, hand surgery was not a popular course and I was not aware of it. I thanked him and went to Dr. Kleinert's office and talked to the office manager. She asked what year I was looking to participate. I said that same year, starting January 1974. She said they already had twelve fellows for that time and did not have room for anyone else. I called Dr. Polk and told him that they didn't have any spots available. He apparently called them and persuaded them to let me participate, so I was lucky enough to start my hand surgery fellowship in January of 1974.

It was interesting for a person like me who had performed the most extensive and difficult cases of general surgery, head and neck surgery, and traumatic chest surgery to assist hand surgeons in their surgery. In the beginning, they allowed me to only close the skin. They were not happy with my skin closure and took my stitches out. They then taught me their way to close the skin. This was only the beginning. I learned their techniques for hand surgery, which were very different from my previous surgeries. The first thing I learned was that I had to buy magnifying glasses and use them during hand surgery because everything we worked on was small.

I was lucky. A few months prior to my hand surgery fellowship, Dr. Kleinert went to Shanghai and worked with the first surgeon in the world to perform a replantation of amputated fingers and hands. During my fellowship, I learned the replantation of fingers and hands, too. Dr. Kleinert told the fellows that anytime we were working on an injured hand where one of the arteries or even a vein of the finger was cut, even if the finger was not amputated, we had to do a micro- repair of the cut artery or vein. That way we were able to constantly practice how to do micro- anastomosis of the tiny blood vessels of the finger.

One day, the nurse at the hand surgery institute announced that someone wanted to see me and told me the name of the person. I didn't recognize the name, but I walked to the door and saw the lady, whose face was very familiar. I still couldn't figure out who she was. I told her I remembered her face, but couldn't remember where I had met her. I asked her what I could do for her. She started laughing and said that she didn't blame me for not recognizing her. She told me she had lost 190 pounds within the last seven months. I realized then that it was my bypass patient. Fortunately, the bypass operation was very successful on this patient, but later on I read that this operation had so many bad side effects that these type of surgeries were discontinued. At the present time, there is a different bypass procedure for obese individuals which is generally successful.

One month after I started the hand surgery fellowship, the orthopedic surgeon from Shanghai came to Louisville and was the guest of Dr. Kleinert. During a dinner party for the doctor from Shanghai, I learned that every doctor in China had to go to the villages and take care of the poor patients every five years, regardless of his specialty. He said that the last time he was in a village, a man came to him because he had cut off his finger. The Chinese doctor told the man that he did not know how to reattach the amputated finger. The doctor said that after he returned to Shanghai, he started to take rabbits to the lab, cut a part of their ear off, and then try to put it back together using micro-anastomosis of cut blood vessels. After several attempts, he was able to reattach the cut ear of the rabbit successfully. That was the beginning of reattaching amputated fingers and hands successfully in China.

The Dr. Kleinert fellowship was very interesting. All the hand surgery was done at the Jewish Hospital of Louisville. There were three operating rooms for hand surgery from eight A.M. to five P.M., two operating rooms from five P.M. to eleven P.M., and one operating room from eleven P.M. to eight A.M. In each operating room, there were two operating tables and two hand surgeries being done simultaneously. This hand surgery center was so famous that patients with hand injuries were brought there from different cities in Kentucky, Indiana, and Ohio.

One day a woman was brought to the operating room with multiple amputations and crushed fingers. This lady was working as an instrument specialist for General Motors for 25 years. She never took one day of sick leave in all her career until the last day before she retired. That day she was teaching a young technician to work with a press machine and she turned her head for one split second. That was when the young worker brought the powerful press machine down over her hand by mistake. Me and one of the professors spent five hours saving a thumb and one finger of her hand using microsurgery.

One night I received a call from the Emergency Room. When I arrived, there was a woman who was brought from her home after her house was hit by lightning while she was on the phone. She was dead and her entire body was burned by the lightning strike. I never read about such a disaster and never before saw such a victim with that type of injury. I gently touched the dorsum of her hand and saw the dead dried skin was coming off. After that, I never talked on the phone during a lightning storm!

Everyone, including Dr. Kleinert, worked very hard in those days. I remember seeing Dr. Kleinert sometimes fall asleep on a stretcher while he was waiting to go to the operating room. One night after midnight, I was so tired that after I dictated an operating note I fell asleep at my desk. Dr. Kleinert woke me up and said I had to help him complete some charts or the hospital would not allow us to perform surgery the next day. So I sat with him and completed charts until three A.M.

I noticed in some conferences that after dinner, Dr. Kleinert was asleep in his chair, but if somebody asked him a question, he opened his eyes and answered the question perfectly.

In the beginning of Dr. Kleinert's hand surgery practice, an Emergency Room physician called him to see the original owner of Kentucky Fried Chicken, Colonel Harlan Sanders, in the Emergency

Room. After examining him, Dr. Kleinert told Col. Sanders he needed major surgery on his hand. Dr. Kleinert was not yet famous. Col. Sanders asked Dr. Kleinert to put a dressing on his hand and he would think about it. Col. Sanders left the Jewish Hospital and flew to Rochester, Minnesota, that same night and went to the Mayo Clinic where he was admitted in the hospital. The next day, a surgeon came to see Col. Sanders. Col. Sanders told the surgeon that he looked a lot like the doctor that he had seen in the Jewish Hospital Emergency Room the day before. He was right. In those days, there was no hand surgeon at the Mayo Clinic, so the Mayo Clinic called Dr. Kleinert to come and see Col. Sanders. Dr. Kleinert told Col. Sanders that he was right, that he was the same surgeon Col. Sanders saw the day before at the Jewish Hospital of Louisville. Dr. Kleinert also told Col. Sanders that the cost of his surgery at the Mayo Clinic would be much higher than at the Jewish Hospital of Louisville because he had to pay for Dr. Kleinert's trip to Rochester.

In 2012, I attended a hand surgery fellowship reunion in Las Vegas. There was a dinner meeting of the Kleinert & Kutz Hand Care Center which I attended, and I was happy to see Doctors Kleinert and Kutz again. The occasion was the celebration of Dr. Kleinert's ninetieth birthday.

Unfortunately, Dr. Kleinert died on September 29, 2013, so I was glad I had a chance to see him one last time.

Plastic Surgery Residency at George Washington University

When I started my plastic surgery residency, I was on call every other night for patients who came to the Emergency Room and needed a plastic surgery consultation. I was also told I that I would have to scrub as the first assistant with Dr. Calvin Klopp. The Chief Resident of plastic surgery told me that Dr. Klopp did not allow him to do any part of the surgery, even closure of the skin, during his first-year residency of plastic surgery. Of course, the Chief Resident had not finished his general surgery residency before he started his plastic surgery residency, so he didn't have as much surgical experience as I did. Also, the Chief Resident told me that I would be the first assistant, and the third-year resident of general surgery would be the second assistant, and the surgical intern would be the third assistant for Dr. Klopp. I told the Chief Resident that I had done a lot of head and neck surgeries as well as mastectomies (complete removal of breast tissues) during my general surgery residency, so I did not need to learn those types of surgeries.

Surgery with Dr. Calvin Klopp

The first day I scrubbed with Dr. Klopp, he had a patient for a radical neck dissection. This is a major surgery, because the surgeon has to remove the entire lymph glands and major vein along with the major muscle of one side of the neck. Dr. Klopp started to draw the line of incision by making a small hole in the patient's skin and used the draining blood to draw the lines. After making multiple incisions, he removed his glove, and told me, "You finish the case." I just stood there. The third-year resident of general surgery asked me if I had heard him. I answered that Dr. Malcolm Paul, the Chief Resident of plastic surgery, had told me that Dr. Klopp always does the surgery himself. The third-year resident said that it was true before, but Dr. Klopp just told me to finish the surgery. So, I started the surgery and completed it satisfactorily. From that day on, anytime Dr. Klopp had cases for surgery, he asked me to do the surgery by myself. He also taught me a very special technique for radical neck dissection which was not published by any other surgeon and was a completely different technique.

One day, Dr. Klopp had a mastectomy patient. He asked me to do the surgery. I told the third-year resident that he could do the surgery and I would help him. Near the end of the surgery, I noticed that his knife was coming toward my right hand. I pulled my hand away quickly, but still a superficial cut was made in the skin of the dorsum of my right little finger. Fortunately, only my skin was cut.

At the end of my first-year residency of plastic surgery, Dr. Klopp invited me for dinner at the Cosmos Club of Washington, a very important club in Washington, DC which only allowed men to be members at that time. I had heard it was very difficult to be a member of that club, and when I went there, I saw pictures of Presidents, Cabinet Secretaries, and some high-level military leaders. It was a great achievement and an honor for me to be invited to dine with him there.

Dr. Klopp was a professor of surgery at George Washington University from 1946 to 1976 and was one of the greatest surgeons with whom I have ever worked. He died from cancer at the age of 89.

First Replantation of Amputated Hand and Wrist in the Washington, DC

The Chairman of the Department of Orthopedics of George Washington University was one of two surgeons in the Washington Metropolitan area who knew hand surgery. He made an arrangement for the physician in the Emergency Room at George Washington University Hospital to call the orthopedic surgery residents (on call) for any patient with a hand injury who came to the Emergency Room.

Two weeks after I started my residency for plastic surgery, I got a call from the Emergency Room to see a patient whose right hand was amputated at the wrist. Apparently, they tried to reach the orthopedic resident on call but he did not respond. They worried about the patient and called me. Of course, they did not know me personally, but their next choice was the plastic surgery resident.

When I went to the Emergency Room and saw the patient, I asked him how his hand had been amputated. He said he was a college student at George Washington University and in the summer, he worked as a waiter in a restaurant. He said he had gone to the cook to tell him that he had brought a lot of orders and the cook had not prepared any of them. The cook slapped him in the face. My patient said he responded by slapping the cook back. Then another man who was talking to the cook picked up a big knife and cut his hand off at the wrist.

Fortunately for this man, I had learned replantation of fingers and hands at the University of Louisville before I started my plastic surgery residency. I asked the Emergency Room physician who was the plastic surgeon on call for that day because I was only a resident and had to call the attending physician. Dr. Scott Teunis was on call so I contacted Dr. Teunis and told him about the patient. Dr. Teunis asked if I had ever done such an operation. I told him I had and he said to please take the patient to the operating room and start the work, that he would join me shortly. Dr. Teunis came later and assisted me, but I had already successfully replanted the hand and wrist. The patient went home five days later.

Plastic Surgery Residents or Orthopedic Surgery Residents for Treatment of Injured Hand

After my successful replantation of the amputated hand, the Emergency Room physician called me frequently for hand injury cases. One day I received a call from the Chairman of the Department of Orthopedic Surgery. He said the orthopedic residents had to learn hand surgery, so they needed to see some of the patients with hand injuries who arrived in the Emergency Room. I agreed, but also said the plastic surgery residents needed the same thing, although I personally did not need it because I had already finished a hand surgery fellowship. I told him I thought the best way would be to share Emergency Room hand injury cases between the orthopedic and plastic surgery residents. He agreed with me and made those arrangements.

Malignant Melanoma

Another patient I saw was a 24-year-old woman who had some skin lesions on her arm. After examining her, I called my professor, Dr. Thompson, to examine the lesions. He asked if I looked at the skin of her entire body. I said no. He said I should check the skin of her entire body. I said I could not tell this young lady to take off all her clothing. He told her to take off her clothing. The young lady resisted and it took more than 30 minutes of talking until she agreed to take off all her clothing. Once she did, the professor started to look everywhere. He showed me a couple of light yellowish skin lesions on her left lower back and asked me what I thought. I told him the lesions did not appear to be malignant. He said he thought it was malignant melanoma. When you read about malignant melanoma, it says it is a pigmented dark skin lesion. The professor told the patient the lesion was suspicious and had to be biopsied. It took a long time for us to convince the patient that she needed the biopsy. One week later we did the biopsy. The pathology report indicated the lesion was malignant melanoma level four (the worse kind of malignant melanoma). We had to take her to the operating room a second time to do a wide re-excision. Six months later, she died because of multiple metastasis of malignant melanoma.

Another day I saw a 26-year-old newlywed woman who had earned a Ph.D.; she had a large pigmented lesion on her scalp, right above the left ear. This lesion was suspicious for being malignant melanoma. I suggested a partial excision for microscopic examination. The pathology report indicated the lesion was malignant melanoma level four. My professor and I recommended a wide excision of the melanoma and subsequent skin graft to cover the defect of the scalp after the excision. We also recommended a radical neck dissection (removal of all lymph nodes of the neck associated with the largest vein of the neck) on the left side.

The patient and her new husband agreed to this major surgery and I successfully performed the operation. The pathology report indicated two out of 33 lymph nodes which I had removed were positive for metastatic malignant melanoma. After everything healed, I saw the patient every month. I told her that any time she had a question, she could call me. After six months, she called me one morning and said that when she woke up, she saw many black skin lesions all over her body. I asked her to come to the office that same day. When I saw her, unfortunately there were multiple metastases scattered all over her body and there was nothing we could do. Sadly, she died five weeks later.

My Second-Year Residency of Plastic Surgery

I learned to repair cleft lips and cleft palates and do all other pediatric plastic surgeries at Washington Hospital Center and Children's Hospital in Washington, DC. I also saw many congenital abnormalities, some of which were very difficult to fix. One day I saw a one-year-old baby who had a defect in his palate (cleft palate). I asked the nurse who brought him to the hospital why the child did not move his head. She said the child had a lot of problems, he was blind and could not eat. She showed me the permanent tube which was put into his stomach to feed him. I went to my professor of Plastic Surgery and asked him why we should repair the cleft palate of a child who could not eat, see, or hear. He said that he agreed with me that such a child would not survive and should not have any type of surgery, but he said that if we refused to fix his cleft palate, we would be sued. That was the first story about malpractice lawsuits that I had heard. We had to do an unnecessary surgery on a child just because of lawyers.

Second Successful Replantation of the Amputated Hand

I got a call from the Emergency Room of Washington Hospital Center for another case of a hand amputation. I called the orthopedic surgeon on call, he came to the hospital and, after I took the patient to the operating room, he did not assist me. I successfully reattached the amputated hand by myself.

Job in Iran

Two months before my residency of plastic surgery was over, one professor said he had found a job for me. He knew I had been planning go to Iran after completing my training, and he said he had found a job for me in Iran. I thought he was joking. Then he opened up the most recent issue of the Plastic and Reconstructive Surgery journal and showed me an advertisement from a new hospital in Iran. The ad was signed by a very famous plastic surgeon in Iran, named Dr. Osanlou. I knew him because his house was close to my parent's house in Tehran. The advertisement said the government was looking for a plastic surgeon to work full-time in a hospital in Tehran. Furthermore, the ad said they would pay $3000 a month salary, tax-free, as well as provide a one-bedroom apartment, and a one-month per-year vacation.

I thanked my professor and wrote a letter to Dr. Osanlou. I sent a copy of all my documents regarding my general surgery, hand surgery, and plastic surgery training. Two weeks later, I received a letter in the Persian language from Dr. Osanlou, accepting and welcoming me.

I was very happy and made arrangements to return to Iran. I put all my important furniture and other belongings in a container and had it shipped. After my arrival in Tehran, I called the hospital and made an appointment to see Dr. Osanlou. My visit was short, and when I asked him about the apartment and other things that were promised, he told me to visit the Hospital Administrator. I went to the Administrator's office. He told me my salary would be $1000 per month and I would have to pay tax on it. Furthermore he said they would not provide an apartment. I was stunned and showed him the advertisement in the Plastic and Reconstructive Surgery journal. He said those promises were for foreign plastic surgeons, not Iranian ones. He also said that with a salary of $1000 per month, I would not be able to find an apartment in Tehran. That was a quick end to the promised job in Iran. The advertisement had not said it applied only to foreigners. Iran typically treats foreigners better than its own citizens. I thought about opening a private practice in Iran, but found out how expensive it was. Private practice physicians had to buy part of the hospital at which they worked. I could not afford that. I could not find another government job that paid any better, so I was forced to return to the United States and build a life here. All of my plans to return to Iran to practice medicine were in ruins.

Return to the United States and Start of Practice

A famous Iranian plastic surgeon, Dr. Bahman Teimourian, who was in practice for fourteen years before me, saw me at a Plastic Surgery Society of Washington Metropolitan meeting when I had just begun my practice. He congratulated me, then asked if I had privileges at Prince Georges Hospital Center in Maryland. I said that I didn't. He suggested that I get privileges there and then he could put me in as a back-up for himself to cover the Emergency Room. I told him I appreciated the offer, but after all these years of training, I would either make it as a hand and plastic surgeon or I would die. He probably meant that if a patient in the Emergency Room had insurance, he would cover it. If not, he would tell them to call Dr. Matini.

After my return to the United States, I joined the practice of an older surgeon who claimed to be both a hand surgeon and plastic surgeon, although he never had formal training in either of those fields. He had offered me a job before I went to Iran. He told me he had been in practice for forty years and wanted to quit in three years. He further said that if I joined his practice, he would give me his practice after three years. Unfortunately, he lied to me.

Usually when an old surgeon hires a young surgeon as an associate, the older doctor asks the young surgeon to cover the Emergency Room. This man was covering the Emergency Room himself. When he had a patient for a major plastic surgery, he asked me to go and see the patient with him. Then, on the day of surgery, he asked me to do the surgery. When the patient woke up, he lied to the patient and told him or her that he had done the surgery.

At the end of the second year of working with him, I found out that he was not planning to retire. Because of his terrible conduct toward me, I told him that I was leaving his practice.

This surgeon was the most unusual person I had ever met in my life. He was a multimillionaire and owned one-third of an island in the south of Florida. He showed me pictures of the island and a six-bedroom mansion he also owned located there. He told me that ever since he had bought the mansion, he had rented it and had never gone there himself to enjoy it.

Clinical Assistant Professor of Plastic Surgery

When I started to practice plastic surgery with this same doctor, I also became a clinical assistant professor of plastic surgery at the George Washington University Hospital. I taught plastic surgery residents at the George Washington University Hospital, Children's Hospital, and the Washington Hospital Center. All the residents seemed to like to work with me.

Buying a Town House in Old Town, Alexandria

After returning from Iran, I bought a townhouse for myself and started to furnish it little by little with very good furniture. Although I bought furniture, I did not buy a television because I wanted to study and prepare myself for the Board of Plastic Surgery examination. I brought a wonderful full silk Persian carpet when I came back from Iran. When I arrived in New York, I presented the Persian carpet to a customs officer who said he had never seen a carpet like that in the last 25 years he had been working there. He was so impressed that he called his colleague to see it.

Bringing My Nephews (My Second Brother's Sons) to the United States

I encouraged my second brother to send his two older sons to the United States and I found the best available boarding schools for them. The eldest was a good student and I was able to find him a good school in Connecticut. The younger nephew was a wonderful boy but his grades were weak, so I had to put him in a different school. Anytime the schools were closed, I made arrangements for my nephews to fly to Washington to stay with me. While they were staying with me, I rented a television for them. The oldest nephew was able to go to Georgetown University and finish college; the youngest one only finished high school. My brother, the father of these two boys, used to come to the United States once a year to see his sons. When he did, I made arrangements for all of us to travel together for a nice vacation.

Falling in Love with a Beautiful Dentist

When I arrived at the operating room of George Washington University Hospital one day, I saw a lady who was in the anesthesia section of the operating room. Of course, she had an operating room scrub suit and a mask, so I could not see her face, but I could see her beautiful green eyes. After the surgery was completed, I kept looking at her until she took her mask off. I saw that her face was also beautiful. After a few days, when I had a chance, I introduced myself. She said that she knew me, and thought I was a good plastic surgeon. I asked her what kind of work she did. She said she was a dentist, that she had finished dental school in South Carolina and after practicing for a couple of years decided to get anesthesia training so she could do more surgical dentistry with anesthesia in her office.

I asked her out for lunch. When I went to pick her up from her apartment, I knocked on the front door, she was not ready. She invited me in. After she got dressed, she asked if I wanted to have a drink before we went to the restaurant. I said sure. She asked me what kind of drink I wanted and I said bourbon on the rocks. She got a bottle of bourbon and a large glass. She put one ice cube in the glass and filled it to the top with bourbon, then handed the glass to me. I said thank you, but was wondering what her plan was because she had given me so much to drink. Then I noticed that she fixed the same drink and same amount for herself. I realized that there was no plan against me. I find out she was a very nice lady. We had a very good time together and every time we went on a date, people looked at her so much that it made me really shy and a bit embarrassed. I found out later that she had been Miss South Carolina when she was in college. Even after she became a dentist and was practicing, she was chosen again as Professional Miss South Carolina.

After nine months, I proposed to her. She told me that she loved going out with me and had a good time with me, but that she was not ready to get married. She said she'd like to keep dating me. One night, I went to pick her up from her apartment and while she was getting ready, her telephone rang. She talked for a long time. I could hear her side of the conversation and could tell she was talking with a man. She was on the phone for more than twenty minutes. I just put my jacket on and left her apartment. I didn't go out with her again.

Senator Kennedy versus Governor Jimmy Carter

In 1976, when Ted Kennedy was running against Jimmy Carter in the Democratic primary for the presidency of the United States, Larry King had a radio program about these two candidates and asked people to call to give their opinion. Most people supported Jimmy Carter. That day, I felt compelled to call. I kept calling and calling and finally got through. I told Larry King that when you're talking about politics, it doesn't matter if the person you want to elect went to church and never did anything wrong or was someone who made social mistakes, as Ted Kennedy had done. I said that Ted Kennedy had been a Senator and was more familiar with the politics of the world. I told Larry that we also had to think about how a candidate would run the United States, not to mention the entire world. I mentioned that Jimmy Carter, who had been governor of a small state, did not have the experience to deal with world politics, which he had demonstrated during his first term presidency of the United States. In spite of Ted Kennedy's issues with women and the Chappaquiddick incident, he could be a successful President.

Mr. Carter didn't know anything about the world. For example, Iran had been a close ally of the United States and Israel. With the help of the United States and England, the Shah of Iran, who had previously been kicked out of Iran by the people of Iran, was brought back in to lead Iran. The Shah was a good friend of the United States. At that time eighty percent of the economy of Iran was connected to the United States; Iran gave practically every penny it earned from selling its oil to purchase military weapons from the U.S. and the Shah had supported this and been a good friend to the United States.

At that time, Iran's Army was the fifth largest in the world. There was a close relationship and friendship between Iran and the United States, and between Iran and Israel when Jimmy Carter became President. There were American listening devices on the border of Iran and Russia and there were a lot of American military members in Iran. As a matter of fact, our house was located in a neighborhood where several American military families were our neighbors. Unemployment in Iran was nonexistent; everyone who wanted a job had one. More than 20,000 foreign nurses worked in Iran. About 50,000 Americans worked in Iran and got their salary from the Iranian government. Iran invited Jimmy Carter to visit Iran, which he did, and Jimmy Carter invited the Shah of Iran to the United States. The Shah accepted Jimmy Carter's invitation in November of 1977.

Right before the Shah arrived as an official guest of the United States government on November 15, 1977, although it was completely illegal, every street in Washington, DC was covered with protestors against the Shah. In my opinion, the protests were part of the United States government's efforts to destroy the Shah. There was a big demonstration around the White House during the Shah's visit. The demonstration turned violent and many people were injured. I watched on TV as the demonstrators broke through police lines and came close to the welcoming ceremony at the White House. Tear gas thrown by the police reached the Shah. As a result of the tear gas, I could see tears rolling down from his eyes.

The worse President of the United States was President Carter. He was the one who brought Khomeini to Iran and kicked the Shah of Iran out. We all know what happened after that in Iran.

Before the presidency of Carter, no American was killed in the Middle East. The American Embassy was invaded by Iranian people who were the servants of Khomeini. Unfortunately, there is nothing in the news media about President Carter's performance which caused so many deaths of Americans.

Friends from Richmond and Meeting a Persian Woman

One of my cousins in Iran called me and told me that some of her best friends had left Iran and were now living in Richmond, Virginia. My cousin said they would like to come and visit, so she gave me their phone number. I invited them to visit one weekend. The man was a dentist who was getting a master's degree and his wife was a dentist who was not planning to practice. After we met and got along well, we saw each other frequently. They were a wonderful couple. One day when they were in my house and we were planning to go out for dinner, my friend's wife said she had a cousin who was a thoracic surgeon living in Maryland. The cousin complained that they came to Alexandria frequently, but never went to Maryland to visit him, so they wanted to go and visit him and they invited me along. I said I didn't know him, but they encouraged me to go anyway. They said we would just stay for a couple of hours and then leave.

That night, we went to visit him at his house. I saw a young lady there who was very beautiful and had a beautiful smile. I found out she was the first cousin of this thoracic surgeon. He had married an American lady a few years earlier and they had three children, two boys and a girl. He found out that his wife was going out with different people, and he was so surprised that he hired a private investigator to document her activities. He was able to divorce her without giving her a penny. He also got to keep their children. Because he had nobody to care for his three children, he asked his cousin, the beautiful lady, to come and help him.

The beautiful lady and I started to date and I became very interested in her, although I had so much education and she hadn't finished high school. Apparently, she had married an Iranian when she was only sixteen years old. Her husband, who lived in Germany, took her back to Germany. They didn't have a good marriage, but her mother convinced her to get pregnant, hoping that would fix the marriage. It didn't. She had a son and when the boy was only three years old, she divorced her husband and gave up custody of the child. While she was in Germany, she studied to become a cosmetician.

My First Marriage

I fell in love with her and decided to marry her, even though I had always wanted to marry someone as highly educated as I was. Two days before the government of the United States was going to deport her, we went to a lawyer's office in Alexandria and got married. The witnesses were my second brother and his wife. Of course, after we got married, I applied for a green card (permanent residency) for her. A couple of months later, we made plans to go to Iran to have a wedding ceremony and big party. Since I had applied for her green card, she could leave the United States and also return.

One of my cousins was a fantastic dressmaker. She made an unbelievable wedding dress for my wife with beautiful stones. My cousin didn't charge me anything for making that dress. We had a Persian wedding ceremony in the early afternoon at my wife's parents' house. Then we had a big dinner reception in a famous hotel in Tehran, with more than 400 people in attendance. At the reception, we had two different orchestras. A few days after the wedding, we returned to the United States.

Interesting Events with My Senior Partner

One night I invited my senior partner and his wife for dinner which I made myself. After drinking one glass of wine, he explained that he had a major medical problem and he went to our guest room to sleep while his wife had dinner with us.

A few months later, he invited me and my wife, and the senior plastic surgery resident and his wife for dinner in his fancy apartment located in Chevy Chase, Maryland. He and his wife had expensive and beautiful furniture. After serving each of us one glass of wine, one small plate of salad, two very thin layers of roast beef, and one small potato each, he took the rest of the salad and roast beef to the kitchen. None of us who were their guests had enough food, so as soon as we left their apartment we went to a restaurant and ate another dinner. He brought the remaining pieces of that roast beef for his lunch to the office for about one month. He was the cheapest millionaire I ever saw. And even though he hired me as his young associate, he was taking all the calls of the Emergency Room himself.

Injury to My Right Hand

In the beginning of our marriage, one day my wife told me that the disposal was not working. I told her to call someone to come and fix it, which she did, and he fixed the problem. The same thing happened again and the repairman came back and fixed it again. It happened a third time and my wife told me that the repairman spent less than five minutes each time. I thought it must be simple to fix, so I went and checked the disposal. I put my right hand inside of the disposal and removed some waste. Then I took my right hand out of the sink, turned on the water with my left hand, then turned on the disposal. I stopped the water, turned off the switch of the disposal, and again put my right hand inside the disposal and picked up any residual waste. I did this maneuver multiple times. Apparently, my actions got mixed up in my head. So, the last time I put my right hand in the disposal, I then turned on the disposal switch with my left hand. I immediately turned off the disposal off when I felt the pain in my right hand. I did not dare to look at my right hand; I was pretty sure I had amputated my fingers. That was the most terrible feeling in my entire life. Fortunately, when I finally looked at my hand, I found no blood and I counted my fingers, all of which were still there. And I was able to move my fingers. I was very, very lucky! From that day on, I never tried to fix anything at home or in the office because as a surgeon, my hands are the most important part of my body and I couldn't take the chance of hurting them. The non-surgical physicians had a joke about surgeons. They said that whenever a surgeon was trying to prevent an elevator door from closing, instead of putting his hands between the closing elevator's doors, he put his head!

My Plan to Return and Stay in Iran!

In 1978, two months before the Shah was deposed, and in spite of my plans to make a new life in America, I went back to Iran intending to stay for good, not knowing the events that were right around the corner. The Vice President of the Department of Health and Education of Iran had visited the United States and asked some of the well-trained Iranian physicians to return to Iran because the Shah was planning to build a huge university and medical center. The medical center was going to be called the Mayo Clinic of the Middle East. When the Vice President of the Department of Health and Education came to talk to me, I told him that two years prior to his visit, after I finished my residency in plastic surgery, I went back to Iran but was unable to stay because they would not pay me enough to live comfortably. I told him I was not going to try it again. He showed me the architect's plan for building the new medical center. It was so huge that he told me it cost $1.2 billion just for the drawing. He told me that if I accepted his invitation, I would be the Chief of Plastic Surgery of that huge new medical center. In the meantime, if I did return, I would be the Chief of Plastic Surgery of Iranshahr Hospital (the Imperial Medical

Center). My wife, who was Iranian, was not happy with the prospect of going back to Iran, but I decided we should go. We sold our house and shipped all of our possessions in a big container to Iran.

When we got to Iran, we had planned to rent a house and have our furniture and other belongings delivered there. Because of strikes around Iran, no shipments were delivered, so our container of goods was held in a neighboring country. We only had two pieces of luggage and no choice but to stay with my wife's parents.

Heart Attacks in Iran

During my early years of medical school in Iran, heart attacks were rare. When a patient was admitted at the university hospital for a heart attack, the doctors had every student go see the patient. However, when I returned ten years later, I heard of so many people dying from heart attacks, which surprised me. I started to investigate and found out that more people were having heart attacks because of improvements in their financial status. Before I came to the United States, most people did not have cars, so they had to walk everywhere. Office buildings did not have elevators and people who worked there had to climb the stairs to get to their offices. As their financial status improved, they ate more meat and drank soda, which had not been present in Iran when I went to medical school. When I was growing up, Iranians usually drank concentrated grape juice mixed with water.

I remember when I first came to the United States in 1968 and went to a restaurant for the first time, I was surprised at the size of my steak, potato, and piece of cake. I couldn't believe that you could go to a salad bar and get all the salad you wanted. I also could not believe how the American people drank so many soft drinks and alcoholic beverages.

Enemies of Iran

In that two months of 1978, when I returned to Iran and before the Shah of Iran was deposed, I can tell you Iran's worst enemy was England. There was an English radio station broadcasting in Persian that lied to the Iranian people about the Shah. It said that many students had been killed at Iranian universities, a lie to get people to revolt against the Shah. The government of England also sent money to make lots of videos and tapes against the Shah and had them mailed to every resident of the big cities of Iran. The Prime Minister of England tried to influence President Carter in hopes he would bring the Shah down and, unfortunately, he succeeded.

My Practice of Plastic Surgery in Iran

When I went to Iran, it was only two months before the Shah was deposed. I worked at a large hospital which was a temporary hospital being used until the major medical center being planned was built. In that hospital, every physician had been trained in either in the United States or Europe, but most were trained in the United States. Even the nurses who were working there were able to speak English, so we wrote all of our orders in English. It felt like I was still working in the United States. The type of surgery that I did there was unbelievable, I never saw those types of patients during the rest of my career. When the Shah was in power, every Iranian had health insurance, which either had been purchased privately, or was provided by the government or an employer. While in Iran, I saw many interesting and unusual cases for plastic surgery.

Fusion of Joints between the Skull and Jaws

One day, a couple brought their 5-year-old daughter to my office at the hospital. The father had heard good things about this medical center. When I asked what was wrong with his daughter, he said she could not open her mouth. When I examined her, her teeth were together, and she couldn't open her mouth. They were feeding her via a small spoon in the back of her mouth. I sent her for a tomogram (special type of X-ray), and found out that the joint between the skull and the jaw (temporal mandibular joint) was not present on either side. Her parents told me that when the girl was about a year old, she had fallen down. I guessed that when she fell, she broke her jaw right at that joint. Because the parents didn't know she was severely injured, she was not taken to a medical facility for treatment and the non-treated fracture caused the fusion of the jaw to the skull on both sides of her mouth. Because of the disappearance of the joint between the skull and jaw, she could not move her jaw and, therefore, could not open her mouth.

The only thing I thought I had to do was create new joints between the skull and the jaw on both sides of the jaw. I had to remove a piece of bone from each fused area and replace it with a silastic joint so she could open her mouth. I explained this operation to the parents and they agreed to the surgery.

I talked to the anesthesiologist and told him that they could not put a tube in the patient's throat through the mouth, so he had to do it blindly through the nose. The anesthesiologist was worried and asked what would happen if he was not able to put the tube through the nose. I told him I could open the trachea in the front of the neck and he could put a tube in there. We took the girl to the operating room and the anesthesiologist was able to put the tube through her nose successfully, and I did the surgery as planned.

The surgery was successful; however, two or three hours after surgery, the girl didn't wake up. I was very worried and did not leave the hospital until the next day when she finally woke up. Apparently, this happened as result of a concussion which probably occurred because I had to use a hammer to break a portion of each jaw bone out and the hammer was used so close to the brain. Fortunately, the effects of the concussion disappeared in under twenty-four hours after surgery. I asked the girl if she could open her mouth and she did. Her parents were so happy that they were crying. They told me I had performed a miracle. I had never seen this operation performed before, nor had I ever read about it.

The Most Extensive Cancer of Scalp as Result Of Radiation

Another day I saw a beautiful young lady, about 30 years old, with a history of a bleeding wound of the scalp. When she removed her kerchief and the covering dressing from her head, I noticed she had no hair. The entire scalp was replaced by skin grafts, and a large portion of the grafted area was ulcerated and bleeding. Apparently when she was a child, she had developed an infection of her scalp from ringworm, then quite common in Iran. To treat that disease they shaved off her scalp hair and used a low dose of radiation for three days. Apparently the radiation machine that was used when she was a child had mechanical problems and she received a tremendously high dose of radiation which caused permanent hair loss. She also developed multiple skin cancers on her scalp which required excision and replacement with skin grafts. I explained to her that she had extensive skin cancer and I had to find out if the cancer had invaded her skull, so I sent her for an x-ray. The x-ray showed the outer layer of the skull were completely dead and infected (osteomyelitis).

I knew that in addition to excising the ulcerated skin cancer of her scalp, I had to remove that portion of her skull and reconstruct it. Because this involved an area close to the brain, I asked a neurosurgeon colleague to come and work on this case with me. He had also finished his training at George Washington University, then married an American woman before returning to Iran.

On the day of the surgery, I removed the huge ulcerated portion of her scalp and the neurosurgeon used an instrument to lift out a large portion of the bone of her skull (the outer portion). We found that the inner portion of the bone of her skull also was infected, and was therefore not viable. This was not visible on the x-ray. The neurosurgeon agreed that we needed to remove that entire infected portion of the skull, and he proceeded to do that. There is a sheath of soft tissue around the brain and underneath the skull; unfortunately, that was also invaded by cancer and had to be removed. Now you could see a large portion of the brain because there was no coverage by the soft tissue sheath, no bone, and no scalp. At this point, the neurosurgeon said that his work was done, the rest was up to me and he left the operating room.

I prepared her left thigh, and took a large portion of fascia of the thigh (the sheath which covers the muscle) to use as a sheath to cover her brain. I sewed it to the edge of the remaining intact sheath to cover the brain. Then I had to cover the large defect of the scalp. Since the rest of her scalp had been removed on multiple previous surgeries and replaced by a split thickness skin graft, I had to bring tissue from another portion of her body. This was a major reconstructive procedure. I raised a large pedicle skin flap from her left arm (a skin flap is a rectangular piece of skin that has been cut on three sides, leaving the fourth side attached to the flesh). We also freed that portion of skin from its underlying muscle (we call this part of skin a flap). Then I took a skin graft (thin layer of thickness of skin from her thigh) to cover the skin defect of the arm which was created by raising the large skin flap. This skin graft was sutured to the edge of defect of the arm.

I brought her left arm over her head and sutured the edges of the arm skin flap to the edge of the defect of her scalp. I immobilized the arm, which was attached to her head, with a plaster splint (a form of cast).

I kept this patient in the hospital for three weeks with her arm attached to her head. After that period of time, I took her back to the operating room and cut a portion of the attachment of the skin flap of the arm to the skull. I saw good circulation had been established from the scalp to the skin flap of the arm. A few days later, I cut the rest of the base arm flap and separated the arm from the head completely. At this point, I sutured the cut edge of the base of the skin flap of the arm to the edge of the defect of the scalp. When the arm became free, I brought the arm down. The large defect of the scalp which was reconstructed had completely healed. The entire cancer was removed and the patient was sent home in satisfactory condition. I told the patient she had to return in four months at which time I would rebuild the defect of the skull using a rib graft (this means taking a few ribs, splitting them and fixing them to the edge of the defective of skull using wire).

These are the types of operations I had never seen during my training in surgery and plastic surgery in the United States, but the training I received in the United States had been so great, it allowed me to successfully perform those types of unusual surgeries in Iran.

Treating Multiply Injured Patients in Iran: Last Demonstration Prior to the Shah's Departure

Before the Shah left, there was a big demonstration in Tehran against the government, police, and military soldiers for four days and nights. This paralyzed the country. The entire surgical staff of our hospital worked day and night to take care of the wounded. There were many patients, both civilian and military, with gunshot wounds. I slept only two and half hours of each 24 hour period. The rest of the time, I was doing surgery and I was able to save everyone I operated on.

At three A.M., a military officer who had been protecting the Shah's palace was brought to our hospital with a gunshot wound to his left arm. His main artery had been cut off by the bullet, preventing circulation of blood to his forearm and hand. I told the nurse anesthetist that we had to do an axillary block anesthesia on his arm (this involved numbing the whole arm by injecting medicine through the axilla) because I had to reconstruct the artery to return blood flow to the forearm and hand. The nurse anesthetist's response was that we didn't have to do anything since the patient worked for the Shah. I looked at him and said that I was a doctor and when I finished medical school, I took a vow to take care of any patient, friend or enemy. I told him we had to fix the patient's arm and then if he had done something wrong, he would be taken to court and put on trial. If he was convicted, he would be punished by the court. I told the nurse anesthetist that if he did not perform the procedure that I would kick him out of the hospital. At that point he cooperated. I was able to reconstruct the artery and bring the flow of blood back to his forearm and hand. It saved his arm.

American plan to get rid of the Shah of Iran and Replace Him with Khomeini

In 1978, President Jimmy Carter met privately with the President of France. They decided that they had to get rid of the Shah and asked him to leave Iran. At the time, the Shah was suffering from malignant lymphoma and because he was a servant of the United States, he listened to his "boss" and left Iran in exile on January 16, 1979. I arrived in Iran two months prior to the arrival of Khomeini. I left Iran and returned to the United States five and half months after his arrival.

President Carter brought Khomeini to run the government of Iran. President Carter had never met Khomeini and did not know anything about him. Khomeini had been exiled by the Shah and was living in Iraq. A few months prior to the Shah's ouster, Khomeini had been brought to Paris. President Carter sent Ramsey Clark, former Attorney General of the United States under President Johnson, to Paris to meet with Khomeini. Clark talked to him; of course, Khomeini was smart enough to lie to please the American government so they would help him get to power. Afterwards, the Shah was deposed and Khomeini was brought to Iran.

I repeat that before Jimmy Carter was President, never had an American soldier died in the Middle East. After Khomeini came to power, one of the first things he arranged was an attack to the embassy of the United States in Tehran. Embassy personnel were captured and the embassy was closed down. This was the first time in history that an embassy in Iran had been attacked by the people of Iran. The Iranians went through all the files in the embassy and found shredded papers that they were able to reconstruct and print.

From that point on, Iran regressed dramatically. Two million sophisticated and highly educated people from Iran escaped and came to Europe and the United States because of Khomeini.

Four years after Khomeini was brought to power, in 1983, 249 Marines were killed in a terrorist attack by Khomeini's agents in Lebanon.[2] This was the first time in history that American soldiers were killed in the Middle East.

Departure of My Oldest Brother from Iran

My oldest brother, the past President of Meshed University and Vice President of the Academy of Etiquette and Art, had to leave Iran after the Shah left and Khomeini came to power. Of course, he did not want to leave because he had not done anything wrong. His close friends convinced him that the situation in Iran was dangerous for him.

When Khomeini came into power, he tried to capture and imprison everyone who had been appointed by the Shah to important positions. When the Shah was in power, it was customary that when a person was appointed as president of a university, the Shah would write an appointment letter. Khomeini ordered the arrest of anyone who had received such an appointment letter from the Shah. When they heard this, my brother's friends realized that it was urgent for my brother to leave Iran and told him so. My brother reserved a plane ticket to the United States through Europe for the following Friday. My brother-in-law, who was in business and planning to go to Europe as well, asked my brother to accompany him on Wednesday rather than wait till Friday. My brother changed his ticket to leave on Wednesday. On the day they left, I went with them to the airport. While we were sitting and waiting, one young new soldier came to us

---

[2] "Beirut Marine Barracks Bombing Fast Facts," http://www.cnn.com/2013/06/13/world/meast/beirut-marine-barracks-bombing-fast-facts/index.html.

and asked my brother for his identification card, which was not then a customary practice. Fortunately, my brother had a card in his wallet like an I.D. card. He showed it to the soldier and, fortunately, the soldier did not stop him from leaving.

The day after leaving Iran, a security officer in the new regime came to his house to arrest him. My brother had left his three children in Iran. The only thing my brother had of value was a big library that included a lot of original handwritten books. The Khomeini regime took the entire library. This is just one small example of what the Khomeini regime did.

Khomeini ordered the execution of more than five thousand people in Iran, including congressmen, senators, secretaries of different departments, and major generals. He also ordered the forced rape of captured teenaged girls in the prison before they were killed because they were part of the Mujahedeen (a group of religious Iranians who supported Khomeini in the beginning and then started opposing him). This group of people later on started to fight with government and many of them were forced to escape to Iraq. At the present time, some of them are in the Europe and United States.

If this was a fair world, Jimmy Carter should be tried in international court. The President of the United States never acted against Khomeini, or put pressure on his government, even after he arranged for the invasion of the American Embassy in Iran and arrested American diplomats. The attack of any embassy is equal to an invasion of that country; the embassy is like the land of that country.

A few months later, President Carter arranged for American Special Forces to invade Iran secretly in order to rescue kidnapped American diplomats. The plan had to be aborted due to mechanical failures. As the forces were leaving, a helicopter collided with an airplane and exploded, destroying both aircraft and killing eight.[3]

For example, fifty years after the terror of the assassination of President John F. Kennedy, the files of that murder have never been opened up to the American people.

A few years ago, Mr. Carter had a book signing event in Los Angeles for a book he had written. Many Iranian people who were forced

---

[3] Lambert, Laura, "Operation Eagle Claw," Encyclopedia Britannica, http://www.britannica.com/event/Operation-Eagle-Claw.

to leave Iran and come to the United States screamed at him for his crime in bringing Khomeini to Iran. Mr. Carter left quickly and never responded to his Iranian critics. I believe one of the problems of the United States is that we sometimes elect Presidents that have no experience in dealing with the politics of the world.

Even after President Carter, the subsequent Presidents of the United States, including Presidents Reagan, George H.W. Bush, Clinton, George W. Bush and Obama, have been quiet about the crimes that were done by Khomeini and the leaders of Iran after him. Two years after President Obama was elected, the young people of Iran demonstrated against the reelection of President Ahmadinejad. The government attacked the demonstrators and killed many young people. President Obama did nothing in response. I believe the current regime of Iran was brought by President Carter and has been supported by all the subsequent presidents of the United States. I do not know why they have supported this regime but hope there are important reasons for them to do so.

Even after the sick Shah was forced out of Iran by President Carter and came to the United States, I think the Government of the United States planned to get rid of him. If Henry Kissinger had not helped the Shah, I believe the Shah would have been killed in America. Instead, Mr. Kissinger helped the Shah go to Egypt and the President of Egypt, Hosni Mubarak, allowed him to stay there until he died.

Request for New President of our University Hospital

In Iran, it was customary that the presidents of hospitals were also physicians themselves. The president of our hospital was in France in 1979 when Khomeini came to Iran and he decided not to return to Iran. The name of our hospital and medical center was the Imperial Medical Center of Iran. We knew this name had to be changed under the new regime. All the physicians got together and chose one of our physicians as the new president. They appointed me to meet with the new Secretary of Health and Education to get his approval. I called and made an appointment. After Khomeini took power, it was required that in order to have a representative of the hospital visit the Department of Health and Education, that representative had to also bring a medical student and one of the lower class working people of the hospital.

When I met the Secretary of Health and Education, I explained about our hospital and our practicing physicians. I further explained that because the president of the medical staff of the hospital was not returning, the medical staff had voted unanimously for a new president. I told the Secretary the new president's name and his specialty. The Secretary said he knew our hospital well and knew that its medical staff of the hospital had the best-educated physicians and had been doing good work. He approved our new election. Just as soon as I went to thank him and leave his office, one of the medical students who came with me started to speak against me. He said that I constantly talked negatively about our new government. I thought this was going to put my life at risk and that I was going to be sent to prison. Fortunately, the Secretary acted like he did not hear anything the student said. He rose from behind his desk and shook hands with me and we left.

That event opened my eyes about the danger I was in because I could not keep my mouth shut. I decided I had to leave Iran. I talked to my wife and my in-laws about departing, I obtained a plane ticket and made arrangements to leave two days later. I also made arrangements to ship my container which had been dropped on a neighboring country's island back to the United States.

Leaving Iran Again

The day I went to the airport, I wrapped all of my framed certificates and diplomas together and carried them with me. I did not put them in my luggage because I was afraid that if I lost my luggage, I would lose all my important diplomas. A young security man came to me and asked if I was leaving the country for good. I told him I was a surgeon and that I had done some research work and the United States asked me to present it at a conference there. I told him they wanted to see my diplomas as well. Fortunately, this young man believed me. He called a few of his coworkers together and told them they should be proud of their doctors. A few minutes later, my plane took off. Since then, I have not returned to Iran. Not only did I become a citizen of the United States, but later on, I applied for permanent resident visas for both of my brothers and their families, and my sister and her family.

Returning to the United States

When I returned to the United States, I had no house, no job, and no money. I talked to Dr. Houchang Sendi, an Iranian plastic surgeon who had been in practice for eleven years. He suggested that I open an office close to Inova Mount Vernon Hospital and practice there. While I was looking for a house and office to rent, Dr. Sendi called me and asked me to lunch.

During lunch, he suggested that I join his practice and work with him on salary for three years. After three years, I could be his full partner. He recognized that I had a negative experience with my previous partner for the first two years of my practice, and assured me that I would have a good experience working with him. I decided this was a good way to start practice again in the United States. Dr. Sendi then told me to look for a house and he would co-sign the mortgage. I found a house near Sherwood Hall Lane (close to the Inova Mount Vernon Hospital) and reached an agreement with the seller. Dr. Sendi co-signed the mortgage as he had promised. I called him and made an appointment with him on a weekend morning. When I called him, I thought he was sick. I asked if he was all right. He said he was not sick but that he could not sleep the previous night. Then he said that unfortunately he had changed his mind and did not want to take me as an associate. That surprised me because he had been the one who had suggested it in the first place. I told him that there were no hard feelings. I left his office, cancelled my offer to purchase the house, and found a rental house instead.

Starting a New Life in Alexandria, Virginia

I started to look for a rental house, and fortunately found a one-level house close to Inova Mount Vernon Hospital. At the same time, I was looking for a rental medical office. Unfortunately, none was available, although there was one small office in the Sherwood Hall Medical Office Building close to the hospital, where another plastic surgeon had signed a letter of offer. The realtor said that if the other plastic surgeon did not come and purchase the office within 48 hours, the offer would be released and I could buy it. Well, 48 hours came and went and the plastic surgeon did not buy the office. The realtor called and said the office was available. I immediately went to sign the papers and write a check for the down payment. The realtor called the next day and said the other plastic surgeon had finally called her and said he was ready to buy the office. She had to tell him that the office was already sold.

Immediately, I went and bought used office furniture for the office. Then I looked for a full-time secretary. All my previous furniture and other belongings, which had been in the container that I sent to Iran, arrived at last and I was able to fill my new rental house with it.

In order to set my office, I had to borrow fifty thousand dollars from my second brother. I used it to pay the down payment on the office, and to purchase office furniture and equipment. I also used it to pay my secretary, buy food, and purchase a car. Of course, I had to pay interest to my brother. I showed the loan document to my attorney, who knew my brother well, and he was surprised. He said he could not believe that my brother would ask me to sign such a document when I had helped him and his family come to America, and helped him buy a house, car and anything else they needed. I said I needed the money and would sign the document. Within one year, I was able to pay my brother back the money that I had borrowed.

Sherwood Hall Medical Center Office Building

In November, 1979, a few months after I had purchased the office, the owners of the offices within the building held a meeting which I attended. After electing a president and vice president, they asked who was interested in being secretary-treasurer. Nobody else volunteered, so I did and was voted in.

This office building was built in such a way that none of windows of the offices could be opened; therefore, we had to have a good heating system for cold weather and a good air conditioning system for hot weather.

When I started to review the bills from the firm that was managing the building, I found we were being charged monthly for maintenance of the heating and air conditioning system. We were also being charged for the health insurance of the working members of their firm. We had frequent problems with our heating and air conditioning system, and received high bills for repair. I decided to get a consultant to look at our heating and air conditioning system. After the consultant came and looked at our system, he told me the reason for the frequent problems was that we had not had routine services on the system for more than two years. At the next monthly meeting, I asked the representative of the management company questions about our system. She lied telling us they had been providing services monthly. I showed her the statement from our hired consultant, then told her that her firm was fired that we did not want to work with a bunch of thieves.

I had to look for someone else to manage our building. I talked with a retired friend of mine, General George Forschler. He was doing the same type of job for another office building, so I hired him. He spent a lot of time and fixed our problems properly. I saw him frequently in our building. No one had ever seen a member of the previous firm in the building.

General Forschler told me if the owners of the offices were interested, he could arrange a Christmas dinner party for us at the Fort Belvoir Officers Club. At that time, I was the president of the Sherwood Hall Office Building. After talking with the other office owners, I learned that everybody was interested. We had a big dinner Christmas party at Fort Belvoir that year and had a lot of fun.

Difficulty of the Emergency Room Coverage

Every hospital has an Emergency Room. Those patients who are sick and cannot wait to see their own doctor come to the Emergency Room. Also, those individuals who are involved in an accident are brought to the Emergency Room. Emergency Rooms are open 24 hours a day. Many hospitals require a doctor be a member of the hospital for two years before they would put him or her on Emergency Room coverage. This was the case for both Inova Alexandria Hospital and Inova Fairfax Hospital when I was starting out. I was lucky that many older plastic surgeons at those hospitals liked me and gave me some of their coverage days, so I started to get a lot of patients. In Inova Mount Vernon Hospital, there was only one other plastic surgeon. He had started one year before me. The Emergency Room at Inova Mount Vernon Hospital was not busy. There was a small hospital in Alexandria, Circle Terrace Hospital, and I also had privileges there.

I also got privileges at another hospital in Alexandria, Jefferson Memorial Hospital. It is closed now. One Sunday, I received a call from Jefferson Memorial Hospital to see a patient there. I went and saw the female patient; who was not an emergency and had no major problems. She said she had been in the hospital for the last few days. Her primary care doctor called me in to take a look at a scar over her buttock. When I checked with a couple of other doctors later on, I learned that they had a policy that every patient got a consult from every specialty, so that all the doctors would make money. When I heard that, I stopped practicing there.

At the time I started practice more than thirty-nine years ago, more than ninety percent of patients who came to the Emergency Room had health insurance. And the insurance companies paid more than ninety percent of the doctor's charges. Today the situation is completely different. Many patients who come to the Emergency Room do not have health insurance. And the insurance companies now pay less than ten percent of the doctor's charges, which is why no physician wants to be on call for Emergency Room coverage.

It took more than three years working in different hospitals covering the Emergency Room to build my practice. The physicians at Inova Fairfax Hospital, National Orthopedic Hospital and others realized I was a very good surgeon and started to refer their patients to me for elective consultation and surgery.

Membership on the Medical Executive Committee of Virginia

Although I didn't know elected officials of the state of Virginia, the Medical Executive Committee chose me to review the complaints of the health insurance companies about physicians' charges. I became a member of that committee for several years. When I attended the meetings, I realized that unfortunately some surgeons were overcharging. We reviewed each complaint regarding what procedure was done, how much time it took, and how much had been charged. If the insurance company was correct, we told them how much we thought the doctor should receive, and sent a copy of that letter to the physician. Once I saw the charges of a new surgeon who had an emergency case in which he had repaired multiple tendons and the median nerve in the wrist of one patient. He charged the insurance company more than $10,000. I calculated the charges for each procedure separately and added them up – it totaled about $2,100. After further investigation, I discovered that the surgeon was brand new and was still paying many charges to set up his office. He charged so much in order to cover those costs. We sent a letter to that surgeon and told him he could only charge $2,100 for his surgery. That was how medicine was practiced then.

I was elected to be the Chairman of the Department of Surgery of Inova Mount Vernon Hospital. Also, I was elected to be a member of the Surgical Review Board Committee of the National Orthopedic Hospital.

First Experience in Performing Surgery after Returning to the United States

The first time that I performed surgery at the Jefferson Memorial Hospital (which eventually closed), I was changing my clothes in the locker room when an older surgeon came in to change. I said good morning and introduced myself. We shook hands and he welcomed me. He asked me what my specialty was and I told him plastic surgery. He said that was very good and asked where I was from, so I told him. That was during the invasion of the American Embassy when American diplomats were taken as hostages. The physician got red in the face and became angry. He started to scream at me and I couldn't get a word in edgewise. He finally stopped screaming at me and I told him that if he had a minute, I could explain to him how what he had said was incorrect. I told him the Iranian people who came to the United States had done nothing wrong. That, in reality, Jimmy Carter was responsible for was happening in Iran. As President, Mr. Carter had decided to get rid of the Shah and bring in Khomeini. I told him that I had been in United States since I was 27 years old. Since then, I had eight years of training and two years of practice, for a total of ten years. I said that I returned to Iran two months before the Shah was deposed and Khomeini was installed. Then I explained that if President Carter had not brought Khomeini to Iran, I would have stayed in Iran the rest of my life because it was a wonderful country prior to Khomeini. The physician realized he had made a mistake and apologized. He explained that he was so upset about what was happening in Iran. I told him I agreed with him and I was more upset than he was. Everything used to be wonderful in Iran and now everything had changed.

Surgical Treatment of Severe Arthritis of Carpo Metacarpal Joint of Thumb

In 1979, in the beginning of my solo practice, I saw a patient in the office with severe pain in his wrist, especially around the base of his thumb. This pain had been present for a long time and was being treated by cortisone injections, however the pain was no longer responding to cortisone. I ordered an x-ray which revealed severe arthritis between the wrist and the base of the thumb.

There are several small bones in the wrist between the hand and forearm. The first small bone of the wrist on the base of the thumb is called the trapezium. The patient developed a severe form of arthritis of this joint (carpometacarpal). The treatment for this problem was surgical removal of the trapezium, then replacement with a Silastic implant, and finally reconstruction of the joint capsule.

This operation had to be done under axillary block anesthesia, which means numbing the arm and not putting the patient to sleep. This surgery is done on an outpatient basis. When I performed this surgery, everything went well. After surgery in the recovery room, I took an x-ray of his wrist and I noticed that not only had I removed the trapezium, but I had also removed a portion of the bone proximal to the trapezium, called the navicular. It scared me so much that I called Dr. Bruce Butler, a hand surgeon who was much older than me and respected in our community. I went to his office with the x-rays and told him my concern. When he looked at them from before, during, and after surgery, he said I hadn't had a choice and had done the right thing since the arthritis involved a large portion of the navicular bone. He said I had done a good job.

Gunshot Wound of the Wrist

A sixteen-year-old boy came to my office with his father because of an incidental BB gunshot wound to his wrist. I ordered an x-ray, which showed the presence of a round bullet in the volar aspect of his wrist. I recommended exploration and removal of the bullet under axillary block anesthesia as an outpatient.

During the surgery, when I opened up the wrist, I could not find the bullet. There are nine tendons in the volar aspect of the wrist. Each finger has two tendons and the thumb has one. I was surprised and ordered another x-ray in the operating room. The x-ray showed the bullet. I started to feel every tendon and I found that the bullet had lodged inside one tendon and was not visible from the outside. I made a small opening in the tendon, removed the bullet, and the patient fully recovered.

Largest Lipoma (Tumor of Fatty Tissues) of Back

Another interesting patient was a 55-year-old lady who came to my office about thirteen years ago because of a large mass on her back. When I asked her how long it had been there, she said fifteen years. When I asked why she had not sought a doctor sooner, she said that she was scared. For many years she could not lie on her back. This mass turned out to be a tumor of the fatty tissue and was really huge. I suggested surgical removal of the fatty tumor and performed the surgery. She had thought that for the rest of her life she would not be able to sleep on her back; she was able to sleep on her back afterward and she was very happy.

My View of Treatment of Skin Cancer

I have been removing skin cancer from patients for so many years. Every time I saw a suspicious skin lesion, I scheduled the patient to be taken to the operating room to remove the lesion with a frozen-section examination. After I removed each lesion, I marked around the lesion for orientation, like a clock, then sent it for frozen-section examination. The pathologist put a different color paint on the edge of the excised skin (twelve to three, three to six, six to nine, and nine to twelve), froze it, then cut it to very thin layers. He then looked at it under the microscope and told me two things: first, whether or not it was cancer, and second, if it was cancer, whether or not I removed it completely. If I had not removed it completely, then the pathologist told me which part was not removed completely, using a clock orientation, like nine o'clock to six o'clock, etc. Then I took some more tissue of that region, marked it like clock again and sent it for another frozen-section examination. I repeated this until the pathologist said the margins were clear, which meant I removed all the cancer. This is the best technique for complete removal of skin cancer.

Of course, after complete excision of the skin cancer, I still had to reconstruct the defect created by the excision of a portion of the skin, and make the patient look normal. This part of surgery is called reconstructive surgery and can be accomplished only by plastic surgeon.

The Behavior of Americans in Response to Invasion of Their Embassy in Iran by Bunch of Crazy Iranian People

The American people were rightfully upset about the invasion of the American Embassy in Iran by a bunch of crazy Iranian people in 1979; however, some Americans stepped over the line and began to attack Iranians residing in the United States. Of course that was not right either. For this reason, if anybody asked me where I was from, my answer was Italy. I did not want to be attacked. I thought the name "Matini" could easily be mistaken for the Italian name "Martini."

One day while I was seeing a young lady patient, she asked where I was from. I told her I was from Italy. She started to speak to me rapidly in Italian. I had to lie to cover my previous lie since I didn't understand a word she said. I told her my father was born in Italy but that he was a diplomat and that I was born in Iran while he was working there. I told her that he gave me a Persian name (Khosrow) since I was born in Iran.

One of my cousins who had also moved to the United States was living in Potomac, Maryland. He had two daughters, one thirteen years old and one ten years old. One morning he noticed the older daughter was upset, which was not normal for her. He asked what was wrong and she didn't say anything. He asked her over and over again, still she said nothing. He finally told his daughter that if she did not tell him what was wrong, he was not letting her go to school. At this point, his daughter started to cry. She pulled her dress up and showed her father how bruised she was. Her father asked her how she got the bruises and she said the American kids attacked the Iranian kids at her school. Of course, my cousin took her to school and talked to the principal to ensure that didn't happen again.

Arranging to Bring My Nephew Out of Iran and into the United States

The children of my oldest brother had stayed in Iran after he had no choice but to leave them. We were worried that the government would force his son into military service. At that time, if you did not finish your military duty, they would not allow you to obtain an exit permit. Finally, we found a couple of Iranians who promised they would take him out of Iran through the Baluchistan state into Pakistan illegally, which meant his passport would not be stamped by the Iranian border authority. My brother sent the couple six thousand dollars to help his son escape. My nephew flew from Tehran to Zahedan, the capital of Baluchistan, and from there, two Iranians who were not supportive of the government took him by car to Pakistan.

I had made arrangements with an attorney to fill out the necessary paperwork for my nephew in order for him to legally obtain a permanent residency visa from an American consulate in Europe. I called the Swiss Consulate in Pakistan and told him the status of my nephew and that his visa for the United States was ready. I asked him to issue a temporary visa so my nephew could stay a few days in Switzerland and go to the American Embassy and obtain his visa. When the consul asked me questions, I answered all of them truthfully. He said my nephew could send the Consulate a request for a temporary visa. The Switzerland Consulate said he would issue a tourist visa. I was happy and made the arrangements to send a letter requesting a temporary visa in Switzerland for him. A few days later, I received a phone call from an Iranian woman who was working for the State Department of Switzerland. She told me to please keep it a secret, but the Swiss Consulate in Pakistan had sent a letter to the State Department of Switzerland asking them not to issue a visa for my nephew.

I made other arrangements through an American attorney to get him a visa to France, where he was able to go to the American Embassy in Paris. They issued him a permanent visa. He finally came to the United States in August 1980 and stayed with his father in Rockville, Maryland. He attended school and got his high school diploma, then graduated from the University of Maryland. He went to the University of Chicago's School of Optometry and I went to Chicago to celebrate his graduation. Since he has returned to Washington, DC, he has been practicing as a wonderful optometrist.

After my nephew arrived safely in to the United States, I called the Swiss Consulate in Pakistan to ask why he had lied to me. I said that I was honest with him and he had lied to me. He would not answer. I told him that unfortunately there are liars like him all over the world.

Learning New Reconstructive Muscle and Myocutaneous Flaps Techniques

In 1979, three years after I had finished my training in plastic surgery and was in practice, I heard that someone had discovered a new technique for using muscle flaps in the reconstruction of defects of the body (defects are a lack, or deficiency, of something necessary for adequacy in form or function). Concurrently, I heard that there was a course teaching this new muscle flap surgery in Norfolk, Virginia so I immediately registered. That technique was both new and difficult. In the morning, we sat in the classroom to learn about the new technique and then, in the afternoon, we went to the anatomy lab to practice different reconstructive muscle flap procedures on a cadaver.

This was the first time since it had been discovered that it is possible to separate a muscle from its many attachments without jeopardizing the blood circulation of the muscle. As long as the attachment to the main blood vessels is maintained, the muscle stays alive in spite of being separated from its multiple attachments. For example, there are usually four muscles in the calf of each leg; to separate one or two of them does not affect the function of the leg. So after separating the muscle from its multiple attachments, the muscle can be moved to cover a defect and exposed bone. After I finished this course, I knew I could do these new procedures. Even today, I believe that learning this new technique was one of the most fascinating things I have done. It helped me to help so many patients in my practice.

The First Muscle Flap Reconstruction in the Washington Metropolitan Region

In 1980, there was a 16-year-old girl who fell and broke her kneecap bone. She was taken to an orthopedic surgeon who did an open reduction of the communed fracture of her kneecap bone and put the pieces of the broken kneecap bone together with wire, then closed the wound and put the young lady's leg and knee in a cast. Apparently, she bled from the broken parts of the kneecap, and this bleeding put pressure on the skin which was covering the kneecap bone. The pressure of the collected blood from one side and the cast from the other side impeded the circulation to the skin that covered the knee joint. Subsequently the skin died which was discovered by the orthopedic surgeon when he removed her cast.

At this point, the orthopedic surgeon called Dr. Scott Teunis, a plastic surgeon, to fix this patient's problem. Dr. Teunis had finished his plastic surgery training at the Mayo Clinic, and was a good plastic surgeon. We became good friends later on. Dr. Teunis took this patient to the operating room and tried to cover the knee joint with a skin flap from the thigh. In this procedure, the skin of the inner aspect of the lower portion of the thigh is cut and moved to cover the exposed shattered kneecap bone. Unfortunately, the patient developed an infection and the skin flap died as well, so it had to be debrided (removed). Dr. Teunis knew I was the only plastic surgeon in the Washington Metropolitan area who had taken the muscle flap course, so he called me in to see the patient.

I was able to take the patient to the operating room and use one of her calf muscles, which I had separated from the heel and freed completely from where it connected behind the knee. Then I made a tunnel from the calf to the dorsum of the knee, brought the muscle through the tunnel to cover the kneecap bone, and used a skin graft from the other thigh to cover the muscle. This procedure was successful and saved the leg of this young lady. Everything healed beautifully.

After everything healed, the girl's parents hired a lawyer to sue the orthopedic surgeon. The lawyer asked me to testify in court and I received money for doing so. A few months later, the lawyer asked me to go to court again. As is customary in the United States, I asked them to pay me in advance for my time in court, but they didn't send payment. I kept receiving a note from the court and ignored it until someone told me that the court could come after me if I didn't testify. I decided to go to court and testified that it wasn't the fault of the orthopedic surgeon that the skin died. I mentioned that I saved the patient's leg and she was now normal. After my testimony, the judge called me to his bench. He told me that because I kept ignoring the court summons, he was planning to arrest me and send me to jail, but when he heard my testimony, he thought I was honest and decided to let me go. He advised me that in the future, I should not ignore a court summons. I learned my lesson and promised that I would never do that again.

First Muscle Flap Reconstruction to Save an Arm

One year later, another orthopedic surgeon named Dr. Jahan Jubin, who practiced in Woodbridge and worked at the Inova Fairfax Hospital, called to say that he had a difficult problem with one of his patients. The patient was a forty-year-old woman who had fallen off her bicycle three and half months prior and had broken her upper arm bone. Her fracture still had not healed.

He further said that when this patient was seven years old, she had received a vaccine in her left upper arm and the needle broke. When they tried to find the needle's nub, they could not find it, so they had to take her to the operating room. Under general anesthesia and using x-rays, they tried to find the needle. Apparently it took two hours for them to find the broken needle. Too much radiation from the x-ray machine had caused necrosis (death) of the skin and muscle of her upper arm, which required removal of the dead skin and muscle and resulted in exposure of the arm bone.

In those days, they didn't know about muscle flaps, so they kept her in the hospital for several weeks, changing the dressing frequently every day until the granulation tissue appeared over the portion of the humerus (arm) bone. They then used a skin graft to cover that part of the bone. The skin graft took well and the exposed portion of bone was covered and healed, but this resulted in an ugly deformity of the left upper arm due to the absence of muscle.

The patient wasn't bothered by the deformity and had lived satisfactorily until she fell from her bicycle and broke her left arm. This orthopedic surgeon was taking care of the fracture, but it wasn't healing after three and half months. The last x-ray they had taken was suspicious for cancer of the bone. He decided to take her to the operating room, get a bone biopsy from the fractured side of the arm bone, and have it examined by a pathologist to see if it was cancerous. If it was not cancerous, he asked me to get some circulation to this portion of the arm bone to help the fracture heal.

Because of my knowledge about muscle flaps, I knew there was a technique for reconstructing a chest wall defect using a muscle flap. Using that technique, we free a muscle of the back by freeing the muscle attachment to the chest ribs, move the muscle from the patient's back and rotate it under the armpit to cover the chest. This operation was typically done for reconstruction of a breast after removal of the breast and its underlying muscle. No one had ever done this operation for reconstruction of the upper arm before.

I went to the anatomy lab at George Washington University Hospital to try this technique on a cadaver. Instead of using a muscle flap to reconstruct a chest wall defect, I wanted to see if we could use the same technique for an upper arm defect. It was successful in the anatomy lab, so I planned this reconstructive surgery for the arm of this patient.

A couple of plastic surgeons who were twenty-five years older than me and much more experienced asked me if they could come to the operating room and watch this new procedure. I welcomed them. After the patient was put under general anesthesia, we lay the patient on her right side on the operating table. The nurses washed the field of surgery and we covered the periphery of the field of surgery with sterile sheets. After the orthopedic surgeon did a needle biopsy of the bone of the arm, he sent it to the pathologist. The pathologist found no cancer in the bone, so I started to do the reconstruction of the left upper arm defect. I took off the thin skin graft which was covering the bone. Then I raised a muscle flap with its overlying skin from the patient's back, getting its circulation and blood supply from blood vessels in axilla. After I closed the defect of the back which was created by moving the remnant skin of back and putting a dressing on the back, I put the patient on the table in a supine position, and the nurse washed the field of surgery. I draped the field of surgery again. Next, I moved the muscle and skin flap, which was still attached to the axilla to the left upper arm and sutured this myocutaneous (muscle and overlying skin) flap to cover the large defect of the left upper arm. The operation was successful and the muscle flap and the overlying skin healed completely.

Within three weeks, the fracture, which had not healed for more than three and half months, healed satisfactorily. The patient was pleased and sent me a nice framed note that I still have. This was the first time an operation had been done in the United States for reconstruction of the upper arm using a muscle flap.

Breast Reconstruction by Abdominal Skin and Underlying Muscle of Abdomen

Reconstructing a breast by using abdominal skin and its underlying muscle is a difficult and complicated, but beautiful, reconstructive breast surgery. This operation creates a breast for patients who had a mastectomy (removal of entire breast). In this operation, a natural-looking breast is created by the skin and fatty tissues of the lower abdominal wall and underlying abdominal muscle. We do not use any breast implants in this operation. Another result of this surgery is a nice-looking abdomen. I performed this five-hour operation at Inova Mount Vernon Hospital. Dr. Sendi, the chief of plastic surgery of Inova Alexandria Hospital who started practice eleven years before me, asked to come and scrub with me on this operation because he had never seen it before. This surgery was done successfully and the patient was very pleased. After a year, the insurance companies reduced their payment for this operation so much ($1500 instead of $8500) that plastic surgeons no longer did it for insured patients.

Birth of my Daughter

In 1980, almost four years after our marriage, I thought my wife and I had worked through our problems. We were living together nicely so we decided to have a child. My wife got pregnant. Four months later, she started to act badly again. I tried to cope with it and thought it might be a side effect of her pregnancy. Before my daughter was born, we bought a new house. When my daughter was born, her mother refused to nurse her and we had to give her prepared milk. My daughter was a wonderful child and when we put her to bed, she never cried.

When my daughter was six months old, her mother was drying her after a bath and my daughter fell down on the floor of the bathroom. When I heard the noise, I picked my daughter up, put her in the car, and took her to the Emergency Room of Inova Mount Vernon Hospital which was about five miles away. A doctor examined her and they took an x-ray of her skull. Fortunately, there was no fracture.

The Crazy Woman Working For the Church

One night when I arrived home in 1983, I saw an elderly woman in our house. My wife introduced her to me and said the woman was working for the church. The elderly lady was interested in staying at our house and, in those evenings when we had plans, she would care for our daughter, so I welcomed her. A few days later, we were leaving the house to go to a dinner party. While I was driving, I remembered we left the hostess gift at the house so I turned around and drove back home. As soon as I opened the door, I heard my daughter crying loudly in the basement. I ran downstairs and saw my daughter standing on the bed and crying. She apparently wanted to go to the bathroom and the elderly woman would not let her go. I realized then that the old woman was crazy. I picked up my daughter and took her to the bathroom. I strongly controlled myself even as I told the woman to leave our house immediately. We did not go to the party. The next day, I called the church and reported her behavior.

Trips to Virginia Beach and Florida

In 1983, when my daughter was nearly two years old, my wife and I went to Miami to attend a plastic surgery meeting and have a few days of vacation. On the first day, we were at the beach most of the day. I brought my daughter into the hotel room for a nap in the afternoon. Around six P.M., we were planning to go out for dinner so we woke my daughter and got her dressed. When I went to pick her up to leave the room, she vomited on my shoulder. We decided to have dinner in the room and, even though we gave her only water, her vomiting continued. I found the name of a pediatrician in the yellow pages and called her. She recommended that I bring my daughter to the hospital. After examining her, the pediatrician said my daughter had some type of virus and had to be admitted to the hospital for intravenous fluid and antibiotic treatment. My daughter was in the hospital for four days and we had to return home the day after she was discharged. That was not much of a vacation.

Later that summer, we went to Virginia Beach on vacation. One day, when we left the hotel room and were in the elevator, the elevator door opened and Muhammad Ali came inside. He looked at my daughter, then picked her up and told her she would be a knock out.

When he did that, he made a little motion with his hand like he was knocking someone out. I still have that picture of them.

Treatment of Longstanding Psychiatric Condition by Plastic Surgery

In 1983, a 40-year-old woman who had lost her left breast at age 21 came to my office. She had been diagnosed with breast cancer at age 21, and the surgeon had removed her left breast, the chest muscle underneath the breast, and a couple of her ribs, then covered the large defect of her left chest with a skin graft. In taking her history, I also learned that after the surgery, she had developed psychiatric problems and had since been on multiple psychiatric medications.

Figure 19: Muhammad Ali and My Daughter

After examining her, I told her I could reconstruct her left breast using a muscle and overlying skin from her back. Her right breast was large, so I needed to use a breast implant as well on the left side. I explained that since her right breast was sagging, I would have to lift her right breast during a second surgery to match the reconstructed left breast. I would also have to recreate the nipple and areola on her reconstructed left breast.

I performed two stages of surgery and she was very pleased how they turned out. Three months after the second surgery, I saw her for follow-up. She told me she had not had to take any more psychiatric medication. I found it interesting that this reconstructive plastic surgery cured a nineteen year psychiatric problem.

Unusual Dog Bite

One night, I received a call from the Emergency Room of Inova Fairfax Hospital. I knew the physician who had phoned me even though I was not on call. He said another doctor wanted to speak to me. The other doctor was a retired anesthesiologist at Inova Fairfax Hospital. He said his 26-year-old daughter had been bitten seriously by their dog. I immediately went to the Inova Fairfax Hospital Emergency Room and examined his daughter. Her left ear was almost torn off, and she had multiple deep avulsed lacerations on the left side of her face, scalp, and left arm. I took her to the operating room and repaired all the lacerations and successfully put her avulsed ear back in its location. I kept her in the hospital for intravenous antibiotic treatment for three days. After discharging her from the hospital, I saw her in the office. She was doing well.

One week later, I received another call from her father. This time his 30-year-old son had been bitten by their dog. Again, I went to Inova, examined his son, and took him to the operating room. He had multiple dog bites on the left side of his face, scalp, and arm. I repaired all the lacerations and kept him in the hospital for intravenous antibiotic treatment. Two days later I discharged him.

A few days later the father told me he had a veterinarian put the dog down. An animal pathologist did an autopsy of the dog and found out that he had a brain tumor. They had that dog for twelve years and loved him. Because they thought they knew the dog, they did not take it to the veterinarian after it bit his daughter. Instead they thought the daughter must have done something to frighten the dog. The dog's tumor was on the right side of his brain which is why all the dog bites were on the left side of his daughter's and son's bodies.

Most Unusual Case of Facial Bone Fractures

Another interesting patient was a gentleman who was a music composer. He had been riding his motorcycle while wearing his prescription glasses when a car hit him so hard that he was thrown more than thirty feet. He was brought to the Inova Fairfax Hospital Emergency Room and examined. Multiple x-rays were taken which showed every facial bone had been broken and his facial bones were separated from his skull. The Emergency Room called me and I admitted him to the hospital and scheduled him for surgery. The surgery was complicated because the attachment ligament between the inner aspects of each eye where the eyes attached to the nasal bone, was separated, and both eyes moved sideways. I had to reattach the ruptured and avulsed ligament of each eye to the nasal bones. The bones that the eyes sit on were also broken on both sides. Those bones are very thin and fragile.

I had to reconstruct the floor of both orbits using a silastic sheet (thin layers of silastic material). The jaw bone was broken and separated from the skull on both sides. It took me seven hours in the operating room to put everything back together, then reattach the separated jaw bone to the skull. I had to put adapting dental arch bars to the upper and lower teeth and then hook the wires together by rubber bands. Fortunately, the patient did very well and after a few days of hospitalization, he was sent home with his upper and lower teeth still wired and hooked together by rubber bands. He was not able to chew for a period of five weeks. All of his fractures healed satisfactorily and the appearance of his face become normal. No one could have guessed that he had such a major injury to his face.

Disaster to My Daughter's Elbow Due to My Niece's Mistake

One day in 1984, my sister and her three children (a thirteen-year-old daughter, and two sons, ages ten and six) came to our house. My niece asked where my daughter was and I said she was asleep. An hour later, my three-year-old daughter woke up and my niece asked if she and her brothers could take my daughter outside in front of my house to play with her. We had a large round grassy area in front of the house with a big tree in the center of it. My niece held my daughter's hand as they left the house.

A few minutes later, I heard my daughter crying. I ran outside, picked her, and asked what had happened. My niece said my daughter was walking on the grass and fell down on her left hand. Because of that explanation, I thought my daughter's wrist was injured, but when I checked her left wrist nothing seemed wrong. To be safe, I wrapped her wrist in an ace bandage, put her in the car, and drove her to the Department of Radiology at Inova Mount Vernon Hospital. I asked the technician to take x-rays of her left wrist. After he took the x-rays, I looked at them and saw that the wrist was fine but because she was so small, a portion of her elbow could be seen in the x-ray. I saw something suspicious in her elbow region and asked the technician to take an x-ray of her elbow. When I looked at that x-ray, I was terrified because I saw that she had a supra condylar fracture of the elbow (the main bone of the arm being broken right above the elbow and with two segments of broken bone severely displaced). This is one of the most dangerous fractures because the edge of the broken bone can cut the main artery or nerve of the arm.

I immediately contacted the orthopedic surgeon on call for that day (Sunday). He came to the hospital and took her to the operating room. Under general anesthesia, he put a big wire through her elbow to be able to put the forearm in traction and she was admitted to the hospital. It took nine days of traction for the broken pieces of bone to come together. Then they took her back to the operating room, removed the wire, put her arm in a cast, and discharged her from the hospital.

Three weeks later, another x-ray was taken which showed that the fracture had healed satisfactorily. The orthopedic surgeon removed the cast. I immediately noticed that her left hand was paralyzed due to an injury to the ulnar nerve, one of the main important nerves of the arm and hand. The surgeon told me it would get better in a few days. Unfortunately, he was too optimistic.

After three days, nothing had changed. I took her to the Department of Physical Medicine and asked one of the specialists to do an E.M.G. (peripheral nerve study). The E.M.G. showed nothing went through the ulnar nerve below the elbow, which was the sign of an ulnar nerve injury. I knew the elbow should be surgically explored and, if the ulnar nerve was cut, it could be repaired. I had done this operation on a few patients myself before, but I did not want to operate on my own daughter. I called the Hand Surgery Center in Louisville, KY, where I was trained for hand surgery. One of my professors made arrangements for her to have the surgery there.

I took my daughter to Louisville, and on the day of the surgery, they asked me to go into the operating room. When the surgeon opened the elbow area, fortunately the nerve was not cut, but it had apparently been hit several times by the wire during her original surgery. Hitting the nerve had resulted in a severe form of scar tissue which squeezed the nerve, caused an hour glass deformity of the nerve, and stopped the conduction of nerve fibers. The hand surgeon opened the sheath around the nerve and removed a portion of it. I brought my daughter back home and three weeks after surgery, the function of the ulnar nerve gradually returned. After six weeks, the ulnar nerve function returned to normal.

Later on, I found out what had really happened. My niece had been sitting on a branch of the tree in my front yard. My daughter was at the age where she wanted to copy bigger kids, so she asked to sit on the branch, too. My niece picked her up and set her on the branch. My daughter fell backwards and broke her elbow. My niece didn't tell me the truth because she realized she should not have put my daughter on that tree branch by herself.

Selling Our House

My wife asked me to add a wall between the kitchen and the family room, and to replace all the carpets and curtains. I did anything she requested even though it cost about $30,000. For a few more months everything was fine, then she started to complain about the location of our house, even though one neighbor was a popular ophthalmologist, another was an otolaryngologist, and a third was a famous attorney. It was the worst time to try and sell a house, interest rates were around eighteen percent. Nobody could afford to buy a house with interest rates so high, but I put the house in the market just to make my wife happy.

The first real estate agent who came to see the house loved it and offered to buy it for herself at the price I was asking. We sold it to her and had to leave.

During the time I lived in that house, I had hired a termite company to check the house every year. A couple of months prior to selling it, they came to check the house and said it was clear of termites. Two weeks after I sold the house, the buyer called me and said she heard I was a good and honest surgeon. She asked me if I knew that there were termites in the house. I told her that I definitely did not and offered to show her documentation of the termite inspections. She said she believed me. She told me that because her husband could not walk and used a wheelchair, she decided to do some construction work on the house so her husband could more easily get around. When the construction company came and looked at the house, they found that the basic wood structure of the house was destroyed by termites and they warned her that the entire house could collapse at any time. After I heard this, I called the termite company and told them what she had said. The company said they were not responsible, and suggested that

I read our contract. After I read the contract carefully, I saw the small print which said they were not responsible. I could not believe it and still feel bad for the couple who bought the house.

Possible Heart Attack

After we sold the house and moved into an apartment, my wife asked for a divorce. I was still living with her and my daughter until the divorce was finalized. During this difficult time, one day I went to my office to see patients, but I was uncomfortable and felt tightness around my neck. At noon, I had to go to a monthly lunch meeting for the office building. I picked up Dr. Frank Talbot, a cardiologist, who was also my friend and a member of the committee. I said how I was feeling and he checked my pulse. He said to come to his office after the lunch meeting and he would do an E.K.G. (electrocardiogram). I told him I had to do surgery after the meeting, but I would come after I finished my surgery. After the meeting, I went to the operating room; during surgery, I did not feel any discomfort.

As soon as the surgery was completed, I felt chest pain. Then I got a call from the Emergency Room to come see a patient. As soon as I finished seeing the patient in the Emergency Room, my chest pain became more severe. I talked to an Emergency Room physician who did an E.K.G. As soon as the doctor saw the results, he told me not to move. He called Dr. Talbot who admitted me to the intensive care unit. Apparently, I was experiencing severe spasms of the coronary arteries (blood vessels) of my heart. Dr. Talbot treated me with different medications and, after twenty four hours, the spasms disappeared and I was released. Fortunately, it was not a heart attack.

The entire episode was terrifying, but turned out to have a beneficial outcome because Dr. Talbot wrote a letter stating that because of my current heart condition, I should not live with my wife. A few weeks later, our two attorneys came to an agreement and the divorce was finalized on July 2, 1985. One of the terms of the divorce was that I pay my ex-wife more money for the first two years after the divorce so she could take care of our daughter instead of having to work. The first weekend after the divorce was final, I found out that she was working six days a week. I suggested that I take my daughter every weekend and my ex-wife agreed.

A few years later, my ex-wife remarried and within the last fourteen years, I have seen both Lily's mother and her husband on various occasions and we have a good time together. I talk by phone with Lily's mother frequently as we both are proud of our wonderful daughter. Occasionally, I have lunch with Lily and her mother, and we even have several pictures together.

Vacations with my Daughter

I took a vacation every summer and traveled with my daughter to Virginia Beach. I usually got a chair and umbrella and sat on the beach. The first summer after my divorce, I let my daughter, then four years old, play on the beach while I watched her carefully. One day, a heavy wave suddenly came to shore and knocked her down. I immediately ran to the water to get her out of the ocean. When I got back to the beach, I realized that I had lost my prescription glasses in the water. I was happy that my daughter was fine, so didn't get upset about the loss of my glasses. To my great surprise, in the afternoon, a huge wave of water brought my glasses back to me on the shore.

My Second Marriage

I had a good friend in medical school who was one year behind me. She had finished nursing school in England before she came to medical school in Iran, so her English was better than mine. She and her brother were my friends while I was in medical school. We were all living in Meshed, Iran. The youngest daughter of this family had gone to a college in Tehran when she was eighteen years old while I was in my third year of medical school. A few years later, this youngest daughter sent me an invitation to her wedding, which I attended with my mother.

During my last year of medical school, I planned to come to the United States, but I had to pass the E.C.F.M.G. examination which evaluates the qualification of foreign medical physicians before accepting them as American physicians. The best way to prepare myself for the examination was to study the Merck Manual, which summarizes all diseases clearly. When I started to read it, I realized quickly that it was going to take forever because there were so many words I didn't know and I had to look up each one's definition.

My friend who was a year behind me in medical school was also planning to go to the United States after she finished medical school. I asked her if she would be interested in studying for the E.C.F.M.G. with me. She said that would be wonderful. It was helpful because she knew English so well. We practically translated the Merck Manual into Farsi. When we finished translating the book, I told her I was thinking of publishing the translation and she said it was a good idea. Unfortunately, two weeks later, somebody else published the translated Merck Manual in Farsi.

After studying so diligently, I passed the exam with flying colors and was able to come to the United States. When I was in the United States for my training after medical school, my friend also came and finished her training in radiology. She became a radiologist and later returned to Iran to practice. She married and had two children.

After the Iranian revolution, when I had returned to the United States for the second time, and opened my practice, she had become divorced and had brought her two kids to the United States on a visitor visa. Her previous permanent residency visa was suspended because she had not renewed it, so she could not stay in the United States as a practicing physician. She asked for my help and I told her there was one thing I could do. I could determine that I needed a nurse in my office who spoke Farsi and English, because my patients spoke both languages. I could then advertise the position and, if nobody else could fill it, I could hire her and request a permanent visa for her. That worked out very well and she obtained a permanent residency visa in the United States. We saw each other once in a while. Later on, she got a job as a radiologist at the Veterans Administration Hospital in Washington DC.

How I Met my Second Wife

Less than two years after my divorce, I was planning to go to a plastic surgery meeting in Toronto, Canada. I called this same friend, told her where I was going, and asked if she had anything she wanted me to take to her sister. I knew her younger sister had divorced her husband and had been in Europe for many years before moving to Toronto. She said no, but gave me her sister's telephone number and asked me to call her and say hi.

When I went to Toronto, I called her sister, who said she would like to see me. We arranged to meet for dinner and when we saw each other, I was attracted to her. She was beautiful and appeared to be very smart. She was an important administrator of a top-notch department store in Toronto. For the few days I was in Toronto, we saw each other several times and I became interested in her.

Later on she visited me a couple of times in Alexandria. We even went together on a vacation to Aruba and had a wonderful time. We started to like each other but, of course, because we lived so far away, it was not possible to see each other more frequently. Because I knew her older sister, brother, and father, I thought she would be as wonderful as the rest of her family and be a good candidate for marriage. We talked about marriage and she was interested. She came to Alexandria; and we married in March 1989. We had a little reception, then went to New York for a brief honeymoon. After New York, she had to return to Toronto and work one more month before she could leave her job.

I didn't know anybody in Toronto. While there, she told me that one of her best friends was giving a party to celebrate our marriage. My new wife took me to the party and introduced me to her friends. Everyone came and shook hands to congratulate me. Because I didn't know anyone, I sat down by myself and just looked around. She talked with all her friends and left me there to sit.

When the party was finished and we were going back to her apartment, she complained that I had looked at her friend who had hosted the party the entire time. I was surprised and asked what she was talking about. I said I loved her and had married her, so why would I be looking at her friend? I told her I looked around because she had left me all by myself and I didn't know anybody.

She told me this funny story about herself after we got married. She said that when she got married the first time, she was still in college. She told her husband that she did not want to get pregnant until she finished her college. Her husband put a crystal bowl full of candy that looked like pills beside their bed. Every night he told her to take two of those pills to prevent pregnancy. Although her father and sister were doctors, she believed her husband and ate that candy every night. A few months after their marriage, she went for her annual checkup to her gynecologist. After he examined her, he congratulated her for being pregnant. She told her doctor she could not be pregnant because she had been taking some pills every night since they got married to prevent pregnancy. She showed her doctor those pills and he recognized that the pills were really candy. He laughed so hard that he fell off his chair.

A New House in Mount Vernon, Virginia

In 1987, prior to my marriage, I tried to find a house to buy in Mount Vernon, Virginia. After showing me many houses, my realtor showed me a new neighborhood and suggested that I build my own house there. I bought land on August 5, 1988, and one year later I signed an agreement with the builder of these large properties to build the house for me. The building was finished in the summer of 1989. When we returned to the United States from Canada, I brought her to the new house.

My Second Wife

During courtship, my second wife asked why my daughter did not live with me. I told her that when I divorced my daughter's mother, she said she wanted to keep our daughter, and since I was busy surgeon, I would have had difficulty looking after a small child. My new wife kept saying that after we got married, she'd like for my daughter to live with us. I told her I didn't think it was possible because her mother wanted to keep her. After a while, my daughter, who was ten years old at the time, said she wanted to come and live with me. I told her that her mother had legal custody but my daughter said she would talk with her mother. I got a call from my ex-wife who said she didn't mind if my daughter came to live with me and that she would see her every other weekend. After talking to my new wife, I happily brought my daughter to our house.

When my daughter finally came to live with us, she was attending a private school. The school bus came and picked her up in front of our house and dropped her off there after school. In the second year, there weren't enough kids to send a school bus near our house, so I had to take her to a bus stop that was ten minutes from my house. I talked with some neighbors whose kids went to the same school and we made a plan that once a week, each parent would take turns taking all the neighborhood students to the bus stop, thus reducing the burden on the parents. I asked my new wife if she would do that, but she refused. Despite her talk, she apparently didn't want my daughter to live with us after all, so I had to take my daughter to the bus stop each morning myself.

It turned out that my new wife had two children from her previous marriage. Her daughter was a college student in Toronto. My new wife said she got an offer from her previous boss in Toronto to work as the office manager at the Saks Jandel in Bethesda, Maryland. Instead, she choose to work as a salesperson, a lower paid job with less responsibility. She constantly complained about her job. I told her that if she didn't like her work, she could quit. She said she had to work because she had to send $500 a month to her daughter in college. I offered to give her the $500 to send her daughter and, of course, she accepted my offer and quit her job.

My Second Divorce

One morning, I heard a lot of noise coming from our bedroom while I was finishing my shower and getting ready for work. My wife was helping my daughter get ready for school so I could take her to the bus stop. I heard them fighting and I came out to see what was happening. My daughter said that my wife was telling her to wear some boots, but she didn't like them and didn't want to wear them. My daughter said that my wife told her that if she didn't listen to her, she could not come back home. I asked my wife if we could talk privately. We went to another room and I asked my wife if she had said this. She said yes. I asked her where my daughter was supposed to go, that she was just a kid. I told my wife that she was the one who wanted my daughter to live with us, but now she didn't do anything for her. I did everything for my daughter. The only thing she was doing was helping my daughter get her clothes on in the morning. She should have told my daughter to listen to her because it was good for her, not because if she disobeyed she could not come home. My wife said that it was too bad, that was the way it was going to be. I told my wife that she should leave the house because my daughter was just a kid and she was treating her badly. We had some problems which I tolerated, but enough was enough and we should get a divorce.

Although we had a prenuptial agreement, she hired an attorney. Of course, the attorney wanted to make money and the best way to do that was to drag things out. So, I had to go to my attorney again. I told my lawyer that we had written a prenuptial agreement to prevent fighting when we split up and she said that, unfortunately, everybody can still fight even with a signed agreement. The only way that this could be cleared up was to go to court and get a judgment in my favor. I asked my attorney when we could go to court. She said that the earliest we could go to court was fourteen months from then. I could just imagine how much money I would have to spend on lawyers during those fourteen months. My wife wanted $2,000 per month for forty-eight months and I decided it was cheaper to settle with her for that amount than to go to court. I arranged for payment and she signed the divorce agreement. The divorce was finalized July 9, 1993.

This is another problem of the legal system in the United States. My wife signed a prenuptial agreement with me prior to marriage. Her personal attorney reviewed the agreement and my soon-to-be wife signed it. But at the time of our divorce, they started a fight with me to make more money for themselves, even though we had a prenuptial agreement.

Moving to a New Office Building

After years of practice in the Sherwood Hall Medical Building, I needed more space. I knew that some plastic surgeons operated in their own office, so I thought if I found a bigger space, I could do that, too. Fortunately, there was an office building close to Sherwood Hall Medical Building where offices were being sold cheaply because the owner had gone bankrupt. I looked and there were two units, one above the other; the top unit was finished and the bottom unit was still a big hole. After negotiations, I bought these two units with the agreement that the bank would build the first unit as I wanted, and then connect the two units with stairs so I could use them together. I decided to prepare one of the upstairs rooms as a possible operating room.

Before proceeding with these plans, I thought it was best to consult with an expert on creating an operating room in a doctor's office. I had heard about a consultant living in Chicago and I called her. She agreed to come to my office and review my practice to let me know if it was a good idea to have an operating room or not.

Cheating Office Manager

The first day this consultant arrived in my office, I introduced her to my office manager. My office manager had worked for me for more than a year and appeared to be good. I told my office manager to help this consultant with anything that she asked. That same day I had to see many patients. Around four P.M., I wanted to talk to my office manager about a patient, but my staff told me that she had not been feeling well and had gone home. The next morning, the consultant returned and my office manager was not in the office. I was worried about my office manager so I called her home phone number and nobody answered. I worried more and called the manager of her apartment building. I told him why I was concerned and asked if he would check her apartment. He did, she was not in her apartment. When I told this to the consultant, she said that this office manager may have been cheating me and was afraid that she would be discovered when the consultant poked around. Apparently the consultant was right. My office manager didn't return. The consultant asked if I had ever received cash from patients. I told her that patients occasionally paid their copayment in cash, but that was usually less than $50. Then I remembered that there was one patient who came for her pre-operative appointment for cosmetic surgery and the office manager came and told me the patient was supposed to pay $3,000 but she had only brought $2,900 in cash. I told my office manager that it was all right; we would accept the $2,900. That was the biggest amount of cash I would have received. I went to the computer and there was no record of receiving the $2,900 cash from my patient. We recognized that the office manager had likely stolen any cash received in the office. I called the patient who paid the cash. She was pleased with the surgery and said she would be glad to testify that she paid the bill in cash to the office manager. I made a formal complaint and a hearing was scheduled with a judge. The day of the hearing, the patient who paid the cash was sick and couldn't attend. When the hearing was rescheduled, the police detective was out of town and the hearing didn't take place. I decided it wasn't worth my time to continue to pursue the case. By then, I was just glad to be rid of my office manager.

The good news was that this consultant reported that the only way I could have a profitable operating room in my office was if I scheduled surgery five days a week. No surgeon operates that much, including me, so I would have had to lease out the space to other surgeons. Since I did not have an associate, she advised against having an operating room in my office. It was worth it to hire her for her expertise, I could possibly have made a large mistake. I continued to use the operating room of Inova Mount Vernon Hospital.

Explosion of Sherwood Hall Medical Center Office Building

In 1990, I went to Louisville, Kentucky for a hand surgery meeting. On Friday afternoon while I was still in Louisville, I called my office to talk to my secretary and see if she had any questions for me. No one was in the office. When I talked to the answering service, I was told my secretary had closed the office two hours before I called. I thought she closed the office early because I was away. When I returned, I found the double glass windows of my office were darkened and some of them shattered. I called one of my colleagues who also had an office in our building and asked him what happened. He told me a psychiatrist who had an office in our building had received a letter bomb and opened it, causing a huge explosion. He sustained a major abdominal injury, had more than 50% of his body covered with burns, and had severe injuries to his hands and arms. He was taken to the best burn unit in Washington DC. He was very lucky to survive. Six months later, after multiple surgeries and extensive treatment for his burns, including multiple skin grafts, he was discharged from the hospital.

Who Mailed the Explosive Letter?

Three months after the bombing, top detectives of both the postal service and the F.B.I. came to my office and said they were investigating who sent the mail bomb to the psychiatrist. They apparently went through the charts of every patient of this doctor and found out one of his patients was the wife of an ex-military man who was an expert in making bombs. They showed me and my staff a picture of the ex-military man. I said I had never seen him. My young secretary, however, said that he had asked her for a date. She said she knew the man was married and told him she would not go out with him. The police were never able to arrest that man because they could not prove he sent the mail bomb.

Lightning Strikes My House

Four years after I moved into my newly-built house, there were not many houses in the neighborhood; there was one house on the left side between my house and the river, and two houses on the right. One night when I came home, there was no electricity in my house and the telephone was not working. A large portion of the tall chimney was missing and there was major damage to the roof of my family room. I called the electric company and the telephone company, both of whom sent repairmen. Both repairmen said my house had been hit by lightning and I was lucky not be at home during this lightning strike because if I had been home and was on the phone, I could have been killed. I had two telephone lines in the house, one of which was completely destroyed. The repairmen were able to restore the electricity and fix one phone line. I had to hire a construction company to repair the house. They found out that parts of the concrete chimney had fallen inside of the chimney and had to remove the fallen bricks piece-by-piece. Some of the concrete pieces were projected about five feet below the grass in the ground, and had to be removed. The construction company had to fix the severely damaged roof of the family room. Because the house was so badly damaged, I felt very lucky to still be alive.

The Major Fire of a New House Being Built

A few years after I built my house, another big house was built on the right side of my house and a primary care physician and his family were living there. After one year, another house was built next to them. One morning, I woke up to see bright light through my window. When I pulled the curtain open, I saw a major fire burning in the new house. My next door neighbor had gotten out his water hose in an effort to try and keep the fire from spreading. After a few minutes, the firemen came and, after several hours, they were able to douse the fire. Unfortunately, the fire and water destroyed the house. My daughter had never seen such a fire before and took a bunch of pictures. After a few months they rebuilt that house.

The Successful Achievements of my Daughter

I started to take my daughter to violin class at age six. I picked her up from school and had lunch with her, then took her to the house of her violin teacher. I enjoyed sitting and watching her take lessons. While I was growing up in Iran, there was no classical music played and so I was not familiar with it. Gradually, I became interested in classical music during her lessons and in the last twenty-five years, I have been going to the Kennedy Center to listen to the National Symphony Orchestra and other wonderful orchestras.

My daughter gradually became a good violin player. When she was sixteen years old, she and thirteen other American children were invited to join the Japanese Children's Orchestra and play Symphony Number Three of Beethoven and the Rhapsody of Tchaikovsky. I went with her to Japan. For one day, these fourteen American children practiced with 86 Japanese children under the direction of a Japanese conductor who could not speak English. The following evening they performed the difficult music of Beethoven and Tchaikovsky in front of 800 people. My daughter was the first violin player. Their performances were excellent. While she was playing in this concert, my face was streaked with tears of happiness because I remembered the injury of her left elbow and paralysis of her left hand when she was three years old. I was thanking God.

While my daughter was in middle school I received a call from the director of the show choir of her school (St. Stephen's and St. Agnes). He told me my daughter had a wonderful voice and he recommended I get her a private teacher. I looked around and talked with a few people and found Mrs. Jennifer Casey Cabot who was a professional opera singer. Fortunately, she accepted my daughter as student and once a week I took my daughter to Old Town, Alexandria, where the teacher lived. Mrs. Cabot taught singing to my daughter for a year and a half. At the same time, I got season tickets for the opera at the Kennedy Center in Washington, DC for me and my daughter. My daughter became an excellent singer and won many prizes. At her high school graduation ceremony, my daughter sang a solo in front of the faculty, students and family of the students. I was a very proud father.

After high school, my daughter attended Oberlin College. While there, my daughter became interested in swing dancing. She collected signatures from parents of other students and convinced the college to provide a concert hall for them to practice, and then she invited some good dance teachers. My daughter became such a good dancer that she became the Swing Dance Champion of the United States before graduating from college. My daughter continues to dance to this day and continues to win competitions. She also teaches dancing every Sunday afternoon.

When President George Bush was elected in January 2001, my daughter was invited to dance with her swing dance partner in front of 16,000 people at one of the Inauguration Balls in Washington., DC. She was the Director of Volunteer Operations for the Presidential Inaugural Committee. The inaugural committee also gave her two additional tickets and she gave them to me. The next day, the Washington Post wrote an article about the celebration and instead of publishing a picture of my daughter, they published a picture of me and my date dancing because we were dancing right next to two cute kids.

How I Fell in Love with a Plastic Surgeon

In April 1996, I went for a plastic surgery conference in Florida. I arrived a few minutes late and the room was dark and the speaker was already talking and showing slides. I took an empty chair and when the speech was finished and the light came on, I saw that I was sitting next to a beautiful lady. I introduced myself and she told me her name. I found out that she was also a plastic surgeon who was practicing in California close to San Francisco. After the conference was finished that day, I asked her if she was with anyone and she said she was by herself. I told her I was by myself too and, if she wanted, we could have dinner together. That was the beginning of our relationship. We started to spend a lot of time together. We were interested in each other, but it was unfortunate that we lived so far apart. We continued to communicate by telephone and e-mail. I usually talked to her after midnight (it was nine P.M. her time) and, after a couple of hours of talking, she told me to please hang up because I had to get up in the morning and go to work. I did not feel the passage of time while I was talking to her.

Many Trips with My Plastic Surgeon Friend

We decided to travel together. The first place we went was Italy, including Sicily in the southern part of Italy in July 1996. When we arrived at the hotel in Sicily, I told the staff that I had heard there was a place that had special water that was good for the skin. They knew of such a place and told me it was located on an island. They said they didn't have anyone to take us there, but that we could rent a car and go there by ourselves. That turned out to be a big mistake. I rented a car and, using their directions, drove on a road beside the ocean. It took about four hours. We finally got to the ferry dock and got on the ferry to go to the island. When we finally arrived, we could only stay one hour in order to catch the last ferry back. We caught the last ferry back and, on the return, I asked someone on the boat about our return trip. I told him that I was told it was only two hours from our hotel to the ferry dock, but that it took us twice as long. He said our trip took longer because we came on the road by the ocean. He said if we go through the mountain route it would be much faster. He gave me the directions for the mountain route. After the ferry was docked and we got in our rental car, we started to drive on the mountain road. I had to drive slowly due to the twist and turns. After a long time climbing the mountain road, we finally started coming down the other side of the mountain. When I applied the brake on one of the curves, the car didn't stop. I tried everything I knew about stopping a car, but nothing worked. I suddenly realized that I had two choices to stop the car, either drive off the cliff or hit the rock of the mountain. I decided to hit the mountain and the car stopped. Thank goodness we weren't hurt. It was about ten P.M. when we finally stopped and I realized we were in real trouble because Sicily was famous for its criminals and violence. I was scared. My friend suggested that we start walking to find a house and explain the situation. I told her that I didn't recommend we do that because Sicily was dangerous. I told her I should turn the car's lights off and, if we saw a car, we could try and flag it down; otherwise, we should wait until morning when it would be safer. It was the fourth of July evening and, while we were stranded, we saw the fire from Mt. Etna, a volcano in Sicily. In trying to calm my friend down, I told her that it was nice of them to give us a fireworks display on the fourth of July!

After an hour, we saw headlights; a car was climbing up the mountain road. I flagged the car down. It was a man and a woman plus their baby in the back of their car. The man didn't speak English at all and we couldn't understand each other. I finally gave up and asked him to call the police when he showed me his badge; he was a policeman. I showed him the car rental document and tried my best to explain our situation. He said that we had to go to the top of the mountain to use his phone; it wouldn't work where we were. He left his wife and his child in our car with my friend and took me to the top of the mountain road where he called the rental company. I was thankful for his help. When we got back to my car, I thanked him and told him that he and his wife could go. He said that he could not go until the car company picked us up because it was such a dangerous area. In saying that, he confirmed my concerns about the area. Finally, the car company came and picked us up and took us back to the hotel.

From Sicily, we returned to Rome and stayed a few days. I shopped in one of the most expensive men's shops (Valentino) which was having an unbelievable sale. For example, a $2,500 suit was on sale for $480. I bought two suits with cash. When we arrived at Kennedy Airport in New York, my friend had to catch a plane to San Francisco, and I had to fly to Washington, DC. I had a full surgery schedule for the next day. When we were in the customs line, a young agent came to me and asked me to come with him to another line. I thought he was trying to move us faster. I showed him my passport and list of my purchases. He kept asking if I was coming from the Middle East and I said no. I told him that I went to Italy and I was returning to my home in Washington, DC. Of course, my passport showed I was a United States citizen. The agent said that he couldn't believe that I bought those suits for such a cheap price and asked for my credit card receipt. I told him I paid cash. He told me he didn't believe me and said he was going to get somebody else to look at the suits I had bought. After waiting and waiting, I was concerned I would miss my flight, so I called him and told him I am a physician and had to be in the hospital for surgery the next morning. I told him he could keep my luggage as long as he gave me a receipt. He couldn't find anyone to support him so he closed the luggage and gave it to me. Fortunately, I was able to get to the plane on time and get back home.

Trip to Brazil and Argentina

In 1997, we made another trip together for an International Plastic Surgery Meeting in Sao Paulo, Brazil. One night, there was a big party for the attendees of the plastic surgery meeting at the most famous club in town. We enjoyed dinner and the live music, and danced until two A.M. Two days later we went to Buenos Aires, Argentina. They had a wide street called Avenida 9 de Julio, a copy of the famous Champs-Elysees in Paris. The hotel where we stayed was like an old French palace. Its décor was unbelievable. The bathtub was made of brass. The price was surprisingly reasonable, about $200 per night. Breakfast was included in the price of the room and was excellent; there were so many varieties of delicious food. One night, we went to a club to watch professional dancers. We had a lot of fun on that trip.

In 1998, she brought her children to my house and I took them to the interesting parts of Washington, DC. One day we went to Georgetown to shop. My friend asked me to stay with her son who was six years old because she wanted to shop with her daughter who was nine years old. While we were standing together, I heard him say the names of different stores. I was surprised. He was reading although he had not yet attended school. He was a very smart kid.

Plastic Surgery Conference in Boston, Massachusetts

One of the last meetings we were at together was in Boston in 1999. After three days of meetings, we were tired and wanted to do something different. We found out there was a baseball game that night between Boston and New York. We decided to go to the game and went to the stadium to buy tickets. The guy in front of us in the line at the box office asked us if we had tickets. I said no, that we were going to buy them. He laughed and said the game was sold out. He said there were some people selling tickets nearby, but that we should be careful not to be caught because it was illegal. He said the tickets would be more expensive. I thanked him and went to another street and found someone who was selling the tickets. I bought tickets and we were in the best seats in that stadium. I was not a big fan of baseball, but we had fun watching that game.

This beautiful plastic surgeon was about 19 years younger than me.

We decided to get married because we were seeing each other about 30 days a year, but were in love and wanted to be together all the time. She agreed to come to Alexandria to join my practice. Unfortunately, when she talked to her attorney, he told her that if she wanted to see her children, she could not leave town according to the agreement she had signed with her ex-husband, because they had joint custody. The whole thing collapsed when we found out that we could not marry. After that, I have only seen her a couple of times. Now we are just friends.

President of Alexandria Medical Society

From the beginning of my practice, I was a member of the Alexandria Medical Society. In 1997, the society chose me as their president. This was just at the beginning of problems in the practice of medicine in the United States. I found out that Blue Cross/Blue Shield (BC/BS) was paying doctors less than they had previously, so I invited the Vice President of BC/BS to come and speak to us at an executive meeting of the society. I asked him why they were paying doctors less. I mentioned that many of my patients had BC/BS and it was a good insurance company that used to pay doctors appropriately. I asked what had changed. He said the changes were due to the doctors. Some physicians had accepted lower payments from other health insurance companies in exchange for the insurance companies sending them more patients. In order to be competitive, BC/BS was matching those insurance companies' payments.

After that, we generally received one-tenth or one–twentieth of what we charged as reimbursement from the insurance companies and there was more paperwork. We constantly argued with the insurance companies and had to answer lots of questions. This continued to the point where, during the last few years of my practice, many physicians and surgeons didn't participate with any health insurance companies. It didn't make sense to work so hard to take care of patients and not get adequately reimbursed for what we were doing.

Largest Skin Cancer of Nose

One day, a gentleman came to my office who had an interesting case of skin cancer. Fifteen years earlier, he had a tiny lesion on the dorsum of his nose which had not healed. The lesion had appeared three months prior to his visit and was not healing. My examination had shown the presence of a tiny ulcerated skin lesion on the dorsum of his nose which was similar to skin cancer and was less than three millimeters in diameter. A few days later, I took him to the operating room and, after injecting local anesthesia, I excised the lesion with a good margin of normal-looking skin and sent it for a frozen-section examination. The pathologist said it was skin cancer and all margins and depths were involved. I took another ellipse of skin around the previous excision and also took the underlying muscle and sent it for a frozen-section examination. Again, the pathologist indicated all margins were involved and were cancerous. I continued this procedure again and again and eventually had to excise the entire skin and underlying muscle of the dorsum of his nose. At this point, I had to reconstruct a large defect of the entire dorsum of his nose which I created. To do this, I had to raise two large skin flaps, one from each cheek, to be able to cover the entire dorsum of his nose. Unfortunately, this entire operation was done under local anesthesia, and the patient received multiple needle injections of local anesthesia medication because I did not expect such a major surgery. The result of the surgery was so good that nobody could guess the skin and muscle of the dorsum of the entire nose was removed. He looked normal.

Neurosurgery at Inova Mount Vernon Hospital

We had three good neurosurgeons at Inova Mount Vernon Hospital who started working there when the hospital opened. They performed all kinds of neurosurgery. Many years ago they left Inova Mount Vernon Hospital and went to Inova Fairfax Hospital because Inova Fairfax Hospital paid them for each night they covered the Emergency Room. Up until nine years ago, two other neurosurgeons still were covering the Emergency Room of Inova Mount Vernon Hospital. One of them was a great neurosurgeon named Dr. Saeed Jamshidi.

Major Neurosurgery on My Neck

In 2000, while the other three neurosurgeons were still working at Inova Mount Vernon Hospital, I developed a severe problem with my right arm as a result of severe traumatic arthritis of the vertebra of my neck. I went to one of the three neurosurgeons who worked as a group and also to Dr. Jamshidi. After all the tests and x-rays were done, both doctors told me that due to a car accident that I had fifteen years before, I had developed an abnormal bone formation at multiple levels in the vertebra of my neck. These abnormal bone formations were pressing the main nerve that came through the holes of the vertebra to my right arm. Both suggested they go from the front of my neck to take out that excessive bone and fuse those joints.

I told them that if they fused the vertebra of my neck, I would not be able to bend my neck anymore and therefore could not perform surgery. Dr. Jamshidi said there was another type of surgery but it was dangerous. He explained he could go from the back of the neck and use a powerful instrument to shave the excess bone formation around the major nerves which came through the neck to my right arm. He further explained it was dangerous to use a power tool around major nerves.

I accepted Dr. Jamshidi's offer and he performed that surgery on my neck. Fortunately, the result was excellent and I was able to continue to do surgery satisfactorily.

A few days after my surgery, on Sunday, I was at home and I felt a severe pain in one small part of the wound of my scalp. I called Dr. Jamshidi and explained my symptoms to him and he said to go to my office, which he was using one day a week to see patients. He came to the office and injected something at the tender point of my scalp and the pain went away. A few days later, my daughter graduated from high school. I went to see her graduate and also to see her sing at the graduation ceremony.

After the ceremony, I took her and a few members of our family out for lunch. I was not feeling good. Right after lunch when I came home, I checked my temperature and I had high fever. I called Dr. Jamshidi again and he said I should go to the laboratory in the morning and get a blood test. My white cell count was very high, which was a sign of a major infection. After I called him and told him the result, he sent me to the radiology department at Inova Mount Vernon Hospital for an M.R.I. The radiologist saw a huge mass pressing against my spinal cord in my neck. The mass turned out to be a huge abscess, from which the radiologist suctioned all the pus. I was hospitalized and put on massive doses of strong antibiotics. I was very lucky to survive.

My Trip to Turkey and Greece

In May 2003, I went to an international plastic surgery meeting in Istanbul, Turkey. My daughter and some close friends of ours came on this trip with me. After the meeting, I decided to spend several days in different parts of Turkey and Greece. When I inquired how to get to Greece, I was told that there was no flight from Turkey to Greece and that we would have to go to the northern part of Turkey and catch a boat to Greece, which we did. The northern part of Turkey was beautiful. The old palace there was magnificent. After I went to Greece, I stayed a few days in Santorini. That island was beautiful and the sunset was so spectacular that many people from other islands in Greece came to Santorini just to watch the sunset.

The day I was leaving Greece, I was at the airport when a gentleman introduced himself. He said he was also a plastic surgeon and had also attended the meeting in Istanbul. He was from Lebanon and now he lived and worked in Florida. He started to talk to me about Israel and said he knew for a fact that there would never be peace in the Middle East between Israel and Palestine. He said that if such a peace occurred, the people of Israel would fight each other because there are so many people with strong differing opinions there. I believed him because he was not a Moslem, he was Christian.

Cardiac Arrest of Patient during Surgery

About fourteen years ago, a salesman for finger splints came to my office with his son, who was sixteen years old. The son had large breasts which embarrassed him. I explained to him and his son how I could reduce the size of the son's breasts using an ultrasound liposuction technique. After I explained everything, the father requested that I schedule his son for surgery.

At this point, the father asked me to look at a lesion of his nose which had appeared a few months prior. When I looked at the lesion under magnification, the tiny skin lesion looked like skin cancer. I told him that after I did his son's surgery, I could remove the lesion under local anesthesia.

On the day of the surgery, I performed the son's surgery successfully and he was transferred to the recovery room. Then I took the father to the operating room. The father had a very small needle point-type of skin lesion on the dorsum of his nose. I injected less than one cc of local anesthesia (numbing medicine) around it and, while we were talking together, I removed the lesion and sent it to the pathologist for frozen-section examination. I continued to talk to him but he suddenly stopped talking. When I looked at him, he was pale. I checked his pulse and there was none. I listened to his heart and no heartbeat was present. His heart had stopped and he was in cardiac arrest! Because I was doing this operation under local anesthesia, there was no anesthesiologist in the room, so I started to resuscitate him myself using mouth-to-mouth resuscitation. The nurses called an anesthesiologist, who arrived immediately. He took over the resuscitation and it was four minutes before his heart started beating again and he woke up. Because of what happened, I didn't send him home, instead I sent him to the recovery room. We obtained a consultation from a cardiologist and ran an electrocardiogram of his heart for three hours based on the cardiologist's recommendation. The cardiologist came to examine him and didn't find anything. After four hours, we sent him home. They didn't know the reason for his cardiac arrest. Before I sent him home, I went to the recovery room to talk to him and tell him he could go home, and he asked me if I knew what had happened to him. I said I knew his heart stopped but we didn't know the reason. He said he was in a tunnel and he almost reached the end of the tunnel when some power pulled him back. I never heard this before. Apparently, he almost died, but we brought him back. He was the only patient of mine who ever had a cardiac arrest during surgery. I was thankful he did not die.

Successful Use of Muscle Flap for Treatment of Unusual Recurrent Fistula of Bladder

A patient was previously operated on by her gynecologist surgeon and urologist many times. These surgeries were unsuccessful in treating recurrent a fistula of the bladder which had resulted from radiation treatment for cancer of the bladder.

In 2003, this patient's gynecologist surgeon called me and said he had heard I had been doing a lot of muscle flap surgery and was wondering if I could help his patient. I said I would be glad to see the patient. After he referred her to me, I examined her. I told her there was a difficult operation that could fix her problem and explained this difficult operation to her in detail.

On the day of the surgery, I raised one muscle with its overlying skin from the inner aspect of each upper thigh and was able to close the donor defect I created at the inner thigh by moving the skin above and below the defect. I then used two skin and muscle flaps in the pelvic area to close the fistula (the leaking tunnel between the bladder and the vagina). This patient, who had a fistula for many years, was completely healed.

The Fantastic Effect of Muscle Flaps

I used the muscle flap technique for so many patients. It was one of the most outstanding plastic surgery techniques that was performed. I saved a lot of legs that would have had to be amputated otherwise. As a matter of fact, during my residency of plastic surgery, I saw a lot of young men who had broken their legs. The front of the leg has thin skin covering the main bone of the leg, so if this bone breaks and the skin which covers the bone is lost (which could happen even after a perfect reduction of the fracture), the exposed bone to the air starts to die, gets infected, and eventually the leg has to be amputated. From the time the muscle flap technique was created and I used it, I never had to amputate a leg. Using this technique, I also saved arms, created new breasts after mastectomies, and rebuilt major portions of the face and neck after radical resections for treatment of cancer. Also, I used muscle flaps to treat a recurrent fistula of the vagina and bladder and pervasive skin cancer of the scalp.

Psychiatric Patients in the United States

There are so many wonderful things in the United States but there are a few things which I believe are wrong. One of them is the lack of a hospital for psychiatric patients. Yes, there are places for their treatment, but after treatment they are sent home on multiple medications.

There is no way to guarantee that these patients take their medications properly. One day I was called for a consultation on a burn patient at Inova Fairfax Hospital. This patient was a gas station attendant who blew up the gas station while he was working there. His past history showed he was a psychiatric patient who had been admitted to the psychiatric unit for one month. When he was discharged, he was put on four different medications which he had to take daily. He was doing well when he was taking those medications daily. Suddenly he stopped taking those medications for four days. In the absence of the medications, his psychiatric condition returned and he blew up the gas station. This patient required several weeks of hospitalization and multiple skin grafting surgery for the treatment of severe burns on his body.

There have been many events within the last two years in which psychiatric patients living at home with their families have turned violent and murdered people. One example was the young man who shot and killed so many people at the movie theater in Denver. Also, there was the incident when a young man killed his mother, then went to a school in Connecticut and killed children and teachers before the police killed him. Of course, everyone remembers the young man from a great family who tried to kill President Reagan several years ago. Events like these happen more and more frequently.

In other parts of the world, they keep psychiatric patients locked up forever. In reality, even when a nurse gives a medication to a psychiatric patient, the nurse asks the patient to open his or her mouth, so the nurse can be sure the patient swallowed the medication.

Another Iranian Woman in my Life

There was a couple that I occasionally saw at parties. One day, the wife called me and said she was sorry to call me so late, but she wanted to invite me to a dinner party. She said one of my second cousins who was living in the United States for years and went to Iran and got married had returned from Iran, and was coming to town. That second cousin had apparently asked to see me so I agreed to go.

When I arrived, my cousin was not there yet. I didn't know anyone at the party except for one friend and we both went to the bar in the basement of the house. We got a drink and were talking. My friend, who was married, asked me when I was going to re-marry. I told him that unfortunately, I couldn't seem to find the right person and due to the type of work I did, I couldn't go out with my patients, or the nurses at the hospital, so had limited exposure to women I could date. I told him I was OK with that. At that moment, a beautiful woman arrived at the bar along with the hostess, who introduced her to me. We shook hands and talked a bit together and she asked me why a good-looking plastic surgeon lives alone. I told her I had two unsuccessful marriages, but I had a wonderful daughter. She told me she was married once, but was divorced three years ago. She said she had a son who was living with her. She gave me her telephone number and asked for mine. We talked again by phone and began seeing each other. I gradually became interested in her.

One night, she invited me to her apartment and introduced me to her mother. She said her mother lived in Iran, but had visited her sister in England and had now come to visit her. She said her mother was going back to Iran in a few months. We kept going out and the more we went out, the more I liked her. I kept asking to see her son so I could get to know him, and she kept saying that he wasn't around much because he spent a lot of time with his father. After a few months, we got engaged. We even looked for a venue for the wedding ceremony and I gave the venue a down payment. She came with me to parties, and gave several parties in her apartment and invited me and my family.

Prenuptial Agreement

I told her that before we got married, we needed to sign a prenuptial agreement. She kept agreeing to do it, but kept putting it off. Finally, we were having dinner one night and I told her if she didn't get her attorney to look over my prenuptial agreement, then I was not going to marry her.

A couple of days later, the hostess from the original party where I met this lady, called me and said she wanted to invite us to have a drink so we could talk. We met for a drink and she told me that my fiancée was worried about the prenuptial agreement. I told her it was nothing against my fiancée and I didn't want a dime from her. I explained that after marriage, if we got divorced, we would share what we made after marriage, but whatever each of us had before marriage, we would keep. She looked at my fiancée and asked her what the problem was. I was not trying to take anything from her. She asked my fiancée why she didn't want to sign the prenuptial agreement. My fiancée said she had made a mistake and would sign it. A few days later, she brought me all the gifts I had given her and said she was not going to sign the prenuptial agreement upon the advice of her mother. I told her it was just as well we didn't get married. Forty-eight hours later, she called me crying and saying she shouldn't have listened to her mother. She told me that she still wanted to get married. I told her it was over. Later on, I found out that her first husband had been an alcoholic and, after their divorce, her husband had not seen their son. Also, her mother was not planning to go back to Iran and was staying in the United States, so she was not truthful with me.

A few months later, I heard she married someone else and a few months after she married, she developed breast cancer and had to have a mastectomy.

Another Persian Woman in my Life

I saw a patient in my office who was Persian. She came for two major cosmetic surgeries. As usual, I showed her the before and after pictures of my previous patients who had those operations and explained those surgeries to her. My nurse and I gave her the fee for each surgery, including the surgical, operating room, and anesthesia fees along with the cost of hospitalization. When she came to sign the consent form, she paid for the surgery. The surgery was performed successfully. About three nights after surgery, she called to say her brother had come to her house and fought with her. It caused the dressings to come off and caused bleeding. I told her to come to the office right away. I saw her at ten P.M. in my office. After examining her, I found that nothing major had happened and calmed her down because she was crying. I gave her some medication to calm her and re-dressed all her wounds.

After she completely recovered from surgery, she invited me for dinner to thank me for both the surgery and taking care of her after she fought with her brother. I went to dinner and noticed she was interested in seeing me not as a surgeon but as a friend. I became interested in her as well. Friends told me she had a very good job importing wine from Europe and made $700,000 per year. I thought this was the first Iranian woman who didn't want to be with me because of my money. Of course this was my mistake. I don't know why I was attracted to her because, as I think back, I recognize that I was very, very stupid and was not paying attention to what this woman really was. For example, she had two grown-up children from her first marriage to an Iranian man. I never knew that man, but I heard he was a multimillionaire and a successful businessman. His house was like a palace in Potomac, Maryland. When I saw her daughter, I observed that she acted immaturely and rarely came to see her mother. I saw her son a couple of times. The second time I saw her son, he and his mother were talking and he got upset. He started to say bad things about his mother in front of me. After ranting for 15 or 20 minutes, he left the house. She also had a young daughter from her second husband who lived with her mother.

A Wonderful Trip to Africa

On March 2006, I went with her to Tanzania and South Africa. We flew from Washington on a jumbo jet to the Netherlands. After we landed, we were supposed to fly to Tanzania on the same plane within ninety minutes. We heard nothing about our second flight. When I went to the desk and asked for the status of our plane, an airline employee said the plane was covered by frozen ice and they were cleaning it. I did not believe the employee for two reasons: one, the weather was not bad, and two, I could see the plane and there was no ice on the plane. After a few more minutes, another passenger and I went to the desk and asked them to tell us the truth. They announced the plane had mechanical problems and we would have to wait for another plane. We waited more than three and a half hours until the new plane took off. I was concerned because the travel agent who had made the arrangement told us that when we arrived at the Tanzania airport, someone would be there to meet us and take us to our hotel. I did not have the phone number of that person to notify him that we would be delayed and was worried that if he was not there, we would be stranded. Although the plane arrived three and a half hours late and it was after midnight, the person was there.

It took more than one hour to drive on a two-lane road to reach the hotel. We had to go through a locked entrance secured by multiple police officers. Our room was wonderful, the food was excellent and we were told we could eat any type of food while staying at that hotel and not have any health issues. I paid $800 to an internist before leaving the United States for multiple immunizations and pills because he told me they were necessary for going to Africa.

The hotel had wonderful shows every night. The beach was beautiful and we could walk more than 400 feet in the water because the depth of the water was not more than five feet. One day after swimming in the ocean, I felt a burning sensation in my forearms and, when I looked at my forearms, I noticed discolored bands. I went to the hotel and showed my forearms to the front desk. They told me those resulted from some kind of fish bites. They gave me a bottle of vinegar and told me to soak a towel with the vinegar and wrap my forearms. After a couple of hours, the burning sensation disappeared.

After three days, a car took us to another part of Tanzania where a minibus came and took us to the part of the country which was home to all kinds of wild animals. Unbeknown to me, we went during the season of animal sexual activity. We were sitting in a minibus and the driver was telling us about all sorts of things. The rule for our safari was that the cars could not blow their horn and, while driving, if any animal was in the road, the driver had to wait until the animal left the road. Because of that rule, the animals were not scared of the cars and many times came very close to us.

One day the driver stopped because there was a lion about twenty feet from us. He explained to us that this was the sexual season of animals and the lion had one week of sexual activity. He said the male lion had sex with a female lion every hour for one week, and that his sexual activity only lasted one minute each time. The female lion, after three days of sexual activity, went hunting to bring meat for her mate. I also saw a lot of different species of monkeys having sex.

On our drive, we saw the most wonderful scenery with different kinds of animals who were near each other but not hurting each other. For example, one day I saw ten lions together playing. So many other wild animals passed by them and the lions didn't bother them at all. I told myself that I wished human beings would learn from wild animals. Human beings steal and cheat to make more money, no matter how much money they have and no matter how old they are.

During a short period of rain, the animals stayed in the same position until the rain stopped. The elephants were the most destructive animals I observed. While they were walking they destroyed everything they passed through. I saw one rhinoceros and the driver said there were only seven more rhinoceros in that region of Africa.

One day, we paid $100 and a tour guide took us to the center of the region where more wild animals were living. In that region, there were African natives (both men and women) who cut their hair short and dressed the same. When we looked at them, we could not say which one was male or female. They welcomed us by special dancing. They sang and jumped up and down in a straight line. Then they allowed us to go inside one of the small huts where they lived. I had to bend over to get into their home; it was similar to a tent but had something on top which secured it firm. In the center of that tent was a fireplace used for cooking and heating. There was a corral beside the tent for their baby animals. I asked the tour guide how those people safely lived around those wild animals. He said the wild animals were scared of them, not vice versa. They also made a lot of handmade crafts and sold them. I bought some of them. They showed us one classroom full of their children who welcomed us.

We flew from Tanzania to Pretoria, South Africa and stayed for a couple days. Then we went from Pretoria to Cape Town on The Blue Train, which was the best train I ever rode. I felt like a king in that train. When we arrived to our room on the train, there was one attendant in front of the room who brought our luggage and said whatever we wanted we could take out of our luggage and he would take our luggage to the storage room. He said if we needed anything out of our luggage during the trip, he would bring our luggage back to us. The room was excellent; there was a television and tape player, and so many varieties of shows on tapes.

There were two huge dining rooms, one for smokers and one for non-smokers. There were huge bars and we could order any type of wine or alcoholic beverages, and we could drink as much as we wanted for no extra charge. The food served in the dining rooms was wonderful and delicious.

This was the best travel by train in my life and I recommend that anyone going to South Africa use that train.

The scenery we saw was unbelievably beautiful. They told us that a lot of poor people from other African countries came illegally to South Africa and were living in some of those wild areas we saw.

When we arrived in Cape Town, South Africa, we stayed in a wonderful hotel. They told us we could only go to certain parts of Cape Town safely by using arrangements made by our hotel. That meant that we told the hotel where we wanted to go and they made the arrangements. We went and saw their Congress, the house of Nelson Mandela, and different parts of the city. The best steak I ate in my lifetime I ate in South Africa.

Other Things about This Woman

The woman I was seeing and traveling with had a second marriage to an American lawyer, who, according to her, had been in Iran for a period of time. She was divorced from him and had a fourteen-year-old daughter from that marriage who lived with her.

I found out she had a couple of loans on which she was paying 24% interest. I loaned her money to pay off her loans which she later paid back to me. She told me so many things about her second husband that seemed unbelievable. I found out later that few things she said were true. When she finally decided to sell her house and successfully sold it, she decided to come and live with me. I stupidly thought that she was moving into my house because she wanted to marry me. I helped her in every way possible, including packing, moving, etc. We brought everything she had to my house. Her fourteen-year-old daughter from her second marriage decided she wanted to live with her father, which surprised me after all the horrible things this woman told me about her second husband, this girl's father.

One day I talked to the daughter on the telephone and invited her to come live at my house instead of with her father. She responded that she respected me but she didn't want to live with her mother anymore, not even for one day. She said she loved her father and she was going to live with him. Unfortunately, I still didn't wake up after hearing all this negative information about this woman, even after troubles had begun to arise in our relationship.

Travel to New Zealand and Australia

I was planning to go to a plastic surgery meeting in Australia and to visit New Zealand. She wanted to come with me, but I told her I'd rather go by myself because we weren't happy together. She told me she still wanted to come. I wasn't interested because I had so many problems with her. I said I was going by myself. She said she would buy our tickets and pay for them if she could come. She called my travel agent who told her we could get two first-class tickets for the price of one if she used her platinum American Express card. She gave her credit card number to the travel agent and bought both tickets. We flew to Los Angeles and then to New Zealand, where we stayed a week before going to Australia. I attended the plastic surgery meeting. The trip didn't change my attitude toward her and we had a major argument on our return.

I took several trips with her and on the last trip, she behaved so badly that I planned to split up with her and not let her live in my house any longer. I realized that she had told me so many lies and was not planning to marry me. She was just using me.

When we finally got home, I told her to leave my house as soon as possible. Fortunately, she did.

After she left, I was happily living by myself, then I received a call from a detective in Maryland. That lady accused me of stealing her credit card to buy our tickets to Australia and New Zealand. The detective asked what happened and I told her. I spent more than an hour talking to the detective. I told her the lady was a liar. The detective said the woman told her that she was my patient and had paid for her surgery with her credit card and I had taken the number of her credit card and used it to buy the tickets. I told the detective that I was going to check the chart and, when I did, I found out that this lady paid for her surgery by check. I made a copy of the check in her chart and faxed them to the detective. I also gave the detective the phone number of the travel agent. The detective called the travel agent who told the truth and confirmed my statement that the lady called the travel agent and gave her credit card number to pay for the tickets. The detective called me back and apologized. She said that it was unfortunate that some people lie and wrongfully accuse others. The case was closed. That didn't stop this woman. She went to some of my best friends and misled them about what happened between us.

My Last and Best Marriage

In my life, I have realized one very important thing: I really admire American women. I have been involved with only four American women; the first one was a registered nurse, the second one was a dentist, the third one was a plastic surgeon, and the fourth one is my current wife who is a federal government senior executive. Each of these women shared living and travel expenses with me versus the Iranian women I dated who always wanted everything for free. The best of these four American women is my current wonderful wife.

Since I had pursued so many women, hoped to get married and have a life together, but it didn't work out, I came to the conclusion that God gave me a lot of talents in regard to medicine and surgery, but he didn't give me the skill of knowing which women told the truth and which told lies. I decided that I was not going to go out with any more women the rest of my life because they made me suffer too much.

One day, I was seeing one of my long-time patients in my office. We were talking about something and she suggested that I go somewhere with my wife. I told her that I was not married, and she asked me why. I told her I couldn't go out with my patients, nor with the people I worked with, and I wasn't the type of person to go to a bar to meet people. She started to laugh and said that her daughter lost her husband two years ago and told her the same thing. We laughed a little bit and then she wrote the name and phone number of her daughter on a piece of paper and said I could call her daughter if I want to.

After she left my office, I remembered that I had already told myself that I had no chance of finding the right woman, so I shouldn't call this lady's daughter. Then, after several days, I finally decided it wouldn't hurt to call. I called and invited her out for dinner. It was not love at first sight, but the more we kept seeing each other, the more we were interested in each other.

After a few months, she was staying at my house every weekend. She then accepted my invitation to live with me and rented out her own house. I came to the point that I was deeply in love with her and she felt the same, so we decided to get married.

On September 22, 2012, we were married. The night before our wedding, her parents had a dinner for us at the Fort Belvoir Officers

Club. We got married at our house and had a reception there with close friends and family afterwards.

Her father is a retired Navy Captain aircraft carrier pilot who accomplished a lot of things for this country. Her mother was an excellent elementary school librarian. The children at her school loved her so much that they named the library after her. My wife was born in Italy, but was raised in the United States, and I was born and raised in Iran, so this was unexpected. We have a wonderful relationship and I am very thankful to God that finally he has given me the right woman for the rest of my life.

My wife is the smartest person I know and is a big sports fan. Every weekend, we love to play tennis together. We also like to watch sports together. I have never met another woman who liked to watch football, baseball and tennis. I taught her rummy and now she is so good at it, she beats me as often as I beat her. I have been going to the National Symphony Orchestra at the Kennedy Center for the last twenty-eight years and I was lucky that when I took her there, she also loved it. We are very compatible and I love her for so many reasons.

My Wonderful American Wife

Every trip with my wife, either prior to marriage or after, has been among the best trips of my life. We have a wonderful time together. Our favorite trip so far was a cruise through Northern Europe, including Stockholm, Copenhagen, and St. Petersburg.

Loss of Coverage of Surgical Subspecialty in the Emergency Room of Inova Mount Vernon Hospital

About fifteen years ago, when the malpractice insurance companies started to raise their premiums for malpractice insurance more than forty percent for surgeons who cover the Emergency Room and 90% for neurosurgeons, Dr. Jamshidi, the excellent neurosurgeon I mentioned previously, wrote a letter to the CEO of Inova to ask him for help in paying a portion of his malpractice premiums. Dr. Jamshidi was on call for the Emergency Room every other night. The CEO of Inova did not respond. Dr. Jamshidi talked to me because I was the Chairman of the Department of Surgery at the time. I talked to the President of the Medical Staff of our hospital and he said he could not do anything. Dr. Jamshidi left Inova Mount Vernon hospital altogether and went to Providence Hospital in Washington, DC where they helped him pay his malpractice insurance costs. After that, he did all his neurosurgical cases at Providence Hospital and also covered the Emergency Room of that hospital for neurosurgery. That is why we did not have any neurosurgeons covering the Emergency Room of Inova Mount Vernon Hospital.

Another problem has resulted from changes in the practice of orthopedic surgery. For example, we have a good group of orthopedic surgeons who only do knee joint or hip joint replacements. They said they could not cover the Emergency Room for general orthopedic surgery.

Inova, unfortunately, has always given the best support to Inova Fairfax Hospital. Now, because of low insurance payments for taking care of Emergency Room patients, and an increase in malpractice insurance premiums for surgeons who cover the Emergency Room, no surgeon wants to cover the Emergency Room unless the hospital pays him or her to cover it.

Inova pays to the surgeons of Inova Fairfax Hospital to cover the Emergency Room, but Inova refuses to pay the surgeons of Inova Mount Vernon Hospital to cover the Emergency Room. A lot of patients who come to the Emergency Room of Inova Mount Vernon Hospital are transferred to Inova Fairfax Hospital because Inova Mount Vernon Hospital has no roster of neurosurgeons, orthopedic surgeons, plastic surgeons, hand surgeons, urologists or ear/nose/throat surgeons.

In 2012, while I was the Chairman of the Department of Surgery at Inova Mount Vernon Hospital, I tried to establish a roster for orthopedic surgeons to cover the Emergency Room and tried to convince Inova to pay the orthopedic surgeons for that coverage, like they did at Inova Fairfax Hospital. Inova did not want to pay our orthopedic surgeons what they were requesting. If someone fell and broke his hip and was brought to the Emergency Room of Inova Mount Vernon Hospital, after the Emergency Room physician examined him, got an x-ray, and diagnosed the fracture, the patient had to be transferred to Inova Fairfax Hospital.

My Work as the Biggest Supporter of Inova Mount Vernon Hospital

Throughout my career and especially when I was the President of the Medical Staff at Inova Mount Vernon Hospital, I was the biggest supporter of the hospital – not just as a physician, but also as a member of the Mount Vernon community.

I called the Washington post newspaper in 2002 when Inova wanted to close Inova Mount Vernon Hospital in 2002. At that time, I put notices I every doctor's office in Mount Vernon for patients to read and sign that they were against Inova's plan to close Inova Mount Vernon Hospital. I also called Mr. Steven Pearlstein at the Washington Post and informed him about Mr. Singleton's plan to close Inova Mount Vernon Hospital. Mr. Pearlstein wrote about situation in the paper. I also contacted Mr. Gerry Hyland, The Mount Vernon Supervisor on the Fairfax County board of Supervisors, and explained the situation to him. He was skeptical until I met him and showed him the evidence. Mr. Hyland arranged for me to meet with previous congressman from Virginia, Mr. Herbert Harris Jr (who had helped pave the way for building Inova Mount Vernon hospital and had a stoplight installed at the intersection of Route 1 and Sherwood Hall Lane) and a previous Mount Vernon Supervisor, Mr. Warren Cikins.

In the meeting with Mr. Hyland, Mr. Harris and Mr. Cikins, I presented Mr. Singleton's plan for closing Inova Mount Vernon Hospital. Everyone was surprised and became upset. Mr. Hyland arranged a meeting with Mr. Singleton. During that meeting with Mr. Singleton Mr. Hyland told him that Inova Mount Vernon Hospital was the property of the Fairfax County and he could not close it. Mr. Singleton established a committee to review the problems of Inova Mount Vernon Hospital and recommend solution. Mr. Singleton invited me and Mr. Cikins to participate on that committee. Mr. Cikins was an excellent man and was very helpful.

Mr. Singleton was forced to establish the Southeast Health Planning Task Force (a new committee) and asked me to participate. Inova hired a consultant to review the problems of Inova Mount Vernon Hospital and to participate on the task force. After several months of research, the consultant said that Inova had two choices, either to make Inova Mount Vernon Hospital a full service hospital or close the

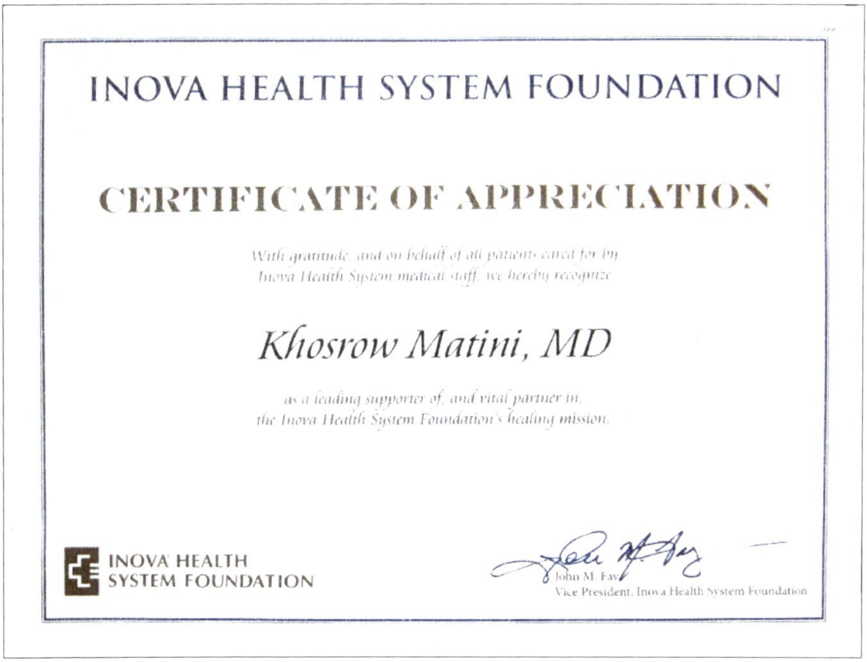

INOVA HEALTH SYSTEM FOUNDATION

CERTIFICATE OF APPRECIATION

With gratitude, and on behalf of all patients cared for by Inova Health System medical staff, we hereby recognize

Khosrow Matini, MD

as a leading supporter of, and vital partner in, the Inova Health System Foundation's healing mission.

INOVA HEALTH SYSTEM FOUNDATION

John M. Fay
Vice President, Inova Health System Foundation

Figure 20: Certificate of Appreciation from Inova Health System Foundation

Mount Vernon Hospital and build another full-service hospital in this region.

The Mount Vernon Voice newspaper published an article on April 2, 1998 entitled, "Is IMVH facing Death by Attrition?" The paper wrote another article entitled, "Doctors Worry about Hospital's Future; Doyle Counters Concerns." The latter article said that doctors were wondering whether, despite the highly-touted renovations to Inova Mount Vernon Hospital, Inova was undermining the facility's future as a full-service hospital by reducing the number of beds.

On June 4, 2003, Mr. Singleton the C.E.O. of Inova Health System invited seventeen active senior members of the medical staff of Inova Mount Vernon Hospital, including me, to a meeting. At this meeting, he outlined three choices for Inova Mount Vernon Hospital: closure, expansion of services, or building a new facility eight miles away. He stated that the board would not approve expansion and indicated he wanted a new facility. He said that the new facility would

Figure 21: Plaque of Appreciation from Inova Health System

be a full-service hospital which had obstetrics, gynecology, neonatology and pediatric services. He further said neonatology would make money for this new hospital. He said he already bought land located 7.5 miles from Mount Vernon Hospital and had investors who were willing to pay two hundred million dollars to build this new hospital.[4] As a member of the Mount Vernon community, I was happy that, for the first time, he was planning to build a full service hospital for the community.

It turned out that this new hospital could not be built because its

---

[4] "Doctors Challenge Inova: Medical Staff at INVH Suggests Ultimatum," August 5, 2003, the Connection.

helicopter landing site would have jeopardized the security of Fort Belvoir, the local army installation. After the plans to build a new hospital failed, Mr. Singleton promised to expand the services of Inova Mount Vernon Hospital. Unfortunately, not only were no new services added, but he decided to take fifty beds of acute care and transform them to long-term care services for all four hospitals of Inova, further reducing the availability of beds for members of our community. The medical staff of Inova Mount Vernon Hospital was against this decision.

A heated town meeting later that month was described in a newspaper article that quoted Lee District Supervisor Dana Kauffman as telling Susan Herbert, Inova Mount Vernon Hospital administrator, to convey to Inova Health System how disappointed she was that Inova did not send a representative to the meeting. She further stated that, "Since they are not represented here, it is one more indication that Inova has already made up its mind to close Mount Vernon Hospital."[5]

Further fueling the fire, in July 2003, it was announced the Inova Health System would be "laying off 113 employee and cutting the hours of 33 more in an attempt to trim $22 million from its 2003 budget" and address what one official called "significant financial challenges."[6] It was reported that Inova had "come under intense criticism from local leaders and residents of southeastern Fairfax County after Inova officials let it be known that they might move Inova Mount Vernon Hospital, which has been losing money, to capitalize on the county's rapid population growth to the west and south."[7]

By August, the Inova Mount Vernon Hospital medical staff "threw down the gauntlet."[8] By then, I was the head of the Planning and Programming Committee at the hospital. I worked with the Executive Committee of the medical staff and we developed five policy changes

---

[5] "Frustrations Boil Over: Town Meeting Draws Officials and Citizens Together, The Connection, June 24, 2003.
[6] Smith, Leef, "Inova Cuts 113 Staffers, Reduced Work Hours," The Washington Post, July 1, 2003.
[7] Ibid
[8] "Doctors Challenge Inova: Medical Staff at IMVH Suggests Ultimatum," The Connection, August 5, 2003.

and 14 service improvements that would reverse Inova Mount Vernon Hospital's downward financial trend. We sent a letter detailing our suggestions to Inova Health System, its Board of Trustees and local county politicians. The consensus in the letter was that Inova Mount Vernon Hospital should remain open with new programs added to the services.[9]

Over a month later, Inova Health Systems responded to the letter and noted that "Inova Mount Vernon continues to be a vital part of the Inova family."[10] At that same time, I put notices in every doctor's office in Mount Vernon for patients to read and sign that said they were against Inova's plan to close Inova Mount Vernon Hospital.

Inova Health System hired a consultant to review the problems of Inova Mount Vernon Hospital and to participate on that Task Force. Unfortunately, some members of the task force reported the Inova Health System had not been open with task force members regarding its plans. A former County Supervisor reported that the Inova Mount Vernon Hospital medical staff, nurses and patients fear that the hospital will be closed.[11]

The South East Health Planning Task Force issued a report after 13 months of discussions stating that Inova Health System should continue to enhance services at Inova Mount Vernon Hospital and work to eliminate financial losses. The report also recommend that Inova Health System should work at building greater community trust by utilizing a more open dialogue and by continuing the Task Force.[12]

The bottom line: Inova Mount Vernon Hospital remained open but no new services were added - no obstetrics, gynecology, neonatology, nor pediatric services.

Another threat of shutdown occurred in 2008. Inova Health Systems announced that 50 of the 140 medical-surgical beds were to be converted to another company for long term acute care. I said at the time that there were only two options for the future of Inova Mount Vernon Hospital: either strengthen it as a full-service community hospital or close it and I believe that Inova Health Systems was headed

---

[9] Ibid.
[10] "Doctors Digest Inova Feedback: Response to Letter Shows Both Hope and Concern," The Connection, September 9, 2003.
[11] Meeting Summary, Health Care Advisory Board, September 8, 2003.
[12] Task Force Tells IHS 'Keep it here', The Connection, March 2, 2004.

for closure.[13] I asked Inova Health System in a letter if they knew how many families when faced with an emergency would tell the ambulance not to take them to Inova Mount Vernon Hospital because either they or their family had a bad experience. Either they would have to resort to staying in an Emergency Room bed because there were no longer any more beds available in the hospital, or our hospital would not have surgical specialists available for Emergency Room coverage to take care of them. Any member of this community who had head injuries, such as subdural hematoma (bleeding inside of the skull), who once would have been seen by a neurosurgeon on call at Inova Mount Vernon Hospital, would now have to be transferred to Inova Fairfax Hospital for treatment. Some of these patients would not survive this trip due to the severity of their injuries. As before, I was just as vocal in telling Inova Health System and community leaders that we need to keep strengthening Inova Mount Vernon Hospital. The conversion of hospital beds thankfully never occurred.

In 2012, while I was Chairman of the Department of Surgery at Inova Mount Vernon Hospital the orthopedic surgeons of Inova Mount Vernon Hospital presented a proposal to cover the Emergency Room of Inova Mount Vernon Hospital which was rejected by Inova.

This story is a great model of how a community can come together to make a difference. Today, Inova Mount Vernon Hospital is home to the nationally recognized Inova Joint Replacement Center and Inova Rehabilitation Center. In November 2014, Inova Mount Vernon opened up a new tower with all new private patient rooms and specialty areas designed especially for the community. In November 2015, Inova Mount Vernon Hospital broke ground on a new Emergency Room.

---

[13] "IHS Intentions Questioned: Hospital's Bottom Line, Number of Beds in Juxtaposition," The Connection, April 10, 2008.

The Truth about Me and Members of My Family

My Oldest Brother (13 Years Older Than Me)

I wonder why, from the same parents come very different children. My oldest brother, who has a Ph.D. in Persian literature and a law degree, was the associate professor of the oil engineering school in Abadan, south of Iran, and the professor of the Faculty of Letters at the University of Meshed in Iran. He was also the Vice Dean and later the Dean of the Faculty of Letters, Vice President and later President of Meshed University. He has written many books and articles on Persian literature.

In 1965, he edited the oldest available handwritten medical book in the Persian language which was written by Dr. Abu Bakr Rabib-Ahmad al-Akhawaini al-Bokhari for his son one thousand years ago. The name of the book was "Hidayat al- Mutallmin." This was a complete medical book and contained all known diseases and their available treatment at that time. When the book was written, there were no medical schools in Persia. At that time, every book was written in the Arabic language in Persia. The father was trained as a physician by Zac Aria Razi, the famous Persian physician. Handwritten copies of this book were found in libraries in Oxford, England, Istanbul, Turkey and Tehran, Iran. My brother won the highest prize of the Editorial of Literature for editing that book. He also received the highest prize from the Shah for his work.

My Oldest Brother's First Wife

My oldest brother married a woman who I only met after they married. The city where I went to medical school was where she was born and raised. One year after I was in medical school, my brother and his wife came to that city so I saw her frequently then. She was the principal of a girl's high school which had about 800 students, and the most popular woman in the city of Meshed (Khorasan State), which had more than 100,000 residents. I had a wonderful relationship with her and always admired her. The people of that city even offered to make her senator or governor of that state but she refused.

Unfortunately, she developed breast cancer and, when they performed a mastectomy, they found that several lymph nodes in her arm pit were involved. At that time, I was at the beginning of my first- year residency in general surgery in New York, so my brother sent all her medical records to me and I presented them to the Tumor Board of the Jewish Hospital of Brooklyn. The Board suggested that she needed radiation treatments and offered to do the radiation for her. I told my brother and he made arrangements right away for them to come to New York. When they arrived, I picked them up at the John F. Kennedy airport and took them to a hotel.

When she was on the plane and needed to go to the bathroom, one of the flight attendants offered to help my sister-in-law. They took good care of her and kept asking if she needed anything. She and my brother thought that I had asked the airline to do that because of her recent surgery. After the plane landed in New York, she and my brother were the first passengers taken off the plane. Again, they thought I had requested special treatment for them. The airport officials took them to a special office and they were told that they were under suspicion perhaps because they believed she had hidden jewelry since she couldn't move normally. The officials had been told that someone was smuggling a lot of expensive jewelry to the United States. My brother told them that she just had a mastectomy and that's why she wasn't moving normally. The officials had a woman officer check her out and, when they found it was true, they apologized. My brother said he realized I had nothing to do with any of the special care on the plane. Later on, I took her to the hospital for radiation treatment.

While they were in New York, I heard there was a really good Broadway show named "Oh, Calcutta!" and, because this was my first year in New York, I wasn't familiar with everything. I got tickets and took them to the show. This Broadway show was unusual; there were a bunch of naked men and women, and they were even having sex on the stage together. I apologized to my brother and sister-in-law and offered to leave if they wanted to, but they said they wanted to stay and watch it. It turned out that they liked the show.

After the radiation treatment was completed, my brother and sister-in-law returned to Iran. I stayed in frequent contact to found out how she was doing because I loved her. Later on, she developed a rib fracture, which was likely the result of cancer having spread to the bones. They recommended that her ovaries be removed, which was done. After a few months, sadly, she passed away. I knew she was very popular woman in Meshed, but something my second brother told me surprised me.

My Second Brother (11 Years Older Than Me)

When my second brother was going to the funeral of our sister-in-law, he flew from Tehran to Meshed, then got a taxi to go to our oldest brother's house. As they approached the address, the taxi driver asked which house he was going to and my brother responded that he was going to his brother, Dr. Matini's house. He said that his brother's wife had passed away. The driver stopped and said this lady was the most fantastic, lovable lady in this city. He said everybody was going to miss her. He told my brother that she was supporting so many families that were poor and needed help. She was giving them money for food and living expenses. He said she had done this all her life. I was very close to my sister in-law and I did not know about this. She was one of the most fantastic women I knew in my life and I still miss her.

My second brother was completely different from me and my oldest brother. My mother told me that when he was in the eleventh grade, he got into an argument with the Vice President of the high school and slapped the Vice President's face. My brother never returned to school, so he never got a high school diploma. If anyone needed anything, my second brother did it for them. For this reason, he was the most popular member of our huge family.

My second brother started to work for the company that was owned by my oldest aunt's husband. He worked as a salesman, but because he was talented in business, he gradually moved up the ranks to become president and became a major shareholder of that company. He was the first child of our family to get married. After he married, he brought his wife to my parent's house and they lived in the upper level of my parent's house for one year, which was common in Iran at that time. He eventually divorced his first wife, re-married, and came to the United States.

After the Iranian revolution, the Khomeini government tried to take the property of the rich and successful people in Iran who weren't living in Iran anymore. My second brother was one of those people. The government took his house and everything else he had. His ex-wife fought with the government of Iran and got my brother's property and other belongings back, saying that it was the property of her children. She was able to get everything back and gave it back to my brother.

A few months ago my brother become sick and he was admitted in Inova Fairfax Hospital. He was not able to eat anything. I went to see him in Fairfax hospital several times. Neither the x-rays nor the MRI did not show any abnormality. The put a gastrostomy tube for him and he was fed through it. After four weeks he was sent home. I went to his house and saw him six days before he passed away. No diagnosis was made for his condition, but I believe those were side effect of diabetes.

Death of my Nephew

I had not seen or talked to my second brother for a few years. One day at 4:30 A.M., I received a call from my brother saying that his youngest son had just had major car accident and was in the operating room at George Washington University Hospital. I immediately went to the hospital and found my brother. A few minutes after I arrived and was talking with my brother, a gentleman came toward us. He asked us" who is the father of the young patient in the operating room". My brother said he was and introduced me as his brother. The gentleman said he was an investigating police officer. He said he could not find any evidence that my nephew put on brakes prior to the accident. I told the police officer that since childhood, my nephew had suffered from seizure disorders and he had been on several medications and could not drink any alcoholic beverages while taking the medicine. I theorized that most probably he had a seizure while he was driving. The officer agreed with my theory.

A few minutes later, they brought my nephew out of the operating room and were taking him to the Intensive Care Unit. I followed him. Of course, he was not awake. After a few minutes, I came out of the Intensive Care Unit and sat with my brother. Shortly, I saw two persons in scrub suits coming toward us. One was a neurosurgeon and the other was an anesthesiologist. The surgeon said that unfortunately, half of my nephew's brain was seriously damaged and he was not hopeful for his survival. We were all so sorry to hear that prognosis. My nephew died at two P.M., later that day.

That evening, I went to my brother's house to sit with him and we cried together. Later on, I found out that my nephew emptied his two computers completely and also left a few bills on his desk that were due. I went to his burial; my daughter who was a law school student in Virginia Beach flew home to attend his burial, too. I went and sat with my brother every night for seven nights, as was the custom in Iran.

My Sister and Her Husband

I have a sister who is two and a half years younger than me. She didn't go to college after she finished high school; instead she started working as a secretary in one of the companies owned by my aunt's husband. My sister gradually advanced in that company. One night, when I was in Tehran for a visit, I invited a few family and friends to a restaurant for dinner. My sister came with a young man and introduced him as her friend. That was a little bit unusual because, at that time in Iran, young men and women did not publicly date. After a few months, she and her friend decided to get married and their marriage took place in my parent's house. When she was in high school, my sister always argued with my mother. Even when I was a kid, I sat down privately with her and told her she knew our mother was one of the best women in the world. I told my sister that everything my mother had done in her life, she did to make us better and to give us a better life. I suggested that if she did not agree with something my mother said, there was no reason to argue with her. She could just listen and not do it, if she didn't want to do it. My sister never listened; she kept arguing with our mother. This was completely different from my relationship with my mother. Even when I was 25 years old and a graduate of medical school, I loved to sit and talk with my Mom. She was one of the most wonderful people I've ever known.

When my sister first got married, her husband was in college, so she paid for all of their expenses. They stayed in my parent's house and when my mother passed away shortly after my sister got married, they continued to stay in my parent's house with my father. They now have three children. When her husband finally finished college, he got a job in government and started working.

A few years later, when my father passed away, my sister and her family continued to stay in my parent's house. My two older brothers gave their share of the house to me and my sister. Of course, I was in the United States.

I loved my sister and her children. I was the one to encourage them to come to the United States. I arranged for them to obtain visas to stay in the United States. I helped them every way I could. My sister's husband, who promised he would come and stay in the United States after two years never did.

Mr. Lewis Johnson

In 1979 when I came back to the United States after the revolution, Mr. Lewis Johnson invited me to his house for dinner one night. This gentleman was a very interesting man. Mr. Johnson had come as a minister to Meshed, Iran, where I was going to medical school and where my brother taught at the university. He knew the Farsi language very well, and since he wanted to learn more to advance Farsi's literature, he asked my brother to teach him about the literature of the Farsi language. My brother was learning English from him at the same time. While my brother was the Dean of the Faculty of Letters, the college was short on English teachers, so my brother asked this gentleman to teach in that college.

Later on, I found out that this man had several Ph.D.'s, including one in law, he knew five different languages, and was originally from Kentucky.

In 1972, when I was a resident in general surgery in Louisville, Kentucky, my brother called me and told me Mr. Johnson was coming to Kentucky to visit his mother. Mr. Johnson asked my brother for my phone number, so when he came to Louisville he could call me. Mr. Johnson called and said he was going to pick me up the next weekend and take me to his mother's house. Apparently, they were a very rich family, because his mother's house, which was about 1½ hours from Louisville, was like a mansion the likes of which I had only seen in movies. We went through a gate and drove for several miles before we could even see the house. When we arrived at the house, I noticed the house was full of excellent Persian carpets, all quite valuable. His mother's servants served us lunch; afterwards, we went back to Louisville. He took me to the Louisville Boat Club. I had never been inside that Boat Club before.

This man, who presented himself as a minister in Iran and tried to push Christianity in the strong Moslem city of Meshed, was an excellent gentleman. His American wife passed away in Iran and he eventually married an Iranian woman. When Khomeini came and the revolution occurred, he presented himself as a lawyer to represent American businesses in Iran. After many months, he finally came back to the United States and started his law practice in Washington, DC.

At that time, the Iranian people were thinking that Khomeini couldn't last for more than a year because he was so horrible and the people would get rid of him. Mr. Johnson invited me to his house in Arlington for dinner. He was an excellent and knowledgeable gentleman. At his dinner party, two American generals were present. I went to Mr. Johnson and asked to be introduced to the generals so I could ask them some questions about the situation in Iran. He told them I was a good friend and asked them to answer my questions. I asked them about Khomeini and asked how long they thought he would be in power. They looked at each other and said they would tell me the truth, but asked me not to disclose what they would tell me. They said this new regime would stay a minimum of twenty five years. At that time, I couldn't believe what I heard, but today, as you know, Khomeini and his cronies have been in power more than thirty years.

Helping my Sister and her Family

When I heard what the generals said, I was concerned. In those days, it was dangerous to talk by phone to your family in Iran because all the phones were tapped. My sister, who worked for a big private company, was forced to keep working there, even though she didn't want to work after the revolution. I sent her a note asking her to come to Paris for a weekend so that we could talk. We made arrangements and she came to Paris. I wasn't wealthy at that time, but I thought this was so important I was willing to do it for my sister.

When we met each other in Paris, I told her what I heard from top government officials that the new government in Iran was going to last for many, many years. I told her I didn't know about her financial situation, but because she had three young children, I would be glad to apply for United States permanent residency visas for her and her family. I told her to talk to her husband and let me know. At that time, I was still married with my first wife.

My sister's husband came to the United States to stay with us and said he wanted to check everything out to see if it was possible for them to move to the United States. He stayed in our house for several months and, before he returned to Iran, he said that he definitely wanted to come and bring his family. I applied for permanent residency visas for them and they all eventually came to the United States. My sister's husband said that he had to be in Iran for a couple more years to gradually close the business that he was running, and then he could move to the United States. Everybody, including his wife, accepted that. I did everything for my sister and her family. I found them an apartment in a safe place, found a school for her kids and, every time they had a problem, they called me. Although I was a plastic surgeon, they called me for any medical problem her children had.

When her oldest daughter, was planning to get married, I heard she wanted to get married in a big house. I called my sister and offered my house for her daughter's marriage (this was the same niece who had lied to me about my daughter's accident when she fell and broke her elbow). Before she got married, my niece would occasionally stay at my house because I was on call for the hospital. Twenty years ago, the marriage ceremony of my niece was done in the Persian fashion and about fifty people attended that ceremony in the morning of her marriage. That same evening, 150 people attended her wedding reception in my house. I have done every possible thing that I could for my sister and her family since they came to the United States.

My sister's husband has to come to the United States every six months to maintain his permanent visa. Since my sister came to the United States, every time my sister's husband came to the United States, I invited him and my sister to have dinner at my house.

I remember that before the election of President Obama, we watched a football game after dinner in my house. My sister and her husband were supposed to come for dinner at 7:00 P.M. They came at 8:00 P.M. and said they were lost. Later on, she said they were late because they had gone to their daughter's house first to see their grandchildren. Her daughter lived very close to my house. It didn't cause any problem for me once I heard the truth. I served dinner and then we watched the football game.

At halftime, candidate Senator Obama and his opponent, Senator John McCain, each gave a one- minute speech. I said that in my opinion, because Obama had no experience, he was not a good candidate for the presidency. I said he was only a senator for two years and hadn't done anything during those two years. I don't know what happened because my sister never had talked politics before, but apparently she liked Mr. Obama and she started to argue with me. The same night, my daughter was in my house and was helping my sister with her computer. My daughter spent more than an hour helping her. My sister and her husband left the house suddenly without even saying goodbye.

A week later, my nephew (my older brother's son) invited us all out for lunch at a restaurant. When I arrived at the restaurant, my sister and her husband were standing and waiting. I said hello to them and asked why they left my house without even saying goodbye. They looked at each other and did not even respond to my question.

Difference in the Members of One Family

I have discussed my brothers and sister to show that it doesn't matter who your parents are, where you were educated, or where you were raised--people are different. For example, the four children in my family were all raised by the same mother and father and in the same house, same town and same country. But we were different in so many ways. My oldest brother and I obtained the highest level of education. My sister only graduated from high school and our second brother did not even finish high school, but they were successful in their own way.

At age 86, my oldest brother is a very fine man. He is famous for his expertise in Persian literature and is respected by Persian literature scholars around the world. As a matter of fact, he created a journal of Persian literature in the Washington Metropolitan region thirty-four years ago and continues to publish that journal even now. He prepares this 300-400 page magazine himself and sends it around the world. Even the current government-supported office that publishes current Persian literature in Iran asked him to send articles which they publish in Iran.

I have taken care of all my brothers and sister and their families.

Cases of Malpractice Brought Against Me in 36 Years of my Practice

---

First Malpractice Suit against Me

In 2002, I was sued for malpractice by a young African-American woman who was diagnosed with breast cancer after having a biopsy. The general surgeon was planning to do a total mastectomy. A friend of the patient gave my name to her for breast reconstruction after the mastectomy.

After I saw this patient, I explained to her the breast reconstruction procedure, which has two stages. The first stage, which could be done right after the mastectomy, involved the insertion of a saline-filled volume expander under the chest muscle. After this surgery, we would increase the volume of the expander by injecting saline in the volume expander every week until we reached a size similar to the other breast. The second stage of surgery was the removal of the saline volume expander, and insertion of a silicone gel implant, then reconstruction of the nipple and areola.

Upon the patient's request, a general surgeon and I booked her for surgery and performed the mastectomy and first stage of breast reconstruction. After several saline injections into the volume expander, the reconstructed breast reached the size of her other breast. I took her back to the operating room and performed the second stage of surgery, removal of the volume expander and insertion of a silicone breast implant, which would make the reconstructed breast feel like a normal breast. Also, I made her a new nipple and areola. The result of the surgery was excellent. A few months later, the patient gained twenty pounds and came to see me. She was complaining of asymmetry of her breasts. After examination, I told her it was because she had gained weight; her other breast became bigger but her reconstructed breast stayed the same size. I told her she had two choices, either lose twenty pounds or I had to put a larger implant in her reconstructed breast to match her other breast. I further told her that if I put the larger implant in, we would have to wait for a few months and then reconstruct the nipple and areola again. She asked me to book her for surgery, which I did. I removed the previous breast implant, enlarged the pocket, and put the larger implant in to match the size of her other breast.

After everything healed, she sued me before I could perform the second stage of the surgery. In the court, when I started to draw a picture of breast reconstruction, all the members of the jury stood up to watch me draw. The jury found me not guilty. The attorney of the patient asked the judge which members of the jury voted in my favor. The judge said all of them did.

Second Malpractice Suit against Me

In 2009, I was sued for malpractice again. This time I was accused of doing the wrong surgery on the hand of a sixteen-year-old girl. The patient's attorney claimed I did not do the right type of surgery on the injured hand of his client. Just before the trial began, the judge who was scheduled for the case could not attend and they put a retired judge, Alfred D. Swersky, on the bench. During part of the case, the patient's attorney brought a plastic surgeon who did not have any special hand surgery training to testify against me.

Many years ago an attorney sent me the chart of a patient who was operated on by the same plastic surgeon who was then testifying against me. The chart detailed the case of a patient who had a hysterectomy by her gynecologist, and then this plastic surgeon performed abdominoplasty (tummy tuck). The progress notes in the chart, written by surgical residents after they examined the patient every day at Inova Fairfax Hospital, indicated a bluish discoloration of the skin of the lower abdomen. The review of the chart indicated the plastic surgeon never noticed the discoloration of the skin of the lower abdomen and, five days after surgery, he discharged the patient from Inova Fairfax Hospital. A few days later, the plastic surgeon saw her in his office and his office note did not indicate any problem.

A few days after that, the patient became very sick. She was brought to the Emergency Room of Inova Fairfax Hospital. The Emergency Room physician called the plastic surgeon's office and the answering service said the plastic surgeon was out of town. They gave the Emergency Room physician the name and phone number of the surgeon who was covering him. When the Emergency Room physician called that doctor, he said he did not have privileges at Inova Fairfax Hospital, therefore, the Emergency Room physician tried to reach another plastic surgeon. He was successful and told the plastic surgeon about the condition of the patient. The plastic surgeon came to the Emergency Room and saw the patient, then took her to the operating room the same night to do major surgery to save her life. This surgery required excision of a large portion of dead abdominal skin and its underlying fatty tissues. The patient had to be admitted to the hospital for intravenous antibiotic treatment and frequent dressing changes for several days. This surgery was followed by another surgery to reconstruct the defect of the abdominal wall which resulted from the excision of the dead skin.

The patient wanted to sue the plastic surgeon who operated on her originally. Her attorney sent the file of the patient to me and, after I read the file carefully and talked to the surgeon who had saved the life of the patient, I provided my opinion in writing. I indicated that although every surgical resident noticed bluish discoloration of the lower portion of the abdominal wall, this plastic surgeon had not had noticed it in the hospital or even in the first office visit after surgery. Although the patient's attorney asked me to testify, they never called me to testify in court.

A few years later, the same plastic surgeon's license was suspended for one year because he mistreated the patients in his office and improperly used his secretary as a registered nurse. After this plastic surgeon testified against me in the malpractice case, my attorney asked the plastic surgeon several questions which proved his statements against me were incorrect.

The chairman of the Department of Plastic Surgery and Hand Surgery at the University of Virginia was my expert witness and he testified that what I did on that patient was accurate. He said he would do the same type of surgery as I did and said that my follow-up of the patient was also correct. He further said that young patients many times either do not follow the instructions given by their surgeon or do something which they were told not to do. He was such an expert that he prepared the tests for those individuals taking the examination of the Certified Board of Hand Surgery in the United States.

I asked my attorney to present the information I had about the plastic surgeon who was the patient's expert witness in order to discredit his testimony. Unfortunately, my attorney chose not do it and he was sorry after the case was finished. My attorney did ask the plastic surgeon several questions regarding his written testimony against me and got him to practically admit that the complications could have happened to anyone and were not my fault.

After all the testimony was finished, the retired judge told the jury to consider an issue which was not even one of the complaints against me: "not seeing the patient adequately after surgery." The patient's file showed I saw her regularly in my office after surgery. I asked my lawyers to ask the judge to strike that issue from the jury's consideration and, even though they pointed out that I was not being sued for that, the judge let the instruction stand. The jury found me guilty of not seeing my patient adequately after surgery. The jury found me innocent of making the wrong diagnosis, performing the wrong surgery, and providing the wrong treatment during post-operative care.

This is a problem of the United States justice system. Why would you call back a judge who had retired? A retired physician cannot treat a patient. Unfortunately, lawyers are treated special because the majority of our congressman and senators are lawyers. A senator after one term of service receives a retirement salary for the rest of his or her life. A congressman after five years receive a retirement salary for the rest of his or her life. A soldier who was sent to war and returns home often has no retirement. That doesn't sound fair to me.

Appeal to the Virginia Supreme Court

I talked to the malpractice insurance company and asked them to appeal this decision to the Virginia Supreme Court. After the insurance company reviewed all the documents from the case and the decision, they agreed with me that the retired judge made a mistake when giving the jury improper instructions and they agreed to appeal to the Virginia Supreme Court.

Supreme Court Justice J. Howe Brown, Jr. asked how I could see the patient when I was in Hawaii. I never went to Hawaii from the first time I saw the patient until the patient sued me, while the medical record indicated that I had seen the patient regularly and frequently after surgery.

This is the legal system of the United States. This case is one example of a wrongful judgment in the court due to the actions of the judge. Unfortunately, you can't sue a judge for wrongful action.

Review of Virginia Board of Medicine

After the lower court found me guilty, the Virginia Board of Medicine sent me a letter asking me to send them the entire medical record of the patient who had sued me and received a judgment against me. After the members of the Virginia Board of Medicine reviewed the file of the patient and the judgment of the jury against me, they invited me to a hearing of the Special Conference Committee of the Virginia Board of Medicine in Henrico, Virginia, on July 13, 2011. There were three physicians serving on the special Conference Committee: Dr. Wayne Reynolds, Dr. Gopinath Jadhav, and Dr. J. Randolph Clements. After several hours of questioning me, the hearing was concluded.

I received a letter from Dr. William L. Harp, Executive Director of Virginia Board of Medicine, dated July 14, 2011. The Board determined that there had been insufficient evidence to support a violation of law, so the committee dismissed the matter.

Most of the time, when an attorney has contacted me about a possible malpractice suit against a surgeon, I found out that the attorney knew nothing about medicine. This is another problem with the legal system in the United States. There is no specialty training school for lawyers in the United States. When a lawyer finishes law school and passes the bar examination, he or she can participate in any kind of legal case. This is completely different for physicians who finish medical school. Physicians have to go to specialty training which lasts between three and eight years before they are allowed to practice medicine.

In my opinion, patients' complaints about medical or surgical care should be heard by physicians who are familiar with medical or surgical problems, and not by judges or juries who know nothing about medicine. This is not the way that European countries take care of patient complaints. In Europe, malpractice suits are presented to judges and experienced medical specialists who testify about each case and answer the questions of the judge or the attorney of the physician. The judge is the one to make a judgment. It is very easy to fool a jury of people who are not physicians and are not lawyers, but it is very difficult to fool a judge.

The Major Changes of Patient's Care Due to the Legal System

When I was a Chief Resident in general surgery, if we had a patient who was terminal but was kept alive on a respirator in the intensive care unit and given multiple units of blood, I contacted one of the close members of the patient's family. I told the family member the terminal status of their loved one and assured him or her that there was no cure. I suggested that we could let the loved one go peacefully, or we could continue to keep them in their current condition. The family member talked to other members of the family and, after a day or so, called me back and told me they decided they want their loved one to go peacefully. After hearing the family's decision, we reduced the oxygen of the respirator to the same amount in the normal room air and, if the patient's blood level was low, I did not give any more blood transfusions. Within two or three days, the patient passed away peacefully surrounded by his or her family.

Today, no one can do anything because of the legal system. That is why when you go to any nursing home today, you will find at least forty percent of the patients like vegetables because they are fed by tubes or by the help of a nurse. The patients do not even know whether or not they are eating. They have no control of their urine or stool and do not recognize anyone, even their children. Most of these patients are suffering from Alzheimer's disease or dementia. In 1973, when you went to any nursing home, you never saw patients like this. For this reason, twenty-five percent of the Medicare budget is spent for the last year of patients' lives.[14]

I attribute these changes to the legal system in this country. Although my own daughter is a good lawyer, I have strong views against lawyers and the legal system of the United States. We have too many lawyers in this country. The lawyers do not create anything; they get money from everyone else to survive. Three hundred and five years

---

14 Wang, Penelope, "Cutting the High Cost of End-of-Life Care," Money, December 12, 2012.

ago, when there were very few lawyers in England, Shakespeare said that the best thing for the English people to do was to get rid of the lawyers.

My View about Malpractice in the United States

Malpractice is a big problem. There are so many cases of malpractice because lawyers try to make money. When a patient calls a lawyer for a malpractice issue, the lawyer often does not ask the patient to pay a dime. Lawyers say they will present the case in court and if they win, they get a significant cut of the award. I believe that if a physician does something wrong to a patient, he or she has to be punished. In Japan, if a patient sues his or her doctor, if the court finds the physician is not guilty, the patient who sued the doctor has to pay the physician all the costs of the court and the cost of his or her lawyers.

Juries are another problem. In the United States, regular citizens are elected as members of a jury. In Europe, juries consist of judges. Lawyers can fool the regular people, but lawyers cannot fool judges because they are also lawyers. During 48 years of living in the United States, I was called for possible jury duty four times. As soon as the lawyers found out I was a surgeon, I was not selected because they knew it would be difficult to fool a surgeon.

Insurance companies that sell malpractice insurance have to cover their risk, so they charge doctors a tremendous amount of money every year. I paid between $35,000 and $50,000 a year for malpractice insurance and I was only sued twice. After the first case in which I was sued and found not guilty, the malpractice insurance company to which I had paid premiums for many years, wrote me a letter and told me they were not going to cover me for malpractice anymore. When I called them, I told them I had paid them for 20 years with only one lawsuit in which I was found not guilty and they were not going to provide coverage for me anymore? They realized they had made a big mistake. They offered to renew my insurance but increased the premium fifty-eight percent. I cancelled that insurance and went to another malpractice insurance company. The doctor's complaints against such malpractice insurance companies fall on deaf ears.

Retirement of Good General Surgeons Because of Increase of Malpractice Insurance Premiums

There were two wonderful general surgeons practicing at Inova Mount Vernon Hospital; one of them even operated on me. Those two surgeons had to retire at age 54 because their malpractice insurance premiums kept increasing and increasing and they couldn't afford to pay them anymore. Fortunately, malpractice insurance in the state of Virginia has a limitation on patient awards in court cases. With the limitation provisions, you cannot sue a physician in Virginia for more than $2,200,000. In other states, there is no such limitation, including Washington, DC, so a patient can sue a physician for $100 million or even higher.

I wonder why congressmen, senators and the President do not talk to physicians, professors of medical schools, and insurance companies to fix the malpractice insurance problem.

Major Changes in Health Insurance Company Payments to the Physicians

At the beginning of my practice, the insurance companies paid us adequately. The majority of patients who were seen in the Emergency Room had good insurance, which is why I could survive the first three years of my solo practice. After three years, many physicians in the area become familiar with my work and started to refer their patients to me for elective surgery.

In the last thirteen years, no surgeons have been interested in covering the Emergency Room because insurance companies pay the physicians inadequately and malpractice insurance premiums are especially high for these surgeons.

Major Changes in the Practice of Medicine in the United States

In 1978, I would say more than 90% of the patients I saw in the Emergency Room had insurance and the insurance companies paid us well. If I charged $1000 for an operation, I usually received $950 from the insurance company. In those days, I was able to charge the insurance company for post-operative office visits. For example, when I performed hand surgery on patients who were referred from the Emergency Room, I had to see them frequently after surgery for several months and received insurance payments for each post-operative visit. For a person like me who was just starting his practice, even though it was difficult work, it was the only way I could get some patients and have an income.

At the present time, no insurance company pays the surgeon for post-operative office visits or hospital visits for a period of three months after surgery. A good otolaryngologist who performed one of most difficult and complicated surgeries, called total laryngectomy (removal of the entire larynx), told me that since his patients had to stay in the hospital for three weeks after surgery and he had to see them every day, he did not charge the insurance company for the surgery. Instead, he charged for his daily hospital visits because the insurance companies paid so little for surgery, even such a difficult surgery. If he charged for surgery, he could not charge the insurance company for daily post-operative hospital visits for those three weeks.

I have some real concerns about the Patient Protection and Affordable Care Act. It has some plusses and minuses, but is still a contentious and political issue in this country. The Senate passed the Patient Protection and Affordable Care Act (known as Obamacare) along party lines. Thirty-four (34) Democratic congressmen joined all the Republican congressmen in voting against the Obama healthcare plan. Even in December 2015, the Republican-controlled Senate repealed Obamacare in its budget bill.[15] There is much more drama to come regarding Obamacare.

How Religion Can Help

I am not a religious person, but I respect the religious right of every human being. I believe in God. As long as people use their religion as a way to be more comfortable and also to be helpful to others, religion is fantastic. Unfortunately, in this world, there are some people who use religion as a tool to gain personal benefit.

Some use religion as a way to comfort for their losses and deal with their problems. About thirteen years ago, I received a call from the

---

[15] Barrett, Ted, "Senate Passes Budget Bill Repealing Obamacare, Defunding Planned Parenthood," CNN, December 4, 2015.

Emergency Room about a six-year-old boy who had multiple facial fractures resulting from a car accident. I went to the emergency room and saw the boy.

I found out that when his father picked him up along with his fourteen- and sixteen-year-old sisters from school and was driving back home, their car suddenly went out of control and hit a concrete wall. The father and sixteen-year-old sister died instantly while the fourteen-year old sister was alive but brain dead in the hospital. She died shortly thereafter.

After I examined the son and looked at his x-rays, I admitted him to the hospital and started to give him intravenous antibiotics, then booked him for surgery the next day. I knew I had to face this boy's mother, who had lost her husband and two daughters, but I had no idea what to say to her. I gave it a lot of thought and still did not know what I was going to say. I finally saw her the morning of her son's surgery and said that unfortunately I was not born in this country, so it was difficult for me to express my feelings about that horrible disaster. I told her I was very sorry for her loss. She had a heavy southern accent and said I should not worry about her husband and her daughters because that morning they were having breakfast with Jesus Christ. When I heard that, it was like someone pouring cold water on my hot head. I thought she had such a wonderful attitude because of her strong religious belief. I also thought for those of us who do not have such a strong belief, we suffer a lot more. Either way, it's still so sad to lose so many loved ones.

Later on, I took the boy to the operating room and fixed all of his fractures. When I saw the mother after the surgery, she was so calm.

My View about the Political System of the United States

I thought the United States was a democratic country and the vote of the people counted for something, but truthfully, the more I have been in the United States and the more I have studied its politics, I have found out several things I didn't know. In the United States, if the majority of the Congress passes legislation, the President of the country can veto it. If the Congressmen and Senators can get two-thirds of the vote, they can overcome the veto. Two-thirds is not democracy, fifty-one percent of the vote is the real democracy.

Another interesting issue of the politics of this country is the election of senators. The state of California has a population of more than 38 million people but can only elect two senators while the state of New Hampshire with a population of 1.3 million people can also elect two senators. This is not a real democracy. Real democracy means the majority of the people make the decisions.

When you look at most democratic countries of the world, like France, England, and Germany, you find that there are multiple parties in each country and whichever party gets the majority of the votes, the head of that party is the President or Prime Minister. So, if the programs and policies that the party in power initiates are good, they will be re-elected. If not, the next time they are not elected.

In the United States, it is completely different. The President can be from the Democratic Party, and the majority of Congress can be mostly Republican or vice versa. Either party has different ideas and plans for running the country. That sets up fighting between them all the time. This is not democracy because if, for example, the majority of the American people vote for Democrats, then the majority of Congress and the President should all be from the Democratic Party. Then, if the people like what they are doing, they re-elect them. If not, they don't re-elect them and they vote for the other party.

Then there is the Supreme Court and how it weighs in on issues. Justice Antonin Scalia, in a dissenting opinion on the Supreme Court's same-sex ruling, even said, "A system of government that makes the People subordinate to a committee of nine unelected lawyers does not deserve to be called a democracy."[16]

American Football is Dangerous

Everyone in the world calls football a game played with feet, with the exception of the goal keeper. Only the American people call that game soccer and call their own game football, although 96% of football is played with the hands. In the game of soccer, when a player makes a bad fault, he receives a yellow card from the referee. And if that player makes another bad fault, he receives a red card and is out of the game for that game series. In American football, the worse

---

[16] Friedman, Dan, "Antonin Scalia Rips Fellow Justices in Sarcastic Dissent on Same-Sex Marriage Ruling: 'Ask the Nearest Hippie,'" New York Daily News, June 26, 2015.

faults by players receive only 15 yards penalty and the player can repeat that type of fault as many times he wants.

As a doctor, I am aware of so many injuries to American football players. In every game you watch, so many players suffer injuries, many of them serious. There are so many head injuries in American football. Some players have permanent damage as a result of head injuries.

I have seen three young high school students with paralysis from the neck down as a result of playing American football. I have a fantastic suggestion. Let players play the same game but the minute the defense touches an offensive player, stop the game. This would prevent any bad injuries to the players, while still allowing them to play the game. I love to watch American football, but I suffer when I see players sustain bad injuries. It seems unfair that 360-pound players can play against 180-pound players.

There is much discussion around the topic of discussions in America today. The Centers for Disease Control issued an informational pamphlet on concussions, how to recognize them, and how to manage them, with an emphasis on safety for the football player.[17] According to the American Association for Neurological Surgeons, "According to the University of Pittsburgh's Brain Trauma Research Center, more than 300,000 sports-related concussions occur annually in the U.S., and the likelihood of suffering a concussion while playing a contact sport is estimated to be as high as 19 percent per year of play. More than 62,000 concussions are sustained each year in high school contact sports, and among college football players, 34 percent have had one concussion, and 20 percent have endured multiple concussions. Concussions can have a long term effect as well.[18] We have got to figure this out for the sake of our athletes and their families.

Conclusion

After spending 18 months preparing this book, I can say everything in this book about me and my work is true. This is my first effort at writing my life story. My parents were the ones who helpe

---

[17] "Heads Up: Concussion in Football," CDC, available at http://www.cdc.gov/concussion/HeadsUp/pdf/Football_Fact_Sheet_Coaches-a.pdf .
[18] Hadhazy, Adam, "Concussions Exact Toll on Football Players Long After They Retire," Scientific American, September 2, 2008.

me grow and flourish in Iran in those days when there was no clean drinking water, no electricity, and no heating system in the houses. The financial support of my brothers during my education at medical school has been appreciated my entire life. Without their help, I could not have made it through medical school. I have been in this country more than forty-seven years. I am proud to be a citizen of this country. I am proud to call myself an American.

Being able to pass the Educational Commission for Foreign Medical Graduates examination at the American Embassy in Iran and coming to the United State as a doctor, being able to be trained at the best medical centers of the United States, and becoming a successful plastic surgeon and hand surgeon were great achievements for me. One of the best things about this country is its treatment of foreigners who come to this country legally. If foreigners are good in their field of work, they are respected pretty much like those people who were born here. For example, when I passed the E.C.F.M.G. examination, I was treated exactly as an American physician who was born here and finished medical school in this country.

I hope that by reading this book, Americans will appreciate and be proud of what they have in this country. Also, as a person who was born and raised in Iran, I appreciate the Iranian people funding my medical education. I could not have become a doctor without their help.

I am also proud of my accomplishments in the United States. With the help of Dr. Mohammad Atik, I did important research work about platelet function in the University of Louisville. This research work and its finding changed how blood banks save blood and how we use aspirin tablets to keep the coronary blood vessels of the heart open. This discovery helped so many people around the world and continues to do so.

I hope I paid back the American people by performing surgical repair of major hand injuries, surgical removal of different cancers and performing reconstructive surgeries to save their parts of their body. I can't forget that I also performed a lot of cosmetic surgeries to make people look younger and more beautiful.

I am indeed a fortunate plastic surgeon.

APPENDIX

The Biggest Enemies of Iran: Russia and England

Qajar Dynasty[19]

The Qajars were a Turkmen tribe that held ancestral lands in present-day Azerbaijan, which then was part of Iran. In 1779, following the death of Mohammad Karim Khan Zand, the Zand Dynasty ruler of southern Iran, Agha Mohammad Khan, a leader of the Qajar tribe, set out to reunify Iran. Agha Mohammad Khan defeated numerous rivals and brought all of Iran under his rule, establishing the Qatar dynasty. By 1794, he had eliminated all of his rivals, including Lotf'Ali Khan, the last of the Zand Dynasty, and had reasserted Iranian sovereignty over the former Iranian territories in Georgia and the Caucasus. Agha Mohammad established his capital at Tehran, a village near the ruins of the ancient city of Ray (now Shahr-e Ray). In 1796, he was formally crowned as Shah (king). Agha Mohammad was assassinated in 1797 and was succeeded by his nephew, Fath Ali Shah.

Fath Ali Shah, 1797-1834

Under Fath Ali Shah, Iran went to war against Russia, which was expanding from the north in to the Caucasus Mountains, an area of historic Iranian interest and influence. Iran suffered major military defeats during the war. Under the terms of the Treaty of Golestan in 1813, Iran recognized Russia's annexation of Georgia and ceded most of the north Caucasus region to Russia. A second war with Russia in the 1820s ended even more disastrously for Iran, which in 1828 was forced to sign the treaty of Turkmanchai acknowledging Russian sovereignty over the entire area north of the Aras River (territory comprising present-day Armenia and Republic of Azerbaijan).

In order to push the treaty, the Russians created a plan in which they paid an Iranian clergyman to gather a bunch of Russians and

---

[19] From www.iranchamber.com/history/qajar/qajar.php

incite them to attack one of the Russian Consulates and kill their own consul. After that attack, Russia told Fath Ali Shah either he had to sign the Turkmanchai treaty or Russia would attack Iran again. In reality, ten states of Iran (Ghara Bagh, Ganjeh, Shaki, Shirvan, Cuba, Darband, Baku, Talesh, Dagestan, and Gorjestan) were taken from Iran by Russia.

Fath Ali's reign saw increased diplomatic contacts with the West and the beginning of intense European diplomatic rivalries over Iran. Fath Ali's grandson, Mohammad Shah, who fell under the influence of Russia and made two unsuccessful attempts to capture Herat, succeeded him in 1834.

When Mohammad Shah died in 1848, the succession passed to his son Naser al-Din, who proved to be the ablest and most successful of the Qajar sovereigns.

Naser al-Din Shah, 1848-1896

During Naser al-Din Shah's reign, Western science, technology, and educational methods were introduced into Iran and the country's modernization began. Naser al-Din Shah tried to exploit the mutual distrust between Great Britain and Russia to preserve Iran's independence, but foreign interference and territorial encroachment increased under his rule. He contracted huge foreign loans to finance expensive personal trips to Europe. He was not able to prevent Britain and Russia from encroaching into regions of traditional Iranian influence. In 1856, Britain prevented Iran from reasserting control over Herat, which had been part of Iran in Safavi times but had been under non-Iranian rule since the mid-18th century. Britain supported Herat's incorporation in to Afghanistan, a country Britain helped create in order to extend the buffer between its Indian territories and Russia's expanding empire eastward. Britain also extended its control to other areas of the Persian Gulf during the 19th century. Meanwhile, by 1881, Russia had completed its conquest of present-day Turkmenistan and Uzbekistan, bringing Russia's frontier to Iran's northeastern borders and severing historic Iranian ties to the cities of Bukhara and Samarqand. Several trade concessions by the Iranian government put economic affairs largely under British control. By the late 19th century, many Iranians believed that their rulers were beholden to foreign interests.

Mirza Taqi Khan Amir Kabir

Mirza Taqi Khan Amir Kabir was the young prince Nasser al-Din's advisor and constable. With the death of Mohammad Shah in 1848, Mirza Taqi was largely responsible for ensuring the crown prince's succession to the throne. When Nasser al-Din succeeded to the throne, Mirza Taqi was awarded the position of prime minister and the title of Amir Kabir, the Great Ruler.

Iran was virtually bankrupt, its central government was weak, and its provinces were almost autonomous. During the next two and a half years, Amir Kabir initiated important reforms in virtually all sectors of society. Government expenditures were slashed and the Amir Kabir assumed responsibility for all areas of the bureaucracy. Foreign interference in Iran's domestic affairs was curtailed, and foreign trade was encouraged. Public works, such as the bazaar in Tehran were undertaken. Amir Kabir issued an edict banning ornate and excessively formal writing in government documents; the beginning of a modern Persian prose style dates from this time.

One of the greatest achievements of Amir Kabir was the building of Dar-ol-Fonoon, the first modern university in Iran, which was established for training a new cadre of administrators and acquainting them with western techniques. Amir Kabir ordered the school to be built on the edge of the city so it could be expanded as needed. He hired Frenchmen and Russians to teach subjects as diverse as language, medicine, law, geography, history, economics, and engineering. Unfortunately, Amir Kabir did not live long enough to see his greatest monument completed, but it still stands in Tehran as a sign of a great man's ideas for the future of his country.

These reforms antagonized various notables who had been excluded from the government. They regarded the Amir Kabir as a social upstart and a threat to their interests, and they formed a coalition against him, in which the queen mother was active. She convinced the young Shah that Amir Kabir wanted to usurp the throne. In October 1851 the Shah dismissed him and exiled him to Kashan, where he was murdered on the Shah's orders.

The Constitutional Revolution

After Nasser al-Din Shah was assassinated by Mirza Reza Kermani in 1896, the crown passed to his son, Mozaffar al-Din. Mozaffar al-Din Shah was a weak and ineffectual ruler. Royal extravagance and the absence of incoming revenues exacerbated financial problems. The Shah quickly spent two large loans from Russia, partly to fund a trip to Europe. Public anger fed on the Shah's propensity for granting concessions to Europe in return for generous payments to him and his officials. People began to demand a curb on royal authority and the establishment of the rule of law as their concern over foreign, and especially Russian, influence grew.

The Shah's failure to respond to protests by the religious establishment, the merchants, and other classes led the merchants and clerical leaders to take sanctuary from probable arrest in mosques in Tehran and outside of the capital in January 1906. When the Shah reneged on a promise to permit the establishment of a "house of justice" or consultative assembly, 10,000 people, led by the merchants, took sanctuary in June in the compound of the British legation in Tehran. In August, the Shah was forced to issue a decree promising a constitution. In October, an elected assembly convened and drew up a constitution that provided for strict limitations on royal power; an elected parliament, or Majles, with wide powers to represent the people; and a government with a cabinet subject to confirmation by the Majles. The Shah signed the constitution on December 30, 1906. He died five days later. The supplementary Fundamental Laws approved in 1907 provided for freedom of the press, speech and association, and for security of life and property within certain limits. The constitutional revolution marked the end of the medieval period in Iran. The hopes for constitutional rule were not realized, however.

Mozafar al-Din's son, Mohammad Ali Shah reigned from 1907-09 and, with the aid of Russia, attempted to rescind the constitution and abolish the parliamentary government. After several disputes with the members of the Majles, in June 1908, he used his Russian-officered Persian Cossacks Brigade to bomb the Majles building, arrest many of the deputies, and close down the assembly. Resistance to the shah, however, coalesced in Tabriz, Esfahan, Rasht, and elsewhere. In July

1909, constitutional forces marched from Rasht and Esfahan to Tehran, deposed the Shah, and re-established the constitution. Mohammad Ali went to Russia.

Although the constitutional forces had triumphed, they faced serious difficulties. The upheavals of the constitutional revolution and civil war had undermined stability and trade. In addition, Mohammad Ali, with Russian support, attempted to regain his throne, landing troops in Iran in July 1910. Most serious of all, the hope that the constitutional revolution would inaugurate a new era of independence from the great powers ended when, under the Anglo-Russian Agreement of 1907, Britain and Russia agreed to divide Iran into spheres of influence. The Russians were to enjoy the exclusive right to pursue their interests in the northern sphere, the British in the south and east. Both powers would be free to compete for economic and political advantage in a neutral sphere in the center. Matters came to a head when Morgan Shuster, a United States administrator hired as treasurer general by the Persian government to reform its finances, sought to collect taxes from powerful officials who were Russian protégés and to send members of the treasury gendarmerie, a tax department police force, into the Russian zone. In December 1911, when the Majles unanimously refused a Russian ultimatum demanding Shuster's dismissal, Russian troops, already in the country, moved to occupy the capital. To prevent this, on December 20, Bakhtiari chiefs and their troops surrounded the Majles building, forced acceptance of the Russian ultimatum, and shut down the assembly, once again suspending the constitution. Following the shutdown, there was a period of government by Bakhtiari chiefs and other powerful notables.

Ahmad Shah was born January 21, 1898 in Tabriz and succeeded to the throne at age 11. He proved to be pleasure-loving, feminine, and incompetent and was unable to preserve the integrity of Iran or the fate of his dynasty. The occupation of Iran during World War 1 (1914-18) by the Russian, British, and Ottoman troops was a blow from which Ahmad Shah never effectively recovered. With a coup d'état in February 1921, Reza Khan (ruled as Reza Shah Pahlavi, 1925-41) became the preeminent political personality in Iran. Ahmad Shah was formally deposed by the Majles in October 1925 while he was visiting Europe, and the assembly declared the rule of the Qajar dynasty to be terminated. Ahmad Shah died later on February 21, 1930 in Neuilly-sur-Seine, France.

Mohammad Reza Pahlavi, the Shah of Iran

Mohammad Reza Pahlavi was the shah of Iran until 1978, when president of the United State, the president of France and the Prime Minister of England decided to get rid of Mohammad Reza Shah Pahlavi and replace him with Khomeini.

What Khomeini and his followers have done to the Iranian people since then are crimes of Great Britain. History shows how many crimes have done by the British Empire around the world. The British Empire used to assert that the sun never set on the British Empire because Great Britain took so much of the world by force.